ALBERT SCHWEITZER, MUSICIAN

also by Michael Murray

Marcel Dupré: The Work of a Master Organist

Albert Schweitzer, Musician

Michael Murray

SCOLAR PRESS

Published by
SCOLAR PRESS
Gower House
Croft Road
Aldershot
Hants GU11 3HR
England

Ashgate Publishing Company
Old Post Road
Brookfield
Vermont 05036
USA

British Library Cataloguing in Publication Data

Murray, Michael
    Albert Schweitzer, Musician
    I. Title
    786. 5092

Library of Congress Cataloging-in-Publication Data

Murray, Michael
    Albert Schweitzer, musician / by Michael Murray.
        p.   cm
    Includes bibliographical references and index.
    ISBN 1—85928—031—5
    1. Schweitzer, Albert, 1875–1965.   2. Organists—Biography.
    I. Title.
    ML416.S33M9   1993
    786.5'092—dc20   93–37090
                         CIP
ISBN 1 85928 031 5   MN

Typeset in 10pt Sabon by Raven Typesetters and
printed in Great Britain at the University Press, Cambridge

for

Gary L. Garber

The study of the arts in their great manifestations is thus a gradual and deliberate accustoming of the feelings to strong sensations and precise ideas. It is a breaking down of self-will for the sake of finding out what life and its objects may really be like. And this means that most esthetic matters turn out to be moral ones in the end.

Jacques Barzun

Contents

Preface

These essays are token payment of a debt. Because of Albert Schweitzer, whom I began to read when I was fifteen, I decided to become an organist, and because of his link with the French traditions of organ playing I ended up in Paris four years later a student of his friend Marcel Dupré. It was Schweitzer's account of old Walckers and Silbermanns and Cavaillé-Colls, and of the music of Bach and others played thereon, that brought me for the first time under the spell of the instrument which has been at the centre of my life ever since.

My indebtedness is of course not unique. Many persons have been similarly led by Schweitzer to recast their lives, whether by embracing music, medicine, philosophy, the missions, or the cause of world peace, and have been similarly grateful. Many have expressed their gratitude in print.

I do so because there is a gap in the literature about Schweitzer, and trying to fill it seemed an attractive task and a fitting gesture of thanks.

It is remarkable that among the dozens of books in English about him only one looks closely at his career in music. And even that volume, Charles R. Joy's *Music in the Life of Albert Schweitzer*, consisting as it does of Schweitzer's own writings interspersed with biographical sketches, remains, for all its richness, a survey. It is casual rather than complete.

It describes his extraordinary accomplishment as organ recitalist, as biographer of Bach and editor of Bach's music, and as expert on organ building. But it was not within its intended scope to show, for example, how his way of performing Bach was rooted in a stylistic tradition that had come down through generations of masters and pupils from Bach himself. Nor does it show how Schweitzer's playing differed from the traditional – or from his own editions. Nor does it tell why he has for decades been mistakenly viewed as founder of organ reform movements whose ideals he in fact deplored. For although the pertinent questions of style and technique are inherently fascinating and worthy of study, and Schweitzer's work was often seminal, the purpose of Dr Joy's book was other than comprehensive.

And yet the musical vocation of Albert Schweitzer, no less than his philosophic or medical or literary vocations, brought him lifelong satisfaction, and to examine his musical acts and views is to learn much about a personality that continues to intrigue thousands of admirers in dozens of lands. Why, then, this lacuna, given the attractiveness of the topic and an audience ready-made?

One answer is clear. Schweitzer's musical activity centred on an instrument loved by many but understood by few. 'The organ is a mystery to almost everyone,' a journalist rightly complains. 'To the layman, and that includes the average musician as well, the King of Instruments is observed only from a distance, and then through a haze of royal purple.'[1] And to writers trying to explain it, the organ presents all manner of discrepant terms that only pretend to stand for concrete ideas. Quite apart from a dozen words whose very familiarity may mislead – 'strings,' 'oboe,' and 'trumpet,' for example, which name timbres greatly different from the orchestral counterparts the reader knows – such words as 'baroque,' 'classic,' and 'romantic' have been so long misused as to stand now for only the vaguest of notions. 'Romantic' in particular has appeared in print as a synonym for such mutually contradictory terms as formal and formless, attractive and stupid, and heroic and irrational, and has become a catchall word for nearly any artistic style not currently deemed respectable. Thus probably fewer writers have explored the twofold subject of organ playing and organ building than despaired of it as hopelessly muddled by its nomenclature. As for us organists, we tend to argue among ourselves, as Jacques Barzun once wrote of E. Power Biggs, with more heat than light.

Indeed, the art of the organ has hardly been made more accessible by recent decades of polemical exchanges among its practitioners. For as organists contend with organists over such subtleties as mechanical versus electrical action and equal versus unequal tuning, deeper questions of style and technique are ignored – and with sorry results. It is nowadays common, for example, to hear nineteenth-century works played on eighteenth-century organs, although nineteenth-century music takes sound itself as a constituent element and to play Franck on a classical organ is therefore as aberrant as to play Chopin on a harpsichord. If organists themselves can so misconstrue their art, little wonder its secrets elude outsiders.

Confusion thus abounds among ordinary music lovers, who enjoy the thunder of a thirty-two-foot bombarde and the shimmer of a flute celeste, and among professionals. So much so that a respected musicologist can devise, and a respected university press publish, this startling generality: 'There is no other branch of music, except the liturgical, in which all musicians would admit the inferiority of everything written in the last two hundred years, of organ music written after 1750, to that written before'[2] – a statement that errs in comparing unlike things and in so doing belittles Vierne, Reubke,

Reger, and Dupré, not to mention Mozart, Schumann, Mendelssohn, and Liszt.

Accordingly, many a lesson may be learned from Albert Schweitzer's practice of music and from the men in whose work this practice took root, not least because their understanding of the organ and its styles of repertory, like his, was comprehensive and clear.

Further, that very abuse of thought and common sense continues to occur which Schweitzer deplored when writing about good organs and their destruction. 'I have sometimes to look on helpless,' he lamented as late as the 1930s, 'while I see noble old organs rebuilt and enlarged till not a scrap of their original beauty is left . . . and see them even broken up, and replaced at heavy cost by plebeian products . . . !'[3] Such was the effect then of the mistaken belief that progress inevitably means improvement, hence that new organs are necessarily more artistic than old ones, and such is the effect today. As if Schweitzer had never exhorted us to defend craftsmanship and tonal beauty, we continue to replace or rebuild excellent organs deserving of care. Only instead of destroying fine old instruments from the eighteenth century, we now destroy those of the nineteenth and twentieth – a kind of vandalism that ensues from wrong thinking (and from 'craftsmanship' and 'tonal beauty' wrongly defined), since, as we shall hear Schweitzer say later on, the 'struggle for the good organ is . . . part of the struggle for truth.'[4]

Or take again the matter of performance. Although Schweitzer's research, like that of later scholars, confirmed Spitta's in establishing the likelihood of Bach's preference for a basically legato style, above all in works of intricate texture, probably more organists now abandon this discipline than embrace it, resorting in Bach to whatever fingering – which is to say: whatever style – is most expedient. In this, our standards have so declined as to recall that other dark age, the period 1789–1840, when organ playing was corrupted by the *empfindsamer Stil* and by the events and ideas of the French Revolution.

Hence a new look at the work of Kittel, Rinck, Hesse, Lemmens, Guilmant, Widor, and Cavaillé-Coll, all of whom helped to mould Schweitzer the musician, and at the earnestness with which these masters regarded artistic duty, may help to keep us on a better path. As a purely practical corollary, it will as well reveal to the thoughtful student something of the keyboard technique and the timbres in which the works of Widor, Vierne, Dupré, Langlais, and Messiaen were conceived. For Bach's praxis as understood by these heirs of Lemmens, together with the sonority and facility of Cavaillé-Coll's organs, provided the foundation on which they built.

And we shall be reminded that the organ, for all its massiveness and power, is indeed the most fragile of instruments, its beauty perpetually threatened by the foolishness of men.

Notes and References

1. *Musical Heritage Society Review*, 2 (Spring 1978), p. 25.
2. Martin Cooper (1951), *French Music*, London: Oxford University Press, pp. 169–70.
3. *Out of My Life and Thought*, p. 97.
4. Ibid., p. 101.

1 Pupil of Widor

When in the autumn of 1893 the young Albert Schweitzer came to Paris to meet Charles-Marie Widor, the illustrious organist of St Sulpice, the youth brought as credentials a passion for Bach and a mind wholly receptive to Widor's discipline. And yet it was but a scant half-dozen years earlier that Schweitzer had begun to study conscientiously, having first been in music, as elsewhere, 'a poor scholar . . . slack and dreamy.'[1]

It was only when one of his grammar school teachers, a certain Herr Wehmann, showed him how to work properly, Schweitzer tells us, that matters improved. 'But Dr Wehmann's influence over me was due above all to the fact . . . that he most carefully prepared beforehand every lesson that he gave. He became to me a model of fulfillment of duty . . . . In languages and mathematics it cost me an effort to accomplish anything. But after a time I felt a certain fascination in mastering subjects for which I had no special talent.'[2] At the piano as well, although the boy had shown promise early on, his dreaminess made him prefer to improvise rather than to practise. This left his renditions inaccurate, while his shyness at unveiling 'the emotion stirred in me by a lovely piece'[3] left them dry. To his first piano and organ teacher, Eugène Münch, of Mulhouse, whose coaching was to serve so well as basis for Widor's, his ineptitude was exasperating.

'Really you don't deserve to have such beautiful music given you,' Schweitzer recalls Münch saying one day after a particularly slipshod performance; and, setting on the rack a volume of Mendelssohn: 'You'll come and spoil this *Lied ohne Worte* for me, just like everything else. If a boy has no feeling, I certainly can't give him any!' Schweitzer looks on this as a turning point. For a week he rehearsed the piece with care, even going so far as to try various fingerings to find the best. At the next lesson, 'I braced myself up and played the *Lied ohne Worte* just as my very soul bade me. My teacher said little, but putting his hands firmly on my shoulders, he moved me from the piano and himself played over to me a *Lied ohne Worte* that was new to me. Next I was given a piece of Beethoven's, and a few lessons later I was found worthy to begin upon Bach.'[4]

It was his good fortune, moreover, and a fact that set the course of his musical life, that Schweitzer found in Münch a teacher who 'delighted later in saying that Bach's *Well-Tempered Clavier* had been from infancy his daily bread'[5] – to whom, indeed, Bach was a god.

The organ chorales in particular seemed to Münch a wellspring. When tired of every kind of music, he told Schweitzer, he would turn to them for refreshment, above all to the *Orgelbüchlein*, which he thought supernal not only for being founded on Scripture but because he 'felt keenly how much of religious character the masterpieces of . . . music had in themselves by virtue of their beauty.' Yet depth of feeling never led Münch to sacrifice simplicity. Rather, his style was 'majestic,' Schweitzer continues, because he tried to bring out a work's great lines, calling this effort 'the plastic art of organ playing' and likening it to the craft of a sculptor whose mass of stone eventually yields harmonious form. 'All effects which could prevent the unfolding of the beautiful forms in a work were odious to him, all those sonorities which obscured it were proscribed.'[6]

Münch was a consummate artist, according to Schweitzer, and whether he had taken to heart the saying of Bach's – 'I have had to work hard; anyone who works as hard will achieve as much' – or was simply diligent by nature, he attained that rank by 'the perseverance and the indefatigable energy that are the essential conditions of all artistic achievement. More than any other instrument the organ exacts these qualities of those who come to it as slaves, before recognizing them later as masters.'[7]

It was by 'ceaseless toil' that Münch perfected his technique, by 'constant experimentation' that he devised his registrations.

> For some time he kept at his organ a piece of paper on which he noted all the combinations to try, from the simplest to the most exotic . . . . For every theme in the Bach fugues he sought tirelessly the sonorous quality which it required. He was not content, however, to seek the sonorities suitable for the portions; what he wanted most of all was harmony among the sonorities, so that the piece would produce the impression of unity. This effect never ended for him: he corrected, noted, eliminated, only to begin again. One can get some idea of this work by casting an eye on his notebooks. Often one finds five or six registrations indicated for a single piece, and each registration is the result of long reflection and many trials.[8]

That Münch's artistry and its requisite hard work roused Schweitzer to high and lifelong ideals is confirmed by the praise just quoted (from a eulogy composed in 1898, the first of Schweitzer's writings to be published) and by these words from the preface to the French version of *J. S. Bach*: 'When I undertook to write the chapter on the chorales, memories of these first and profound artistic emotions came back to me. Certain phrases came to my pen all formed, and I saw then that I was only repeating the words and imagery by which my first organ teacher had opened my understanding for the music of Bach.'[9]

The eighteen-year-old Schweitzer thus found himself amply prepared to receive not just the discipline but also the esthetic beliefs of Widor, who shared with Münch the view (by no means a consensus among nineteenth-century musicians) that Bach's art had to do with the transcendental.

> Organ playing [Widor was to tell Schweitzer] is the manifestation of a will filled with a vision of eternity. All organ instruction, both technical and artistic, has as its aim only to educate a man to this pure manifestation of the higher will. This will, expressed by the organist in the objectivity of his organ, should overwhelm the hearer. He who cannot master the great, concentrated will in the theme of a Bach fugue – so that even the thoughtless hearer cannot escape from it, but even after the second measure grasps and comprehends it whether he will or not – he who cannot command this concentrated, peaceful will imparting itself so powerfully, may be a great artist in spite of this but is not a born organist. He has mistaken his instrument; for the organ represents the *rapprochement* of the human spirit to the eternal, imperishable spirit.[10]

From the sublime to the practical, however, was a mere step, for transcendent verities were communicable only by technique that was clear. Hence it was in technique, comprehensively defined to include rhythm, tempo, phrasing, and registration as well as the purely physical skills, that Widor proposed to instruct Schweitzer.

The meeting that began their long years of collaboration and friendship has often been recounted. Armed with a letter of introduction, the youth presented himself and asked to play. 'Play what?' – 'Bach, of course.'[11] And although Widor seldom gave lessons outside of his organ class at the Conservatoire, he was sufficiently impressed to take the boy on. 'This instruction,' Schweitzer tells us, 'was for me an event of decisive importance. Widor led me . . . to a fundamental improvement of my technique, and made me strive to attain perfect plasticity in playing. At the same time there dawned on me, thanks to him, the meaning of the architectonic.'[12]

Widor brought him to view certain Bach fugues, for example, as 'late-Gothics in music' whose 'simple, boldly-flung lines' were given unity and vitality by 'the luxuriant detail'[13] – it being in such terms that one could best describe the shape of Bach's musical thought as perceived in the overall proportioning and in the balance of part with part. The implications, Schweitzer concludes, were obvious:

> Just as in Gothic architecture the great plan develops out of the simple motive, but enfolds itself in the richest detail . . . and only makes its effect when every detail is truly vital, so does the impression a Bach work makes on the hearer depend on the player communicating to him the massive outline and the details together, both equally clear and equally full of life.[14]

To achieve this vitality and clarity, it seemed to Widor that rhythm was the keystone, or more precisely the indispensable foundation. Rhythmic solidity alone conveyed that 'will' which made the structure, in both senses of the word, sound. This was so because of the very nature of the organ. Unique among instruments, it must sustain a tone indefinitely and with unchanging intensity and could therefore allow of no accent or phrasing except by means of durations. 'Losing a slight amount of time on certain notes, catching up with it on others,' Widor would say, 'that is the secret . . . . Nevertheless, while this is being accomplished the beat must be respected. The listener must have no suspicion of the means employed in drawing his attention to what you wish to emphasize. It is a very delicate matter, for the slightest exaggeration produces a detestable mannerism.'[15] Shortening a note, then, would accent the note following, only provided the underlying rhythm remained firm. Nor, according to Widor, could any but the steadiest of rhythms accord with the most telling characteristic of the organ, its grandeur.

Thus Widor taught, according also to Louis Vierne, who was in 1890–96 first Widor's pupil and then his assistant in the organ class, and in 1892–1900 his assistant as well at St Sulpice; and thus, Vierne recalls, Widor played:

> He knew how to be majestic without grandiloquence, elegant without affectation, austere without coldness, fiery while remaining absolute master of the rhythm. His playing was 'alive' without being hurried. His staccato was exact, but never too short. He attacked and raised chords with precision, but he studiously avoided detaching them quickly, a practice which degrades organ playing to a lamentable imitation of orchestra or piano. Even in rapid chords he always had 'tone', as he said to us, pressing on our shoulders when we cut them off too short. Never should a short value be curtailed.
>
> 'One ought to be able to pronounce a syllable on each short note,' he would say to correct our fault of 'swallowing' them. He played the pedal marvellously without ever looking at his feet; nor did he look at them when activating the pedal pistons . . . . Motionless in the centre of the bench, his body leaning slightly forward, he drew and withdrew stops with mathematically precise gestures occasioning the minimum loss of time.[16]

With him it was a cardinal precept, Vierne continues, that economy of movement contributed as much to accuracy as to firm rhythm:

> To correct the imperfections of our technique he began by showing us the proper position of the body at the keyboard, forbidding us not only ridiculous gestures, fruitless as well as unesthetic, but also all useless motions, no matter how slight.
>
> 'All unjustified movement is harmful, because it is a loss of time and of strength. Before deciding that a movement is inevitable you must have tried out its utility during the period of slow practice. That period must be very long. If you have the courage and the conscience to make yourself do it, it will be considerable time gained, and then you will play every virtuoso piece in its exact tempo without difficulty.'[17]

Hence that fingering or pedalling was best which required least movement.

Then too, he returned constantly to the question of tempo. 'Bach used two principal tempos,' Vierne recalls him saying, 'one not very fast, corresponding to our *andante*; one rather slow, which was the present-day *adagio*. *Alla breve* was less quick than our *allegro*, call it *allegro molto moderato*. *Vivace* did not mean "quickly" as it does today, but "in a lively manner." *Prestissimo* was our *presto* and *adagissimo* doubled the time values of the *adagio*.'[18] He would add that the instruments for which Bach wrote did not speak with the facility of the modern organ, their mechanism not allowing great speed, and that their characteristics must guide one's understanding of Bach's thought. Besides,

> polyphony does not admit of rapid execution, which only confuses it, and leaves it a breathless caricature of its real self. Except for the Fugues in D Major, D Minor, C Major and G Major, which can be played at a brisk rate, I think that all require moderate and even somewhat slow tempos. The great Fugues in G Minor, A Minor, B Minor, E Minor, when played fast, become stupidly mechanical; likewise the first and last movements of the sonatas and concertos.[19]

With the six sonatas in particular, which he considered sublime music, Widor taught the art of phrasing. As another pupil recalls, he

> always reminded the student that it was necessary to phrase more on the organ than on the piano, and much more decidedly, and this in the interest of clarity, rhythm and accent. From the foregoing ... the following general rules or principles were given to each student: ... In *allegro* or *moderato* tempos, repeated notes in the same voice should be played demi-staccato, the late note in the group being phrased to the following note .... A dotted note, when repeated, loses the value of the dot .... Widor was a great believer in the usefulness of trio playing, and one of the first works I studied with him was Bach's Trio-Sonata in E-flat .... All the other trio-sonatas in the set were handed out to other members of the class .... Widor always phrased the first section of each sonata movement himself, marking it in the pupil's copy, the pupil being required to complete the phrasing from the model given.[20]

Vierne recalls not only the importance Widor gave to phrasing but the master's dismay when phrasing was clumsily done: 'Alas!' he would cry. 'Organists never listen to themselves .... To hear some organists you would think their instrument was exempt from the obligation of making its music intelligible.' The other instruments and the voice brought to their interpretations a series of indispensable devices for translating the composer's intent: articulating, punctuating, breathing, phrasing, shading.

> Should the organ content itself with an insufferable rumble without any artistic significance? But why? Music is a special language, I admit, but it has its requirements of expression just like a spoken language. On the organ repeated notes must be articulated very precisely. If the time values are short, or if the tempo is quick or moderately so, cut short the first note by half its value. If the values are long or the movement slower, cut off a quarter or an eighth. With few exceptions it is reasonable in slow tempos to adopt the smallest time value of the particular piece of music as the fraction to cut from the first of two repeated notes for clear articulation .... For the devices of punctuation and respiration one may proceed by analogy with the bowed or wind instruments, always remembering, however,

the fact that the organ can practise these devices only by mechanical means, and that therefore one should punctuate with moderation, breathe less often, phrase more broadly.[21]

To phrase according to a work's *grandes lignes* would conduce to clarity, given the resonance of the great churches, evoking as well 'the majesty and serenity of the organ.'[22] At the same time, these qualities were best evoked by the player who aimed at simplicity, and Schweitzer merely echoes Widor in contending that 'sheer "personality" playing' would bring to the organ feelings not appropriate there – 'natural human emotion, but not the wonderfully luminous, objective emotion of the last great preludes and fugues of Bach.'[23]

All in all, Widor would say, 'It is a question of discernment. When one possesses a rational organ technique one quickly comes to recognize the possibilities and the incompatibilities. There develops in us a new instinct which makes us reject what is unsuitable and adopt what is in the true style . . . . Leave nothing to chance . . . . Submit everything to the test of reason and, once accepted, express it with a will.'[24]

Nowhere, he felt, was discernment more to be desired than in the art of registration, whose pitfalls were myriad. 'I beg of you, no magic lantern,' Vierne remembers him saying to those who tried to use nineteenth-century timbres for eighteenth-century music. Thus in Bach he 'forbade the use of reeds in preludes and fugues except in the D Minor Toccata and the E Minor Prelude . . . and to justify his position said: "In the orchestra would you double four-part polyphony with trumpets and trombones?" ' As a rule, he gave the class 'rather summary indications, limiting himself to the families of stops in the sonorous plan, rather than entering into details on the timbre of each individual stop. The use of foundations, mixtures, reeds, as justified by the character of the music, the incompatibility of certain combinations of stops, the number of stops to use, the proportion of volume of the different timbres – these were the things he indicated. Like his teacher, Lemmens, he had a horror of frequent changing of stops.'[25] In a word, the simpler the registration the closer to Bach.[26]

Hence Widor recommended a single, eight-foot stop for each voice in the sonatas, suggesting that since Bach had probably written them in the first place for the pedal harpsichord, they should be treated as chamber music and registered as though played by, say, a flute, viola, and cello.[27] He further considered the sonatas, as Schweitzer puts it, 'the *Gradus ad Parnassum* for every organist. Whoever has studied them thoroughly will find scarcely a single difficulty in the old or even in modern organ music that he has not met with there and learned how to overcome . . . since in this complicated trio-playing the slightest unevenness in touch is heard with appalling clearness.'[28] And Widor considered that touch best which cleanly and precisely exchanged one note for the next, without overlap or break, for only against this background of exactitude in legato could phrasings, breaths, and articulations stand out in high relief and only thus could accents be 'placed.' One should depress the key 'with quickness and precision, but without stiffness,' he would say. 'Legato results from the instantaneous carrying over of pressure from one finger to another.'[29]

Like most of Widor's pupils, Schweitzer benefited from the master's wide culture and encyclopedic knowledge of history and art. 'On this background,' a pupil writes, Widor 'drew richly during the lesson hour, stimulating and inspiring his students by personal example and apt allusion, story or incident.'[30] Vierne likewise confirms 'that Widor, in order to make his necessarily complex instruction more intelligible, frequently used comparisons with painting, architecture . . . to make concrete in our minds the forms that we should know,'[31] declining as well to allow that 'the organist should be the only artist exempt from the necessity of knowing the entire literature of his instrument'[32] – or, for that matter, of music at large.

> Once a month . . . he initiated us into . . . Philipp Emanuel Bach, Haydn, Mozart and Beethoven (upon whom he dwelt at some length), Schubert, Mendelssohn, Schumann, down to the modern symphonists . . . . One day the *maître* exclaimed: 'What! you have played the Beethoven sonatas and never had the curiosity to wonder how they were put together? Why, that is the mentality of a parrot, not of an artist.'[33]

As the years passed and Schweitzer returned time and again to Paris, now for a week, now a month, now (as in 1898–99) six months, all the while completing his undergraduate work at Strasbourg University, he found his teacher-pupil relationship with Widor deepening into friendship – and on one occasion even being reversed. It happened that Widor's lifelong study of the Bach organ chorales was based on an edition that omitted the texts, and when one afternoon the master confessed to puzzlement at certain abrupt changes of mood and plan, Schweitzer enlightened him by supplying the poems from memory and translating them into French.

> The mysteries [Widor recalls], were all solved. During the next few afternoons we played through the whole of the chorale preludes [and] I made the acquaintance of a Bach of whose existence I had previously had only the dimmest suspicion. In a flash it became clear to me that the cantor of St Thomas's was much more than an incomparable contrapuntist to whom I had formerly looked up as one gazes up at a colossal statue, and that his work exhibits an unparalleled desire and capacity for expressing poetic ideas and for bringing word and tone into unity.[34]

Schweitzer's own acquaintance with Bach continued to grow in those years, thanks not only to Widor's instruction and to lessons in musical theory from Gustav Jacobsthal, a master of counterpoint and an authority on the eighteenth century, but to having also been engaged by Ernest Münch, brother of the Mulhouse organ teacher, to provide organ accompaniment for the Bach concerts given by Münch's choir at St William Church in Strasbourg. Schweitzer recalls St William's 'as one of the most important nurseries of the Bach cult which was coming into existence at the end of last century'; Münch he describes as 'one of the first who abandoned the modernized rendering of the cantatas and the Passion music which at the end of the nineteenth century was almost universal,' and who strove for 'really artistic performances with his small choir accompanied by the famous Strasbourg orchestra. Many an evening did we sit over the scores . . . and discuss the right method of rendering them.'[35]

Many an evening, too, Schweitzer spent at the opera, for with his

> veneration for Bach went the same feeling for Richard Wagner. When I was a schoolboy at . . . the age of sixteen, I was allowed for the first time to go to the theatre, and I heard there Wagner's *Tannhäuser*. This music overpowered me to such an extent that it was days before I was capable of giving proper attention to the lessons in school. In Strasbourg, where the operatic performances . . . were of outstanding excellence, I had the opportunity of becoming thoroughly familiar with the whole of Wagner's works, except, of course, *Parsifal*, which at that time could only be performed at Bayreuth. It was a great experience for me to be present in Bayreuth in 1896, at the memorable first repetition of the Tetralogy since the original performances in 1876. Parisian friends had given me the tickets. To balance the cost of the journey I had to content myself with one meal a day.[36]

Widor had in fact attended those original performances of twenty years before and been similarly taken with Wagner's music. Nor had he forgotten what it was like to be a student in an expensive foreign capital. Knowing that Schweitzer sometimes lacked money for proper meals, Widor would take him to the Restaurant Foyot near the Luxembourg, where excellent food and congenial surroundings drew a clientele of senators, painters, writers, and musicians, and where the master was an *habitué*. Here at his accustomed table, Widor would present his young friend to the luminaries of politics and the arts, and here, no less than at the organs of St Sulpice and Notre Dame, did Schweitzer learn how it came to be that Widor held to essentially classic principles in an age dominated by the subjective.

Notes and References

1. *Out of My Life and Thought*, p. 13.
2. Ibid., pp. 13–14.
3. *Souvenirs de mon enfance*, p. 54.
4. *Memoirs of Childhood and Youth*, pp. 40–41.
5. Joy, p. 10.
6. Ibid., p. 12.
7. Ibid., p. 11.
8. Ibid., pp. 11–12.
9. *Jean-Sébastien Bach, le musicien-poète*, p. v. Schweitzer studied with Münch from the autumn of 1885 to August 1893.

10. Joy, pp. 168–69.
11. *J. S. Bach*, vol. I., p. viii.
12. *Out of My Life and Thought*, p. 15.
13. *J. S. Bach*, vol. I., p. 273.
14. Ibid., p. 363.
15. Vierne, November 1938, p. 11.
16. December 1938, p. 6.
17. November 1938, p. 11.
18. Ibid.
19. Ibid.
20. Henderson, p. 16.
21. Vierne, November 1938, p. 11.
22. Ibid.
23. Joy, p. 168.
24. Vierne, December 1938, p. 6.
25. Ibid.
26. Joy, p. 170.
27. Henderson, p. 16.
28. *J. S. Bach*, vol. I., p. 279.
29. Vierne, November 1938, p. 11.
30. Henderson, p. 16.
31. December 1938, p. 6.
32. November 1938, p. 10.
33. Ibid.
34. *J. S. Bach*, vol. I., p. viii. Widor apparently knew too little German to decipher the texts in question, which were in any case barely known in Germany, let alone in France, the old chorale having long since been supplanted. The terms 'chorale' and 'chorale prelude' are often used interchangeably, one may add, but not every chorale was a prelude properly so called – meant to be played, that is, as introduction to a congregational hymn.
35. *Out of My Life and Thought*, pp. 22–23.
36. Ibid., p. 23.

2 Biographer

Vast in its sweep of ideas, events, and personalities, the nineteenth century can hardly be defined by single terms or phrases; hence to sum up as 'romantic' its complexities of trend and countertrend is not to unravel but to confuse. As noted above, the very word breeds contradictions, as we organists in particular should long ago have learned. It has been variously used to mean the formal and formless, the real and unreal, the picturesque and bombastic, the frivolous and noteworthy, the conservative and revolutionary, and much else besides, and to many persons it still resounds with overtones of the illogical and the sentimental.

The fact is that the century was rich in men of genius, hence in thought and invention on every side, and to aid in comprehending this richness our minds naturally try to assign form. But the task of definition is made difficult by our tendency to categorize in black and white. We err, for instance, in considering the classical as centred in structure to the exclusion of feeling, and the romantic as feeling only, formless and uncontrolled. They are, rather, polarities – two sides of the human coin, so to speak, at once antithetical and complementary. And if 'romantic' is to be at all useful, we must ignore familiar connotations of the impractical, quixotic, sensuous, vague, and undisciplined, remembering as well that there exists not one species of romanticism but several, and not merely in other centuries than the nineteenth but within the nineteenth century itself.

More precisely, it is the period 1789–1914 that contains the growth and flourishing with which we have to do (together with such offshoots as impressionism and realism) and whose changing musical styles – not to mention political, scientific, and industrial upheaval – provided the setting in which an archaic tradition of playing Bach managed to survive. The first decades of the period were anything but kind to the organ, as Schweitzer's research confirmed when at Widor's urging he began to write 'a little essay upon the chorale preludes' for the Conservatoire students.[1] By the 1790s, what some have called the organ's golden age was just a memory and far from universally revered. The Couperins, Clérambault, Buxtehude, and Bach among the musicians and the Silbermanns and Clicquots among the builders were indeed still respected for their mastery, but with that disinterested respect given a lovely antique whose design is outdated and useless. Hence Schweitzer found that the overt destructiveness of the French Revolution, which had here and there turned churches into temples of reason and melted down organ pipes for scrap metal, accompanied a destructiveness more subtle. 'In the first place,' he was to conclude, 'we must take into consideration the artistic ideal of the men of that epoch; they were too simple to rank the art of the previous generation as highly as that of their own. They were convinced that music was always advancing, and as their own art was later than the old art, it must necessarily come nearer to the ideal . . . . People were weary of fugues and of pieces constructed of obbligato parts, and longed for a music that should be spontaneous feeling and nothing else.'[2] Accordingly, there had come to the fore the *gallant* style in France and its cousin the *empfindsamer* style in northern Germany in both of which intricacy of counterpoint was exchanged for elegance, profundity of expression for fervour.

Week after week in the library of Strasbourg University, applying to musical history the scholarly techniques he knew from philosophy and had used so skillfully in a recent dissertation on Kant, Schweitzer penetrated ever more deeply into the question of Bach's fate at the hands of posterity. He concluded that the

> concept of Nature which, in the epoch of growing rationalism, transformed philosophy and poetry, asserted itself also in music. Answering as they did to the needs of the epoch, the emotional compositions of the day, with their 'tender and pathetic expression,' insignificant as they were in themselves, appealed to thoughtful artists as being nearer to truth than the music of the epoch of rigid rule. That Bach's art in its own way was also true to nature, and that in his strict polyphony a volcanic emotion and thought were embedded, like substances petrified in lava – this the men of the expiring eighteenth century could not see.[3]

True, Bach's art was not neglected entirely. On the contrary, some of his works indeed appeared in print and others, including some of the cantatas, were copied out and performed. Yet not even Carl Philipp Emanuel and Wilhelm Friedemann, superb musicians though they were, saw in their father a greater genius than that of contrapuntist and virtuoso (not surprising, then, the superficiality of the organ works by Emanuel and his laughing boast of not having played upon a pedal in years[4]). And it did not help to promote good organ playing that the Church lost its central place in matters cultural and social, with an attendant decline in organists' prestige and salaries, or that the patrons of music were no longer the upper classes but the middle.[5]

In sum, by the shift from salon to concert hall, the skepticism of the time, the growing democratic sense, the new interest in sound itself as a conveyor of musical meaning, the concomitant perfecting of instruments, the huge popularity of Italian opera, the rise of the virtuoso performer – by all of this the former ways were almost wholly supplanted. Bach could not have seemed more old-fashioned, or the tones of an organ more remote from human passion.

To supply this perceived lack of sentiment, organists fell to entertaining congregations with such imitative effects as bird calls and thunderstorms and to using Napoleon's victories as a timely subject on which to improvise. An old tradition lent respectability to the abuse, for not even such eighteenth-century masters as Daquin and Balbastre had been above portraying the Last Judgement, earthquakes, and the roar of cannon. Indeed, Daquin had once 'evoked such excitement in the hearts of the audience that everyone turned pale.'[6] Thus his descendants merely built on precedent when they accompanied the most sublime moments of the Eucharistic service with gavottes, airs, and rigadoons. 'Organists are weak,' lamented the scholar Fétis in 1830, 'and what they produce is simply beneath criticism.'[7]

As in France, so in Germany. A letter written in that same year by the young Mendelssohn gives this humorous but sobering account of a visit to the organ at Weimar Cathedral:

> The organist offered me the choice of hearing something scholarly, or something for 'people' (because he said that for people one had to compose only easy and bad music), so I asked for something scholarly. But it was not much to be proud of; he modulated around enough to make one giddy, but nothing unusual came of it; he made a number of entries, but no fugue was forthcoming. When my turn came to play to him, I started with the D Minor toccata of Sebastian and remarked that this was at the same time scholarly and something for 'people' too, at least for some of them; but mind, hardly had I begun to play when the superintendent dispatched his valet upstairs with the message that this playing had to be stopped right away because it was a weekday and he could not study with that much noise going on . . . . Here, in Munich, the musicians behave exactly like that organist; they believe that good music may be considered a heaven-sent gift, but just *in abstracte*, and as soon as they sit down to play they produce the stupidest, silliest stuff imaginable.[8]

Yet again, in Widor's words, organists – whose forebears had been the most rigorously trained of all musical workmen – degenerated by the 1830s into 'musicians without brains, performers without fingers.'[9] Little wonder that the essayist Montalembert spurned them in 1839 as 'a special class of thieves. It is criminal to affront intelligent ears with this so-called religious music, a music which instills in the listener any sentiment you wish *except* that of religious feeling and employs in this profanity the king of instruments.'[10] Nor was there much to boast of in the activities of organ builders.

Thus in 1844 F. K. Griepenkerl, in his foreword to the first volume of the Peters edition of Bach's organ works, remarked that the 'pay of organists since 1750 has not been increased, but diminished. On the other hand the necessities of life have been doubled in price and no great artist becomes a candidate for such a place, except from inclination or an enthusiastic love of art . . . . Under such circumstances it is indeed a wonder that even isolated rare traces of the old sublime organ-art have maintained themselves.'

All in all, taking as he did a broad view, Schweitzer was to observe that a 'great deal in the history of mankind is to be explained in the end only by the inexplicable – that a generation has lost its comprehension of something.'[11] Thus it seems in retrospect no more reasonable that organ art should have so decayed in 1750–1840 and the sublimity of Bach been forsaken, than that in our own day the genius of Franck or Cavaillé-Coll should have been held in contempt by otherwise perceptive musicians to whom 'romanticism' was a word full of scorn. No century has a monopoly on misjudgement.

Notice, then, a sad parallel. Until about two decades ago, at the height of yet another neoclassic surge, whole schools of organists took as axiomatic several flawed ideas: that eighteenth-century music had reached a degree of perfection compared to which later music was necessarily inferior; that keyboard technique of the eighteenth century ought to be the model for players of the twentieth; that unequal temperaments were inherently expressive; that none but tracker action could allow sensitivity in phrasing; and that nineteenth- and twentieth-century works sounded best when played on eighteenth-century organs. I have shown elsewhere how these mistaken views, despite being rooted in a healthy respect for excellence, came to crowd out reason and restraint and in so doing undermined once again standards of technique among organists and of craftsmanship among builders.[12] For now, we may just recall that the ebb and flow of artistic trends – those great tides spanning decades and centuries – have to do with the need of artists to level the old ground, as Jacques Barzun puts it, before making a fresh start on a new construction, and that the 'particular relation of nineteenth-century romanticism to twentieth-century anti-romanticism corresponds to a deeper need than that of the children to disown their fathers . . ., for we cannot attack the nineteenth century as the breaker of tradition when we know that before it, in the ninth, twelfth, and fourteenth centuries, previous epochs of expansion and exploration followed upon attempts at fixed systems.'[13] The classic-romantic systole and diastole are apparently permanent in Western man.

For Schweitzer, in any event, the long hours of pondering over Bach, together with other philosophic studies and a cultivated historical sense, led to at least two consequences, one practical and immediate, the other long-term and metaphysical. First, the 'little essay' on the organ chorales lengthened to a book, for after only a few weeks of preliminary studies, Widor recalls,

he wrote to me that it was necessary to include the cantatas and Passions in his essay, since the vocal works explained the chorale works, and *vice versa* . . . . The remarks upon the chorale and the church service in Bach's time grew into an epitome of the history of Protestant church music; the observations upon the nature of Bach's musical expression became a chapter upon 'Bach's tone-speech'; a short literary portrait of the composer was seen to be desirable; then there came chapters on the practical performance of Bach's works.[14]

Second, the collapse of standards among Bach's successors doubtless appeared to Schweitzer as yet more evidence to support his belief that the very notion of progress was suspect – that civilization itself might actually be regressing. This belief was to pervade his thought ever afterward, bringing him to a philosophy of civilization that took as starting point an idea he labelled *Wir epigonen* and that culminated in the all-embracing principle of Reverence for Life.[15]

This culmination lay in the future, however, when in 1903–1904, while lecturing and preaching in Strasbourg, Schweitzer devoted all of his spare moments to Bach. As the young scholar was to recall,

> It was, in truth, a very rash undertaking on my part. Although I had, thanks to extensive reading, some knowledge of musical history and theory, I had not studied music as one studies for a profession. However, my design was not to produce new historical material about Bach and his time. As a musician I wanted to talk to other musicians about Bach's music. The main subject of my work, therefore, should be, so I resolved, what in most books hitherto had been much too slightly treated, namely an explanation of the real nature of Bach's music, and a discussion of the correct method of rendering it. My work accordingly sets forth what is biographical and historical as introductory rather than as the main subject.[16]

For this reason, and despite conceiving his task so comprehensively that the book spans 455 pages in the original French, 844 in the German edition, and 926 in the English – the German being an almost entirely new book and the English being not merely a translation of the German but still another revision – he mentions only in passing how during the very years of Bach's neglect, and amid that tumult of change and mediocrity which we have seen, the essence of Bach's organ style remained intact in the work of a few extraordinary men. Among them were Johann Christian Leberecht Kittel, Johann Christian Heinrich Rinck, Adolph Friedrich Hesse, and Jacques-Nicolas Lemmens. But though Schweitzer took their influence for granted, we shall learn something of him, and something of Bach, by examining their lives more closely.

The first of these revered Bach with a fervour bordering on worship. Kittel was eighteen at Bach's death, in 1750, and had been a pupil residing in the master's house, after the custom of the day, since about 1748. Far from decreasing in the course of his long career, the veneration Kittel showed for Bach's memory grew stronger, as is manifest in a famous passage from the lexicographer Gerber:

He also continued, with undiminished keenness of mind and as the only living pillar of the old Bachian school, to educate many a good organist. As a special form of reward and punishment for his pupils he used an oil painting of Joh. Sebast. Bach – a fine likeness – which he had recently acquired and hung over his clavier. If the pupil showed industry worthy of this Father of Harmony, the curtain covering it was drawn aside. For the unworthy, on the other hand, Bach's countenance remained hidden.[17]

Kittel directed that after his death the beloved painting be enshrined at the organ in his church.[18]

Without ignoring what was of interest in contemporary trends, Kittel's teaching likewise reflected the image of Bach, as we are told in an account based on the testimony of a nephew:

First the fundamentals were clarified – the pupil had to learn to read notes, recognize the various rest values, then go through the teaching of intervals to a study of the different keys. Then Kittel would approach the study of an instrument, usually the clavichord or spinet, which one usually used for the elementary instruction of young people. At this point, the pupil was introduced to the literature. First various minuets were studied and played, then the sonatas of Carl Philipp Emanuel Bach. After six months, Kittel introduced his students to figured bass, still the foundation and primary factor of musical practice at that time. He then went into the study of harmony, and in logical sequence took up the consideration of four-part chorale settings .... The melody was placed in different voices, and was imitated and treated in double counterpoint with the other voices. As a very perceptive teacher, Kittel recognized that boredom and a certain dullness might overtake the pupil at about this stage in his development. Consequently, Kittel himself would play for a pupil, often performing the Fantasies of Johann Sebastian or Carl Philipp Emanuel Bach. The increased enthusiasm engendered in the pupil upon hearing the 'piece as it should sound,' gave him the incentive to approach a long, arduous, and rewarding study of Bach's *Das wohltemperierte Klavier*. With this, the specific study of the clavier literature came to an end, and master and pupil went on to a consideration of the organ and its literature, with particular emphasis on the works of Bach and Johann Ludwig Krebs. As the finale and summation of his studies, the pupil was tutored in fugal composition.[19]

Kittel himself was to state that 'the method which I have tried to employ in my own instruction is based entirely on Bach's principles, and . . . I have tested its excellence in more than fifty years of teaching.'[20]

Indeed, the elements taught and their method of bestowal alike recall Bach, whose pupils, as his sons have informed us, would first be given a rigorous grounding of several months in his particular way of so depressing the keys as to produce a 'clear and clean' touch, and then be plunged at once into the midst of difficulties in thorough bass and chorales. Bach would begin by setting the basses himself, making the pupil invent only the alto and tenor, then lead the pupil into devising the basses as well. Harmony once mastered, the pupil began to study fugue. Bach, too, when he found his pupils losing heart, 'was so obliging as to write little connected pieces, in which those exercises were combined together' or would play whole pieces, saying 'so it must sound.'[21] The story is well known of one such pupil's delight when the master would demonstrate at greater length – when Bach, on pretext of being out of the mood to teach, would sit down at one of his excellent instruments and turn hours into minutes.[22]

Still another kind of demonstration sometimes occurred at rehearsals of choir or orchestra and was to remain vivid in Kittel's memory sixty years later:

> One of his most capable pupils [presumed to be Kittel himself] always had to accompany on the harpsichord. It will easily be guessed that no one dared to put forward a meager thorough-bass accompaniment. Nevertheless, one had always to be prepared to have Bach's hands and fingers intervene among the hands and fingers of the player, and, without getting in the way of the latter, furnish the accompaniment with masses of harmonies which made an even greater impression than the unsuspected close proximity of the teacher.[23]

It is noteworthy, one may add, that Kittel was with Bach soon after that period of Bach's reawakened interest in the organ which saw not only the revising of earlier works but also the fruition of the Eighteen Chorales. Still, Kittel is no exception to Schweitzer's judgement that it is impossible to find among Bach's pupils

> a single one who became a great composer; not even Friedemann, not even Emanuel. They were only talented men. Even Krebs, of whom Bach himself was the most proud, did not rise in his compositions above the level of honest mediocrity. They became orchestra leaders, cantors, or remarkable organists; but at bottom they owed their prestige and their distinction to the fact that they were former pupils of Bach.[24]

Though Kittel was not wholly opposed to the new styles, apparently even permitting them a place in church, he remained linked to Bach's art in his preference for works based on hymn-tunes, in his advocacy of comprehensive pedal technique, in his cautions against playing too fast, and, judging by the markings of his scores, in his use of a fundamentally legato touch.

Indeed, an analysis of the articulation marks in those scores, made by John Philip Anthony, goes to confirm that Kittel's legato increased proportionately with strictness of style. Works of contrapuntal intricacy, having considerable stepwise melodic motion, would for the sake of clarity be played more strictly legato than works freer in form or more open in texture.[25]

That Bach had esteemed the youth warmly – perhaps as warmly as the master esteemed Krebs, with whom Kittel was on friendly terms for many years – is suggested by Kittel's receipt of some manuscripts upon the distribution of Bach's estate. What is certain is that Kittel remained in Leipzig only a few months after Bach died, for in 1751 the young man became organist at St Boniface in Langensalza and began to teach in a school for girls. Hardly half a dozen years pass before we note in Kittel's behaviour shades of

Bach yet again: many disputes arise with town councils and rectors, Kittel having lost his post, seemingly out of dedication to art. We learn from his successor that his love of composition led him to write music during school hours and so come into collision with his superiors.[26] Meantime he had begun to attract pupils from far and wide, one of the first being his nine-year-old nephew, Johann Wilhelm Hässler, who as a keyboard virtuoso was to astonish the world.

Kittel was not long in finding work as organist at the Barfüsserkirche, where he remained until 1762, the year he assumed the post of organist at the Predigerkirche in his natal town of Erfurt. There he stayed until his death, in 1809.

He had embarked near the turn of the century on a concert tour that took him to Göttingen, Hannover, Altona, and Hamburg, giving him the chance to hear and judge the local church music – and to be appalled by what he found: gone almost entirely were the old chorale and the variations, cantatas, and preludes based thereon. Not surprisingly, Kittel received a mixed reception in Hamburg, where he spent several months and where the musical public had long been captivated by Carl Philipp Emanuel and the new elegance. Thus, although pupils and friends thought Kittel a consummate artist, others of more current taste referred to him as 'old, peculiar, conceited, and empty.'[27] Doubtless in reaction to what he saw as the decadence around him, Kittel for his part grew ever more adamant in believing the old-fashioned disciplines necessarily paramount, and in 1801 on his return to Erfurt he accordingly set to work editing and publishing his scores and methods, above all the volumes of *Der angehende praktische Organist*, his artistic testament.

His life may be summed up, then, in these words by the dean of Bach biographers, Philipp Spitta:

> Kittel was an excellent organ player and composer, and a favourite teacher; he taught a great number of the best organists of Thuringia, and, with pious reverence for his own great teacher, did his utmost to transmit the traditions of Bach's art and style.[28]

Although fame was won by such of Kittel's pupils as Karl Gottlieb Umbreit and Michael Gotthardt Fischer, it is in the work of Johann Christian Heinrich Rinck, who left us both a method and an autobiography, that Bach's influence can most easily be traced.

Interestingly enough, the three years of Rinck's studies in Erfurt with Kittel (1786–89) do not represent the boy's first exposure to the style of Bach. Already in 1784 at the age of fifteen Rinck had begun to study with a former pupil of Johann Peter Kellner, Bach's friend and disciple. Significantly, Rinck's first assigned piece on the organ was one of Kellner's that began with a pedal solo.

Yet Rinck soon came into contact with more recent trends too, for another of his early teachers, Kirchner by name, initiated him into the clavier works of Boccherini, Haydn, and Carl Philipp Emanuel. Rinck was to remember Kirchner as a 'conscientious and diligent teacher, a man of great knowledge, experience and insight into art. He had composed much beautiful church music, not in a wholly conservative style,'[29] but it was under his guidance that Rinck made first attempts at composing fugues and chorales.

The setting out of chorales formed the cornerstone of Rinck's work with Kittel. During their years together Rinck devised chorales in two, three, and four parts, thus progressively mastering the technique of figured bass. He was required, for example, 'to learn to invent several basses for a given chorale melody,' after which the 'chorale melody was itself used as the bass, a chorale melody that I first had to work out note for note, then in eighths, sixteenths, and . . . frequently also in various rhythms. [Kittel] proceeded in the same way with three- and four-part counterpoint. I had then to write variations on many chorales, perhaps twenty to thirty times in different ways.' Kittel would admonish him, not without humour, that 'whoever fails to master four-part writing and learn to work out a theme will . . . find his work buried with him, or even earlier!'[30]

Nor did Rinck neglect to master the keyboard, for he became an accomplished organist and harpsichordist and performed at least once as solo pianist in a concerto. Quiet in deportment and dignified in content, his organ playing was notable as well for its clarity – all of this according to the Leipzig *Musikalische Zeitung*, whose reviewers in 1817–19 deemed him 'the first among those who nowadays represent the school of Bach . . . . [Rinck] belongs among the most excellent of contemporary organ players, particularly in fugal pieces, chorale variations and similar works.'[31]

Famous as executant, Rinck attracted many pupils. His biographer remarks that he

> taught harmony, counterpoint, and composition (probably mainly church music), organ, and piano. He seems to have had, like Kittel, a definite gift for teaching. Many dedications of works and a great number of letters to their former master testify to the grateful attachment of his students. Concerning the method of his teaching there was no document to be found. But the organization of his manual on harmony and counterpoint, left unfinished and in manuscript, suggests that he followed Kittel's ideas absolutely.[32]

It bespeaks his regard for his master that Rinck collected virtually all of the prints and many manuscripts of Kittel's music, preserving even simple exercises in figured bass,[33] and it bespeaks his agreement with Kittel's views that Rinck's *Practische Orgelschule* begins with exercises designed to foster precise contrapuntal playing and a comprehensive pedal technique and with an admonition to organists to respect the character of the instrument by playing always in moderate tempo.

Though Rinck was a man of his time, as witness his chamber works and 'characteristic pieces,' the old traditions continued to draw his respect. The library he was to leave behind held quantities of his own and others' works that are all too typical of the day; but in contrast its collection of music for organ consists almost entirely of works by masters from the first half of the eighteenth century.[34] He was acquainted, moreover, with the theoretical works of Marpurg and Kirnberger, the one an admirer and the other a pupil of Bach, and seemed to accept as inevitable the inferiority of later generations: 'Bach is a Colossus,' Widor tells us Rinck once said; 'one can hope to follow him in his domain only at a distance, for he has exhausted all resources, and is inimitable.'[35]

It remains to be noticed that Rinck spent fifteen years as an organist in Giessen, where his post demanded much, paid little, and offered him the poorest of instruments. But he 'studied nights, and played on an inadequate clavichord as well as possible the clavier and organ works of C. P. E. Bach, Mozart, Haydn, and Clementi . . . and composed as time allowed.'[36] In 1805 he moved to Darmstadt, where he was by turns municipal organist, cantor and music teacher in the ducal school, organist of the Schlosskirche, and musician to the court. Here he remained, occasionally journeying to meet fellow musicians and to hear and give concerts. He died in 1846.

Two years earlier, Rinck's pupil Adolph Friedrich Hesse had astonished musical Paris by his technique on the pedals, and Bach had long since returned to public notice. It was now no longer a question of Bach's style making its way intact through a background of changes, but of its absorption and transformation by the romanticists.

Notes and References

1. The 'little essay' was first meant to be a lecture. In 1959 Schweitzer inscribed a copy of *Jean-Sébastien Bach, le musicien-poète* for the organist Jean Bouvard as follows:

   > I owe it to my dear master Widor that I undertook to write about Bach. It was originally to be a lecture on Bach for his students at the Conservatoire. It was he, when I gave him an account of my labours in the research for this lecture, who decided that it ought to become a book.
   >
   > Je dois à mon cher maître Widor que j'aie entrepris d'écrire sur Bach. Cela devait d'abord être une conférence sur Bach pour ses élèves du Conservatoire. C'est lui, quand je lui ai rendu compte de mes travaux pour la documentation de cette conférence, qui a décidé que cela devait devenir un livre.

   Hereinafter, with regard to previously unpublished material, the original German or French will accompany each translation of Schweitzer's words.
2. *J. S. Bach*, vol. I., pp. 227–28.
3. Ibid., p. 228.
4. Ibid., pp. 220–21.

5. See Donald Jay Grout (1980), *A History of Western Music*, 3rd ed., New York: Norton, pp. 448–571; Homer Ulrich and Paul A. Pisk (1963), *A History of Music and Musical Style*, New York: Harcourt, Brace and World, pp. 312–464; and Charles Rosen (1971), *The Classical Style: Haydn, Mozart, Beethoven*, New York: Viking, passim.
6. Douglass (1969), p. 71.
7. Piccand, p. 89.
8. *Letters*, pp. 81–82.
9. Widor, p. 5.
10. Piccand, p. 89.
11. Joy, p. 220.
12. *Marcel Dupré: The Work of a Master Organist*, pp. 88, 148–52, and passim.
13. *Classic, Romantic and Modern*, pp. 135–37. That man seems to delight in tearing down, and to be driven to it by an inner need distinct from artistic or creative exigencies, has been argued interestingly by many writers. See, for example, C. S. Lewis (1967), 'De Futilitate' and 'The Funeral of a Great Myth' in *Christian Reflections*, Walter Hooper, ed., Grand Rapids, Michigan: Eerdmans, pp. 57–71, 82–93.
14. *J. S. Bach*, vol. I., p. ix.
15. Like the book on Bach, *Wir epigonen* sprang from a conversation that took place in 1899. As Schweitzer recalls in *Out of My Life and Thought* (pp. 172–74), his first incitement to examine the questions that led to his *Philosophy of Civilization* came in the summer of that year in Berlin at the house of the Ernst Curtius family. 'Hermann Grimm and others were conversing there one evening about a sitting of the academy from which they had just come, when suddenly one of them – I forget which it was – came out with: "Why, we are all of us just nothing but 'Epigoni'!" [the generation following those who lived in a great age; heirs of a great past] It struck home with me, like a flash of lightning, because it put into words what I myself felt. As early as my first years at the university I had begun to feel misgivings about the opinion that mankind is constantly developing in the direction of progress. My impression was that the fire of its ideals was burning low without anyone noticing it or troubling about it. On a number of occasions I had to acknowledge that public opinion did not reject with indignation inhumane ideas which were publicly disseminated, but accepted them, and that it approved of, as opportune, inhumane courses of action taken by governments and nations. Even for what was just and expedient as well there seemed to me to be only a lukewarm zeal available. From a number of signs I had to infer the growth of a peculiar intellectual and spiritual fatigue in this generation which is so proud of what it has accomplished. It seemed as if I heard its members arguing to each other that their previous hopes for the future of mankind had been pitched too high, and that it was becoming necessary to limit oneself to striving for what was attainable .... One of the clearest indications of decline for me was the fact that superstition, which had hitherto been banished from educated circles, was again thought fit for admission to society .... It seemed to be assumed everywhere not only that we had made progress in inventions and knowledge, but also that in the intellectual and ethical spheres we lived and moved at a height which we had never before reached, and from which we should never decline. My own impression was that in our mental and spiritual life we were not only below the level of past generations, but were in many respects only living on their achievements ... and that not a little of this heritage was beginning to melt away in our hands.' What

was to have been a book entitled *Wir epigonen* became instead a work on the restoration of civilization.

16. *Out of My Life and Thought*, p. 77.
17. Ernst Ludwig Gerber, *Neues historisch-biographisches Lexikon der Ton-künstler* (Leipzig, 1813), quoted in David and Mendel, pp. 425–26.
18. Ibid.
19. Fall, pp. 28–29.
20. *Der angehende praktische Organist*, pp. ii–iv.
21. Johann Nicolaus Forkel, *On Johann Sebastian Bach's Life, Genius, and Works* (1802), reprinted in David and Mendel, pp. 328–29.
22. Schweitzer, *J. S. Bach*, vol. I., pp. 216–17. The pupil was Heinrich Nicolaus Gerber, father of the lexicographer quoted above.
23. *Der angehende praktische Organist*, vol. III., p. 33, quoted in David and Mendel, p. 266.
24. Joy, p. 115.
25. Pp. 265–74.
26. Spitta, vol. III., p. 247n.
27. Fall, pp. 25–26.
28. Spitta, Vol. III., p. 247.
29. Fall, p. 16.
30. Ibid., pp. 17–18.
31. Ibid., p. 21.
32. Ibid.
33. Anthony, p. 104.
34. Fall, p. 66. Rinck's library was purchased in 1852 by Lowell Mason and later given to Yale University.
35. Pirro, p. ix.
36. Fall, p. 19.

3   Heir to a Tradition

When Charles Gounod added to one of Bach's C Major preludes a descant that generations were to love as a setting of the 'Ave Maria,' he intended to arrange music, not to devise a symbol. Yet the act betokens attitudes and practices of the nineteenth-century masters who revered Bach's art but saw it perforce in the light of new ideals. Tausig, Liszt, and Busoni, for example, stretched and coloured Bach's art as transcribers, and Wagner, Franck, and Brahms in myriad ways assimilated something of Bach's art into works of their own.

Paramount among the new ideals – overwhelming in its effects upon thought – was a conception of sound, of timbre, that was profoundly different from anything known before. 'We need only think of the transition from the symphonies, sonatas, or operas of Haydn, Mozart, and Beethoven to those of Schubert and Weber,' Alfred Einstein writes, 'in order to grasp the mighty change . . . . With the first Romantics, sound took on a new meaning. It was a stronger factor in the body of the music than it had ever been before; it won a higher value purely in and for itself.'[1] So it was that when Mendelssohn conducted the *St Matthew Passion* in 1829 he used a chorus of nearly four hundred persons and a revised orchestration, and so it was that when Czerny edited the *Well-Tempered Clavier* in 1837 he had recourse to the *crescendi* and *decrescendi* of Beethoven. For sound was no longer perceived as a mere conveyor of meaning but as inherently expressive, and to these musicians one could render Bach no greater service than that of making his music intelligible by endowing it with the sonorous qualities it lacked.

Indeed, we can today scarcely imagine the force with which timbre affected the sensibilities of contemporary listeners. Mendelssohn relates, for instance, how a stranger 'asked me whether I knew what a wind instrument was? I said yes with a good conscience, and then he said I should try to imagine 30 such instruments together, and fiddles and basses besides, or rather I couldn't imagine it, for such a thing had to be heard to be believed, it sounded as if it came straight from Heaven.'[2] Or as Widor was to exclaim: '. . . the flute in *Orpheus*, the horn in *Oberon* . . . the bourdon bells of Notre Dame . . . what influences! . . . what a marvel!'[3]

The conception of sound as inherently expressive accompanied advances in instrument-making that brought about an unprecedented range of nuance and ease of control. Flutes and oboes were given new key mechanisms, horns and trumpets new valves, and it was Berlioz – that much misunderstood genius whose art Schweitzer esteemed – who was chief among pioneers in using instruments for their particular tones and in considering timbre to be constituent rather than extrinsic. As for the organ, the instrument of the 1840s was viewed as rivalling the Beethoven-Berlioz orchestra itself in varieties of tonal colour and gradations of loud and soft. For thanks to Cavaillé-Coll and other innovators, the organist no longer needed an assistant to change sonorities; a group of pedals let one person manage everything. Nor did one now need Herculean fingers to play *fortissimo* or quickly: the pneumatic lever made the keys no heavier to press than those of a grand piano.

Accordingly, as Schweitzer tells us,

> People still knew what was the eighteenth-century tradition in playing. But they rejected this correct method of rendering the organ works of Bach as too simple and too plain, and believed they were acting in his spirit when they employed in the most generous measure possible the constant changes in volume and character of sound which could be produced on the modern organ . . . . France was an exception. Widor, Guilmant, and the rest held firmly to the old German tradition which they had received from the well-known organist, Adolph Friedrich Hesse.[4]

It was on 18 June in the very year of Widor's birth, 1844, that Hesse played in Paris at the church of St Eustache before a crowd numbering in the thousands – an event of such importance for contemporary organ music in France, and eventually for Bach's music worldwide, that musicians were to speak of it for decades. With the public, however, Hesse was anything but a success. Accustomed to hearing organists play rigadoons or depict thunderstorms, most of his listeners found his discipline incomprehensible. But its significance was recognized by some, including this reviewer: 'The event of the occasion was the appearance that the German organ school made in the person of Monsieur Hesse, the Breslau organist.' As to technique: 'This heir to the traditions of the school of Bach, whose famous *Toccata in F* he played with so much verve, dazzles, as a player, by the dexterity with which he treats the *pedal* part – which we in France have so long regarded as an unimportant accessory.' The reviewer might have added that not even the eighteenth-century masters had given much independence to the pedals. As to registration: 'The effects that one gets by the mixing of various sonorities appear to concern him only incidentally, though he is far from depriving himself of this kind of resource, as he demonstrated in several of his own pieces, among others his *Variations*.' And in sum: 'The German school, so little known among us, and which sends us so worthy an interpreter, seems to have attained a perfection to be hardly surpassed.'[5] 'He is a giant,' wrote

Berlioz of Hesse's performances that week; and, echoing the famous judgement rendered of Bach himself: 'he plays with the feet as many another would be hard put to it to play with the hands.'[6]

Invited to help inaugurate a Daublaine-Callinet of four manuals and seventy-eight ranks in collaboration with some of the most distinguished organists in Paris – Benoist of the Conservatoire, Fessy of the Madeleine, Boëly of St Germain-l'Auxerrois, Lefébure-Wély of St Roch, and, as impresario, Danjou of Notre Dame – Hesse thus carried to France a tradition whose components were neither so vague as to be valueless nor so precise as to defy accurate transmittal. We have already seen them incorporated into the teaching of Widor: a fundamentally legato style, period registrations (including terrace dynamics), steady rhythm and moderate tempi, and the implicit concern for clarity.

The love of Bach had come to Hesse at almost the beginning of his musical life, long before his studies with Rinck, through the training of Friedrich Wilhelm Berner (1780–1827), the organist at St Elizabeth Church in Breslau – significantly a town where more than one classical organ remained intact, and a teacher who had himself not only embraced the old disciplines but campaigned against the gallant style and its jejune virtuosity. Hesse advanced so swiftly in his studies that he had played in public by age nine (1818), heard his first composition performed by age eighteen (1827), and by age twenty given concerts of his own works and Bach's in such musical centres as Dresden, Leipzig, Hamburg, Darmstadt, and Berlin. In Berlin his predilection for Bach was perhaps reinforced by a meeting with Karl Friedrich Zelter (and this within months of the Bach revival led in Berlin by Zelter's Singakademie under Mendelssohn), and in Darmstadt he came under the influence of Rinck.

Their collaboration could not have begun less auspiciously. Rinck had only recently dispatched to the quarterly *Cäcilia* a critique in which he called young Hesse's published preludes and arrangements too dissonant, full of foreign keys, lacking in contrast, untoward. Then the two men met, and Rinck felt obliged to add a postscript:

> After this review was sent to the editors . . ., I had the opportunity of meeting Herr Hesse myself and of hearing him play. With special pleasure I can personally attest that he plays the organ with great facility, and in particular he employs the pedal in such a way as merits respect and amazement. If he endeavours to give his playing greater simplicity and variety, and if he continues, as earnestly as he is now doing, to strive for even greater perfection, he will surely become a very distinguished artist.[7]

To that end, Rinck gave Hesse organ lessons for five months from early October 1828, and indeed welcomed him to Darmstadt as his guest.[8]

'My sudden departure yesterday,' Hesse wrote to him on 4 March 1829,

> may have appeared strange to you, but I simply had to leave, for at table I could no

longer restrain my tears. The Lord bless you and your dear family. You have received me like a son, may God reward you. It would be my most fervent wish to see you someday in the bosom of my family so as to repay you in a small measure for all the kindness which I enjoyed in your house. Your experience and knowledge have had an important influence on my musical education, and through the company of your gracious wife and daughters I hope also to have gained in respect of social graces.[9]

Even allowing for the florid diction of the times, Hesse's letters to Rinck convey a profound affection that transcended the pupil-teacher relationship and the difference in ages. 'With expressions of the highest esteem, I am eternally your friend,' declared Hesse in closing the letter just cited. And again, three years later, 'My dear fatherly friend . . . give a thousand greetings to your dear family. I wish with all my heart that you may live as many years and write as many works as the number of little pipefuls you still intend to smoke . . . . I am in true friendship ever yours.'[10] And again, on 14 October 1829,

Apropos of your organ variations, which you so kindly forwarded to me here in Cassel, I played them last week to much acclaim, they turned out quite exquisitely . . . . I am publishing a new little work: 'Useful Offering for Organists, Especially Those who Wish to Acquire an Appropriate Method of Playing the Pedals.' It contains explanations, applied pedal scales, pedal exercises, exercises for pedal and left hand, three- and four-part exercises, easy preludes . . . with interludes, directions for modulating neatly and tastefully. Förster is printing it handsomely. A picture of the large organ at St Maria Magdalena will appear after the title page. I had the temerity to dedicate the little opus most humbly to you.[11]

In it, as we may expect, Hesse follows the principles of his friend and master by urging the student to strive for 'clean, smooth' technique and to play with quiet deportment: 'the bench must be suitably adjusted,' he writes, 'the upper body erect and motionless.'[12] An independent pedal technique he of course considers the *sine qua non* of contrapuntal style. For this, 'the heels and toes must be kept in contact with the pedals'; 'the pressure applied to the pedals must not be forceful but . . . quiet and smooth'; 'only in this way is it possible to execute fast pedal passages without . . . tiring'; and for conjunct notes at the extremes of the pedalboard, where crossing of feet is impossible, one must 'glide' from key to key so as to avoid 'unevenness.' In sum, 'clear, clean playing of the organ can be achieved only through quiet, gentle treatment of manuals and pedals.'[13]

His own skills were to bring him renown throughout Europe not only as organist but as pianist and conductor. From Breslau, where he had been named music director for the city, he wrote in April 1855 to his friend Ludwig Spohr that 'the winter here has passed with endless music making. The three regular orchestras of forty players each have all together given ninety symphony concerts . . . . Of these, I conducted thirty.'[14] As pianist he was admired above all for his playing of Hummel and Moscheles.

But the organ remained central in his activity. In 1831 Hesse became senior organist at the Bernardine church, where a large Casparini had just been renovated. To Spohr he praised its 'power, clarity and refinement of voicing'[15] and for the next quarter of a century made the church a centre for music both liturgical and secular.

Although his orchestral and pianistic work reflected some of the superficiality of the times, at the organ Hesse remained conservative, and when in later years he visited Prague, Vienna, London, and Naples, he deplored the inept state of organ playing and building.[16] In England he stated his dislike for organs tuned to unequal temperament, and in Italy he noted that even the airs and gallops played at mass were played badly. In Paris as late as 1859 and 1862, when he tried Cavaillé-Coll's new organs at St Clotilde and St Sulpice, he found the instruments excellent but the public still seduced by a mindless repertory.[17] He had therefore observed only the beginnings of change by the time of his death, after a long and painful illness, on 5 August 1863.

It was thanks to his most famous pupil, the Belgian Jacques-Nicolas Lemmens, that the old ways again took root and began to flourish – Lemmens, who taught the young Guilmant and Widor and whose friendship with Cavaillé-Coll helped the builder to see what an organ needs for the apt rendering of Bach.

Unfortunately, the good humour that marked the master-pupil relationship of Hesse and Rinck was absent from that of Hesse and Lemmens. Hesse was quoted as saying, after their few months of working together in 1846–47, that 'I have nothing more to teach Herr Lemmens; he plays Bach's most difficult music as well as I do.' But the remark was pure exaggeration by Lemmens's patron, François-Joseph Fétis, who presumably needed to justify the government grant he had obtained to make Lemmens's sojourn in Breslau possible. In fact, Hesse declared in print: 'The talent of Herr Lemmens turned out to be extremely mediocre, and if he later became the great man that Herr Fétis maintains, it is no fault of mine.'[18] So ended in bitterness a relationship that had begun in cordiality.

Yet it would be wrong to conclude that Lemmens absorbed little from Hesse. In fact the principles of the old Bachian style were, and are, easily grasped: moderate tempi and solid rhythm, the striving for clarity, a simplicity in registrations that has nothing to do with the colouristic nuances of post-eighteenth-century organs, a basically legato touch. For their demonstration a mere lesson or two would suffice even the average pupil.

Lemmens, on the contrary, was greatly gifted. 'Not a person who heard Lemmens,' writes Widor, 'will forget the clarity, the strength, the grandeur of his playing – with the smallest details given weight, but always in proportion with the piece taken as a whole . . . . A consummate musician, as great an artist at the organ as at the piano, marvellous interpreter of Beethoven and of Bach, Lemmens played with clarity, ease, and dignity.'[19] As to his pedal technique, a remark by Guilmant suggests that in this too he followed Hesse: 'No matter how loose or how old the pedals that Lemmens happened to be playing, they were absolutely noiseless when under his control.'[20]

He first played in Paris in 1850, for services at the Madeleine and during visits to the organs at St Denis, St Roch, and the Ponthémont, returning in 1852 to give a recital at St Vincent de Paul that was attended, according to Widor, by such eminent musicians as Alkan, Boëly, Franck, Benoist, Gounod, Halévy, and Thomas. It is not hard to imagine the impression he made, Widor writes,

> interpreting Bach with his style and mastery, in a programme devoted entirely to major works . . . . Born in 1823 in Zoerle-Parwijs (Antwerp province), Lemmens died in 1881. After brilliant studies at the Brussels Conservatory, he received from his government a scholarship that allowed him to work in Breslau with the renowned master Adolph Hesse, heir to the purest classical tradition. In 1849 the young Lemmens became professor of organ in Brussels . . . .
>
> Guilmant had been his pupil. A few years after Guilmant, and following his example, I went to study in Brussels. For a virtuoso, the ideal of foolish youth is speed. Just when I thought my playing achieved that ideal perfectly, profound disappointment: 'It is worthless,' he said, 'mechanical, without will.' What did he mean by *will*? I dared not ask him. But I came to understand: it is the art of the orator, his authority that makes itself felt through the serenity, the order, and the just proportions of the discourse. With us musicians, it is through rhythm that the will mainly shows itself: a player piano keeps our attention no longer than the ticking of a clock; we do not listen to it; whereas the mastery of a Liszt or a Rubinstein, *who did not play fast* [emphasis Widor's], moved everyone. Such, at the organ, was the authority of Lemmens.[21]

His registrations were as discreet as his tempi. 'Be on guard,' Lemmens was to write, 'against that constant changing of stops which is a particular abuse nowadays. Modern building has enriched the organ with a multitude of mechanical devices for changing timbres and . . . many organists sacrifice thought and feeling to material effects.'[22]

For clarity and for rhythm alike he demanded careful articulation, insisting that the release of a note or chord be as precise as the attack and that repeated notes be measured: 'To detach a note from its neighbour,' he writes, 'is to create between them a rest equal to half the first note's value . . . though obviously for long values in slow tempi one must conform to the spirit of the law rather than the letter.'[23] Without such careful measuring of note values, he would say, articulation would not be understood or even perceived, especially in a resonant room.

His precepts were of course taken to heart by Widor, as we have seen, serving as the base on which Widor's own teachings rested – as did those of Guilmant, Clément Loret, and others – and becoming a legacy handed on to yet other generations that included first Vierne, Bonnet, and Dupré and then such of their pupils as Langlais, Alain, and Messiaen. In what ways these artists in turn remained faithful to Lemmens's ideas has been shown elsewhere.[24]

His physical appearance was striking, for Lemmens was a tall, vigorous man whose agility and powerful build left an impression of sovereign control. 'Seeing him at the organ,' Widor would always remember, 'one thought of an animal tamer confronting the beast . . . classic posture, knees and ankles together, the player motionless, hands and feet as near as possible to the keys . . . the minimum of movements.'[25]

Nor was his discipline confined to the technical. The organist 'will mistake his function,' Lemmens wrote in 1862, 'if he has not taken into account the special character of each religious service. Catholic ceremonies have each their particular nature; the competent organist will not fail to make his effects accord with the feelings that the Church means to evoke by her liturgy.'[26]

Lemmens in fact spent much of his later life in helping to reform Gregorian chant as well, and to that end founded a church-music institute, followed with interest the research at Solesmes, and visited Rome. Even here, as he wrote in 1878 to Cavaillé-Coll,

> of religious music, there is none at all. Of infernal music, too much! . . . I received your good letter this morning when leaving Rome, where I seem to have arrived barely in time to keep the new pope from restoring a papal brief to Pustel, the printer of books of plainsong that I think are *barbarous* [emphasis Lemmens's]. I spoke of this with the Holy Father, in the two audiences he granted me, and spoke to him also of the great organ for St Peter's. There are many supporters, but there are also some who say that St Peter's is not the church for an organ.[27]

Indeed, Cavaillé-Coll was never to realize his dream of creating for that basilica an organ worthy of its traditions and size, or his dream of bringing Lemmens to Paris as *titulaire* at St Sulpice or Notre Dame.

But from this friendship, as noted above, came instruments from which composers of genius were to take inspiration and on which the music of Bach could be exquisitely played. For Lemmens cautioned the builder, as Widor explains, to design organs with a 'proper dose' of mixtures and with keyboards of fifty-four notes and pedalboards of thirty.

> To Cavaillé-Coll it was a revelation. He discovered in the master virtuoso the guidelines, the indispensable principles, that until then he had lacked . . . . [Theretofore,] Cavaillé-Coll's pedalboard at St Denis began at *F*, that of St Roch at *A*, of Notre Dame de Lorette at *A* for the foundations, *C* for the reeds. As for that of the Madeleine, it contained only twenty-five keys, dangerously close together. No law, no principle.[28]

Schweitzer himself, writing for German colleagues at the turn of the century, is our witness to the happy result attained by the innovations and workmanship of Cavaillé-Coll as directed in large part by the counsels of Lemmens.

> In general we could learn a great deal about the details of arrangement from the French organ. Its keys are somewhat shorter than ours; the black keys cunningly rounded off; the manuals closer together than ours as they rise above each other. Everything is provided for the most exact blending, and for the easy and sure changing from one manual to another, on which, as is well known, Bach laid a great deal of stress. And as for the French pedals, they cost, indeed, about double ours. But what perfection! All arranged concave and radiating, recently reaching to g^1, and with a really ideal spring . . . . The concave pedal has not yet won its way among us, in spite of its apparent advantages, and in spite of the fact that everyone who has reflected upon the radiating movement of the foot in pedal work must mark it as the only one that makes sense . . . . In a word, it is easier to play well on a French organ than on a German organ.

Indeed, Schweitzer concludes, given these technical advantages, together with 'the beautiful tonal unity of the foundation stops and the mixtures' that Cavaillé-Coll achieved, the French organists therefore 'play the Bach fugues in many respects more simply, clearly, and appropriately than we; because their organs are nearer to the Bach organ than ours.'[29]

As to timbre in general, Schweitzer found the Cavaillé-Coll organ resembled fine old classical organs with their 'round and soft but full tone.'[30] 'In the strength of tone he gave to a single stop he remained conservative. It is true that he constructed high-pressure reeds (*trompettes en chamade*) for the swell organ; for the other stops he sought only beauty. Even his flutes – not simply his principals and gambas – are wonderfully beautiful . . . . The foundation stops are voiced with reference to the tonal unity they should form. Not only those in each manual alone, but also all of them together, form a well-balanced, harmonious whole' in which the mixtures 'enter into the tone colour of the foundation stops to make them light and transparent, that is, adapted to polyphonic playing.'[31]

The art of organ playing, Schweitzer observes, is always the product of the art of organ building. 'Let no one deceive himself: as the organs, so the organists. No other instrument exercises such an influence upon artists. Perfect organs train organists in perfection; imperfect ones train them in imperfection and in false virtuosity.'[32]

Notes and References

1. Einstein, pp. 7–8.
2. Letter of 24 July 1831 to his family (Weiss, p. 232).
3. Widor, p. 6.
4. *Out of My Life and Thought*, pp. 155–56.
5. Stephen Morelot (1844), 'Inauguration de l'Orgue de Saint-Eustache,' *Revue et Gazette musicale* 27 (7 July), p. 231. Hesse had also performed at the industrial exhibition in the Champs-Elysées.

6. *'Exposition de l'Industrie,' Journal des Débats*, series 8 (23 June 1844), p. 3.
7. 'Orgelcompositionen von A. Hesse,' *Cäcilia* 10 (1829), p. 45.
8. Seyfried, p. 13.
9. Hesse's letters to Rinck may be found in the Hessische Landes- und Hochschulbibliothek in Darmstadt.
10. 15 June 1832.
11. *Nützliche Gabe für Organisten, insbesondere solche, welche sich eines zweckmässigen Pedalspiels befleissigen wollen.*
12. Ibid., p. 1. Historically, quiet technique – technique that avoids superfluous movement – has almost invariably been the hallmark of virtuosity. One finds proof by watching a Horowitz or a Rubinstein or a Rachmaninoff, not to mention a Dupré or a Marchal, that the most accurate player is the player who wastes motion least – and this because excess motion both causes fatigue and violates the principle that one cannot incorrectly play a key with which the finger or foot is in contact in advance. Though the fact is self-evident, its subtleties are not so – especially the adjustment of fingerings required to find the one most conducive to economy of motion.
13. Ibid.
14. *Spohr und Hesse, Briefwechsel aus den Jahren 1829–1859*, J. Kahn, ed. (1928), Regensburg: Ratisbonne, p. 283.
15. Ibid., p. 164. The instrument was by Casparini *fils*.
16. Hesse (1853), 'Einiges über Orgeln, deren Einrichtung und Behandlung in Österreich, Italien, Frankreich und England,' *Neue Zeitschrift für Musik* 39, p. 53.
17. An example of which, cited by Widor (Piccand, p. 299), was a teaching method by a distinguished *maître de chapelle* whose model for good organ music was this 'Descriptive Piece on the Resurrection of Our Lord':
    1) *The Mournful Silence of the Tomb*
       (triple meter, A minor)
    2) *Lifting of the Morning Mists*
       (tremolo from bottom to top of keyboards)
    3) *The Earthquake*
       (violent stamping on the pedals)
    4) *Cherubim Remove the Stone from the Door*
       (prestissimo chromatic scales from the highest note of the flute to the lowest note of the contrebasse)
    5) *Our Lord Departs from the Tomb*
       (allegro giocoso ma risoluto)
18. See Fétis (1883), *Biographie universelle des musiciens*, Paris: Firmin-Didot, p. 267. Hesse's rebuttal appeared in the *Neue Zeitschrift für Musik* (37) in March 1852. The rupture occurred after 16 December 1846, when Hesse had written as follows: 'Herr Lemmens, a very talented musician, has been with me since the month of September and has partaken of my instruction in organ playing and composing for this instrument. Herr Lemmens spent this time so diligently that he now performs several of the greatest and most difficult organ works with composure and a true grasp; he has also composed a fugue for this instrument under my direction which testifies to his solid accomplishments in the field of serious music. His knowledge and skill qualify him for a position as Professor of Organ at the Conservatory.' (Autograph document in the collection of Mr Lowell Lacey.) François-Joseph Fétis (1784–1871), the founder of *La Revue musicale*, was variously a critic and historian, librarian of the Paris

Conservatory, musician to the Belgian court, composer, teacher (Widor was his pupil in fugue), and lexicographer. His *Biographie universelle des musiciens* appeared in eight volumes between 1837 and 1844.

19. Widor, p. 6. See also Raugel, p. 88.
20. Carl, p. 4.
21. Widor, p. 6.
22. *Ecole d'Orgue*, pp. 1–3.
23. Ibid., p. 3.
24. See Norbert Dufourcq (1964), 'Les Disciples,' *l'Orgue*, Paris: Presses Universitaires de France, pp. 106–23; Vierne, (November 1938) p. 10; Murray, 'A Legacy and a Prize,' in *Marcel Dupré: The Work of a Master Organist*, pp. 44–54.
25. Widor, p. 6.
26. *Ecole d'orgue*, p. 1.
27. Letters of 13 and 22 November. For these and others, see Norbert Dufourcq (1953), 'A propos du Cinquantenaire de la mort de Cavaillé-Coll, 1899–1949: Lemmens et Cavaillé-Coll,' *l'Orgue*, 65, January–March, pp. 59–61. Musical art at St Peter's had apparently progressed little since the 1830s, when Berlioz visited the basilica and was stirred by the 'solemn silence, the cool, still air, the fine, luminous harmony of colour . . . . It seemed to me that this was really the temple of God . . . . These pictures and statues and columns, all this gigantic architecture, are . . . but the body of the building; music is its soul . . . . Where is the organ?' Alas, his vision of the ideal was shattered when he found the 'organ' hidden behind a pillar – a sort of harmonium on wheels. (*Memoirs*, trans. Ernest Newman [1966], New York: Dover, p. 154.)
28. Widor, p. 6.
29. Joy, pp. 154, 155, 160. Still, the concave, radiating pedalboard was to remain the exception in French organ building rather than the rule.
30. *Out of My Life and Thought*, p. 89.
31. Joy, pp. 158, 159, 160.
32. Ibid., p. 167.

4   Scholar and Stylist

'Thus by an historical paradox,' Schweitzer records in his autobiography, 'the principles of the old German tradition were saved for the present age by Parisian masters of the organ, and this tradition also became known in detail when by degrees musicians again began to consult the theoretical works on their art preserved for us from the eighteenth century.'[1]

A tradition is, however, living. Its custodians are thinking and feeling human beings who each bring to it unique perceptions and preferences. Hence to say that Rinck, Hesse, Lemmens, and Widor played Bach according to a tradition of moderate tempo, steady rhythm, period registration, and legato touch is not to say that they played Bach identically, still less that they played Bach in all respects as Bach himself did. For good organists, as Dupré was to observe, 'although strictly governed by these stern provisos, are clearly differentiated by their taste, their lucidity, and their imagination.'[2] Nor would Schweitzer conform inflexibly to the praxis of Widor.

They agreed, to be sure, on certain essentials, and since his conclusions changed little over the years we may see this agreement in the counsels Schweitzer gives for colleagues, whether it is expressed in the *Bach* of 1905, the editions of 1913, the autobiography of 1931, or the letters of the 1950s. As to speed, for example:

> People cannot be reminded too often that on the organs of the seventeenth century it was not possible to play in as quick a tempo as one might wish to. The keys moved so stiffly and had to be depressed so far, that a good moderato itself was something of an achievement. Since, then, Bach must have conceived his preludes and fugues in the moderate tempo in which they could be played on his own organs, we, too, must hold fast to this fact as giving us the tempo which is authentic and appropriate. It is well known that Hesse, in accordance with the Bach tradition which had come down to him, used to play the organ compositions in an extremely quiet tempo.[3]

Polyphonic music, Schweitzer further explains, which presupposes the comprehension of lines of sound advancing side by side, 'becomes for the listener a chaos, if a too rapid tempo makes this comprehension impossible.'[4] Nor, as we have heard Widor say, can categories of tempo be interpreted in the modern sense: 'Bach's *adagio*, *grave*, and *lento*,' Schweitzer continues, 'are not so slow as ours, or his *presto* so fast; therefore we are easily betrayed into making his slow movements too long-drawn and hurrying his fast ones.'[5]

As to rhythm, Schweitzer reminds his readers of the passage in the Necrology describing Bach the conductor as 'very accurate, and extremely sure.'[6] As to deportment: 'What astonished his hearers, besides the plasticity and clearness of his playing, was his calmness during performance. Scheibe and Forkel refer to this as to something quite exceptional.'[7]

But Schweitzer's advice about the choice of stops only begins by echoing Widor's.

> As a rule Bach kept to the characteristic registration with which he began, getting variety and gradation in his playing by transitions from one manual to another. It is noteworthy, however, that he played a great many organ pieces throughout on the great organ without any change whatever of manuals and without any gradation of tone .... The representatives of the old German organ school, that still preserved some traditions from the Bach epoch, played Bach's preludes and fugues throughout on the great organ with diapasons and mixtures. The pedal was sometimes strengthened by reeds.[8]

Nevertheless, Schweitzer makes 'no *a priori* objection ... to a greater variation in volume and gradations of tone than Bach could manage upon his organs, provided that the architecture of the piece is clearly perceptible .... Whereas Bach was satisfied to carry a fugue through with three or four variously toned degrees of loudness in alternation, we can allow ourselves six or eight.'[9] And here Schweitzer and Widor take different paths indeed.

Schweitzer's intentions are easily discerned when it is a question of rendering Bach on a bad organ. In his suggestions for performance of the *Prelude and Fugue in A Minor*, for example, Schweitzer remarks that in Bach's day a full registration could be used throughout the prelude and that even such powerful reeds as the 16-foot posaune could remain drawn despite the sustained notes, the reed tone being clear and penetrating but not so heavy as to drown the other parts. But – he then suggests – given the strong tone of late-nineteenth-century organs, and especially the more intense tone of their reeds, one is forced to allow changes: 'For the long organ-points the pedal must be reduced. In the *forte* certain shadings must be introduced, that it may not grow intolerable to the listener. No change is to be made in the foundation stops and mixtures drawn; but the reed-groups may be reduced or increased.'[10] He further instructs the player to vary the *forte* not only by withdrawing and adding reeds but by using the swell shades: at first, 'the swell-box is open .... For the beginning of the triplets in sixteenth-notes in the middle of measure 9, the swell-box is closed. It opens again during the progress of measures 10–21.'[11] The long *crescendo* of ten measures which therefore results appears to him to be the lesser of two evils, the other that of subjecting the listener to ten measures of a *forte* whose harshness is unalleviated. Only thus does Schweitzer think it possible to convey Bach's intentions on organs unpleasantly voiced, though this prelude should ideally 'be played from beginning to end on one manual in an equal *forte* . . . . He who hath ears to hear will notice that the natural intensification immanent to the music is most gloriously manifested when no extrinsic aids are employed to bring it out.'[12] In this case, he has explained his departure from Widor's classical style as being required by circumstances.

Yet he appears to have in mind good organs and thus to contradict himself when he writes:

> Archaistic tendencies should not be tolerated in music. Bach would have been the last to set his face against new methods. Many passages – e.g. the conclusion of the A Minor fugue – really demand an increase in the *forte* itself. And how happy Bach would have been could he have got a finer *piano* on his third manual . . . as is possible by means of the Venetian shutter swell! To refuse to make use of this device in the great episode in the A Minor fugue beginning at the fifty-first bar – employing first a *decrescendo*, then a *crescendo* – is to be false to Bach.[13]

But the modern organist must make use of the device without disturbing the architecture of the fugue, Schweitzer adds, and be sure that the divisions of the work come out simply and clearly. Within these limits one may do what one thinks necessary. He moreover underlines the contradiction by stating on the same page that 'the modern swell really does our organists a disservice, in that it is always tempting them to indulge in these gradual *crescendi*. The true cumulative effects in Bach are made by the entry at definite moments of two or three new tone-masses, and the *decrescendo* by their departure.'[14] Thus we are right to be puzzled and to ask which practice he really preferred.

The fact is that Schweitzer interpreted Bach in a deeply personal way, taking as starting point the classical principles learned from Widor and from painstaking research, but adding certain touches wholly his own to phrasing and registration.

Regarding swell boxes, it was an abuse in his time, brought on by the post-1840 convenience with which mechanicals could be managed, to indulge in *crescendi* and *decrescendi* for their own sake, organists taking delight in the recently-found malleability of the instrument; hence Schweitzer in reaction condemns the arbitrary superimposing of such dynamics on Bach while yet hoping to show that the practice is not always without merit. Here, then, contradiction is perhaps more apparent than real. But in this Schweitzer greatly differed from Widor, to whom it would not have occurred to use the swell shades in such a way. Nor could Widor have conveniently done so, since the swell pedal at St Sulpice, as on many French organs, was of the hitch-down variety, located at the extreme right of the pedalboard and having notches for only three positions of the shades: open, half open, and closed.

We may note here in passing that the stylistic disparity between Schweitzer's Bach and Widor's, as seen in the prefaces to the edition on which they collaborated, is accounted for by Schweitzer as follows:

By the publisher's desire our work was published in three languages. The divergencies between the French text, on the one hand, and the German, together with the English which is based on it, on the other, arise from the fact that in respect of the details as to which our opinions differed, Widor and I had agreed that in the French edition his ideas, which fitted better the peculiarities of the French organs, should be dominant, while in the German and the English mine should, taking, as they did, more into account the character of the modern organ.[15]

Schweitzer went his own way too in the playing of ornaments, using neither the inverted mordent, for example, nor the modulated trill, and believing that trills should be rhythmically calculated, the slow trill, he would say, having its place in Bach. Neither did the interrupted trill on a dotted note necessarily end on the dot.

Again, although Widor and Schweitzer agreed in principle in defining legato as the instantaneous exchange of one note for the next, with neither break nor overlap, they did not agree in practice. Schweitzer articulated more often than his master, whether in the subjects of fugues or the themes of preludes or the cantus firmus and accompanimental voices of chorales. He tended to make smaller groupings of notes within periods. And he did not measure articulations with invariable precision: his detached and repeated notes in moderate tempo, for instance, do not always lose half their value. He explains that the rule about repeated notes indeed 'holds good not only for the phrasing of the themes, but for the treatment of the repeated notes in general' and 'cannot be observed too strictly.'[16] And yet nearly 'imperceptible' breaks that give 'clearness and animation' to an otherwise unbroken legato line he deems equally necessary, it being 'quite a mistaken idea that what Bach chiefly wants is a monotonous smoothness. He certainly favoured the legato style. But his legato is not a mere levelling; it is alive. It must be filled by a fine phrasing which the hearer need not perceive as such, but of which he is conscious as a captivating lucidity in the playing. Within the legato, the separate tones must be grouped into living phrases'[17] – as at the beginning of the A Minor prelude, where Schweitzer places tiny breaks after the fourth, seventh, and tenth sixteenth-notes. To him, Bach generally asks for a legato whose liveliness comes from the notes being connected one with the next but in the manner of the violin bow achieving a cantabile line without portamento. Or, as he once put it in a homelier way to his friend Jacques Feschotte: 'A beautifully executed passage at the organ ought to be like a good dish of rice. Each grain ought to keep its form and its consistency, despite the amount of cooking. Otherwise, it becomes mush.'[18]

If he was sometimes taken to task for modernizing Bach's music, his explicit motive nevertheless was to convey Bach's thought. From this same motive he often used well-voiced manual reeds as part of the plenum, reinforcing the foundations and mixtures. Schweitzer inferred from what he believed to be Bach's liking for the metallic tone in orchestral scoring Bach's liking for an analogous timbre at the organ.[19] The French reeds, however, he considered 'in spite of their beauty' too preponderant for Bach playing, though 'the diapasons and mixtures of the Cavaillé-Coll organs seem made for it, this builder having been particularly anxious to avoid abnormally strong and "solid" voicing. On the organs at St Sulpice and Notre Dame, Bach's fugues come out with extraordinary clearness.'[20] Schweitzer tells us Widor concurred in the belief 'that we must go back to the building of reeds which do not dominate the whole instrument.'[21]

Finally, we have already seen that it was Schweitzer who illumined a part of Bach's esthetics previously unrecognized not only by Widor and Lemmens but by the most thorough and devoted of Bach's biographers, Philipp Spitta: the depicting in music of ideas drawn from poetry. Schweitzer as a young man was the first to publish a detailed account of Bach's way of portraying in tone the sentiments of the various texts, and he did so against the then prevailing judgement of Bach as the 'pure' musician whose counterpoints were untainted by the descriptive or the poetic – against the mistaken view, that is, of 'words rendering only actions, painting only images, and music only emotions.'[22] That Schweitzer revealed to contemporary scholarship this essential and theretofore neglected part of Bach's mind would seem to us the astonishing *coup* it was, did not the insight appear to come so naturally and inevitably and had not Schweitzer's later accomplishments also been prodigious. Nor, even if true, does the opinion of some later scholars that Schweitzer attributes to Bach a more precise use of symbolism than could have been the case lessen the value of the accomplishment.

Schweitzer possessed, at any rate, from childhood days in his father's rectory, a thorough acquaintance with the chorale and cantata texts and, of course, with the German language and liturgy; his acquaintance grew, during his young manhood, with his work as accompanist to the St William Choir and the Paris Bach Society, whose performances brought him experience that was practical as well as theoretical. Thus at about age twenty-seven he wrote that 'Bach has a tonal language of his own'[23] and proceeded to describe its nuances. Doing so, and apart from the insight he gave performers of the vocal music, Schweitzer provided for organists the most striking of clues to mood and intention, hence to appropriate tempo and registration, in the organ chorales above all. Indeed, he called the *Orgelbüchlein* a veritable lexicon of Bach's symbols, and in page after page of example and demonstration he gave the proof of his theory.

Not that Bach portrayed a text word for word, Schweitzer decided, rather its ideas and images. Bach 'is satisfied with it if it contains a picture. When he discovers a pictorial idea it takes the place of the whole text . . . . Often he seizes upon a single word'[24] from which springs a rhythmic or melodic motive that captures what is essential, whether this be drifting mists, Schweitzer tells us, or rivers flowing, waves ebbing, bells ringing for the dying, the confident faith that walks with sure steps, or the weak faith that falters insecure. Bach's portrayal is quite specific as to the feelings inspired by the text, feelings that, as Mendelssohn has it, are not too vague for words but too precise.

Among the twenty to twenty-five main motives recurring in the cantatas, Passions, and chorale treatments, Schweitzer considers distinctive the 'step' motives for the expression of firmness, the syncopated themes of lassitude, the theme that depicts tumult, the graceful lines that depict peaceful rest, the serpentine lines that contort themselves at the mention of the name Satan, the flowing motives that enter when angels are mentioned, the motives of rapturous or passionate joy, the motives of noble grief.[25] He hastens to add that 'the wealth of Bach's musical language does not consist in any special multiplicity of themes and motives, but in the manifold shadings by means of which a few general formulae are made to express characteristic ideas and feelings' and that attention to these matters 'is not a mere pastime for the esthetician, but a necessity for the practical musician. It is often impossible to play a work . . . in the right tempo, and with the right accent and the right phrasing, unless we know the meaning of the motive. The simple "feeling" does not always suffice.'[26] To this end, he states, one must study not merely some of the works but all, for they often mutually explain each other, the cantatas especially.

His understanding of Bach's symbolism naturally moulded the way Schweitzer played the organ chorales. But his wish to bring Bach's meaning to light did not lead him into the error of giving too much weight to form at the expense of content. The two are inseparable, of course, except in the abstract. But he would not, for example, distort the melodic shape of a well-formed phrase merely to emphasize a cleverness of construction, or bring out a fugal subject in solo on another manual merely to emphasize a skillful placement within the structure. The importance he attached to keeping a balance was expressed in a telling way when he urged players to remember that the 'piece is not there for the sake of the canon, but the canon for the sake of the piece.'[27] Thus he avoided exaggeration in the chorales as in the free works, convinced also that not even the most expressive pieces should be played too softly or too slowly. In this, needless to say, he and Widor were as one.

Schweitzer's theories of the pictorial and poetic Bach did not so much deviate from the Widorian tradition as restore to it a depth of understanding that had been lost. Nowhere in his writings does Bach refer to the practice of capturing in tone the sentiment of a text. Indeed, only one contemporary document has been found that attributes to him this objective – the recollection by a former pupil that Bach had taught him to play chorales 'not merely offhand but according to the sense (*Affect*) of the words.'[28] Yet the doctrine of affections was almost certainly well known to Bach, who may have taken for granted that in this, as in the playing of certain ornaments, his desires would be understood. As far as he knew, moreover, his works would be played only by his sons and pupils, for few of the works were published or likely to be, and the very idea of the executant artist who specialized in other men's music still lay in the future. Or again, the pictorial treatment of texts may have been with Bach wholly unconscious; certainly Emanuel seems to have been unaware of his father's intention when, in 1765 and 1769, he published collections of Bach's chorale treatments without including the texts. Or Bach may, on the contrary, have been fully conscious of his technique and thought it too obvious to need mentioning. History shows us how seldom the people of an era talk or leave written records about what is to them obvious – and thus how often and how easily a lack of documents will, in a mere generation or two, render the obvious the mysterious.

In sum, then, how did Schweitzer play? To begin with, assuming our best evidence to be his phonograph records, his proficiency should not be judged by the recordings he made in the early 1950s in Günsbach, when advancing years and long absences from the organ had undermined his skill, and where the organ in the village church was really not appropriate to the task. Rather, the definitive recordings are those he made in 1936 at St Aurelia's in Strasbourg. He himself had chosen the instrument, a rebuilt Silbermann whose tone he thought ideal, and he came to the sessions with his technique in excellent form, having just spent a full year in Europe lecturing and giving recitals. He furthermore spent nearly a full two weeks recording at St Aurelia's, completing no fewer than thirty-three disks, of which twenty-five were of Bach. The recorded evidence is the more accurate since the 78 r.p.m. medium permitted no editing, each four-and-one-half-minute side presenting in that respect an unaltered likeness of his playing.[29]

The need to divide Bach's music into intervals of about five minutes seems not to have affected the tempi, for Schweitzer plays neither very slowly nor very fast. One notices that his rhythm is solid without being inflexible; that his ornaments come sometimes ahead of the beat and sometimes with, beginning now on the main note and now on the auxiliary; and that the reeds are prominent in the plenum, Schweitzer adding and removing them in the manner, if not always at the places, indicated in his editions. Overall, his playing is exciting, partly because of his inexorable rhythm and the brilliant voicing of the reeds; poetic, partly because he so moulds phrases as to show their mutual relationships and equipoise; and authoritative, partly because every gesture seems well planned, well thought. Although verbal descriptions of art are necessarily subjective and, as he himself once said, a kind of speaking in parables,[30] his playing may be said to convey a sense of respect for this music and its maker and, perhaps mainly through the loving attention to detail, an implicit acknowledgement that Bach is master and Schweitzer servant.

He would in any case have deemed such an attitude right, agreeing as he did with Widor that the player must renounce self-aggrandizement before the august nature of the organ and its masterworks. When he quotes Widor's definition of organ playing as the manifestation of a will filled with a vision of the eternal, Schweitzer reveals to us as well as to the turn-of-the-century German colleagues whom he was addressing an attitude he thought essential. He elsewhere calls it 'objective,' an attitude not merely detached but supra-personal, not merely respectful but self-transcending – an attitude which Boulanger had in mind when she asserted that the great interpreter is the one who wishes to be forgotten, and which Dupré had in mind when he wrote that the great interpreter has as paramount concern the beauty of the music. 'If the crushing toil found in acquiring a flawless technique gives to him who possesses it independence and authority,' Dupré writes, echoing Widor, 'it remains true none the less that a technique is honourable only if it is . . . scrupulously *respectful* . . . . To serve Bach means not to exploit him.'[31]

Schweitzer's attitude agrees not only with Dupré's and Widor's but with that of many another master interpreter. For great examples suggest that the highest artistry cannot be reached unless self-expression is subordinate to duty. Think of Toscanini, who in the effort to convey the composer's meaning would add a trumpet to Beethoven's horns, or violas to Debussy's violins, only after scrupulous study – and a degree of soul-searching that approached the Carthusian – had persuaded him that an orchestration needed clarifying. Or take Wanda Landowska's kindred attitude toward Scarlatti or Bruno Walter's toward Bruckner. Obviously, the interpreter expresses self. But if the elements of self-expression are not to hinder the work, they must be unwitting; they must come into play only as the spontaneous result of one's inevitably being oneself and not somebody else.

In this, moreover, Schweitzer delineates what is a moral as well as an esthetic principle. Although he would have been the last person to deny that the good interpreter necessarily brings to bear on the work all that is best in his or her character and experience, Schweitzer is in fact embracing an ethic of self-effacement. Not for him, therefore, to ask how music might be considered innately good. To that ancient question he clearly took one answer for granted: the ethical attributes of music are found both in its transcendence and in the behaviour required of its ablest practitioners.

If this truth can be applied to the executive artist, it seemed to him, how much more so to the creative. Little wonder, then, that Schweitzer felt for Bach an esteem bordering on veneration, for the greatest of composers was the very type of the ethical musician. 'In this respect,' Schweitzer declares, Bach may well stand 'highest among all creative artists; his immense strength functioned without self-consciousness, like the forces of nature; and for this reason it is as cosmic and copious as these.'[32]

Indeed, Schweitzer found that music was for Bach an act of worship and was therefore, in some sense, Bach's religion. To begin with, Bach cared little whether his contemporaries understood his works. 'He had put all his devotion into them, and God at any rate certainly understood them.'[33] Then too, 'Bach includes religion in the definition of art in general. All great art, even secular, is in itself religious in his eyes; for him the tones do not perish, but ascend to God like praise too deep for utterance.'[34] And Schweitzer recalls Bach's oft-quoted words: 'Like all music, the figured bass should have no other end and aim than the glory of God and the recreation of the soul.'[35] Accordingly, 'his artistic activity and his personality are both based on his piety. If he is to be understood from any standpoint at all, it is from this.'[36]

Schweitzer further concludes that though Bach was a conservative Lutheran, his

> real religion was not orthodox Lutheranism, but mysticism . . . . This robust man, who seems to be in the thick of life with his family and his work . . . was inwardly dead to the world. His whole thought was transfigured by a wonderful, serene longing for death. Again and again, whenever the text affords the least pretext for it, he gives voice to this longing in his music.[37]

That Bach's point of view was profoundly mystical is shown by his treatment of every pertinent text, according to Schweitzer, and

> nowhere is his speech so moving as in the cantatas in which he discourses on the release from the body of this death. The Epiphany and certain bass cantatas are the revelation of his most intimate religious feelings. Sometimes it is a sorrowful and weary longing that the music expresses; at others, a glad, serene desire, finding voice in one of those lulling cradle-songs that only he could write; then again a passionate, ecstatic longing, that calls death to it jubilantly, and goes forth in rapture to meet it . . . . This is Bach's religion as it appears in the cantatas. It transfigured his life.[38]

If the specifically metaphysical connotations of the word are set aside, the effect of Bach upon Schweitzer was as well a kind of transfiguration, for the person and art of the master infused and enriched and transformed Schweitzer's activity. His biography of Bach brought Schweitzer some of his earliest international acclaim and some of his most significant friendships. His recitals of Bach helped to fund the African hospital. And his knowledge of Bach doubtless reaffirmed for him the acceptability of certain character traits of his own, for both men were strong-willed, often short-tempered, and nearly always incapable of working under direction. Both took endless pains with their work, were in large measure self-taught, and possessed an uncommon ability to see through to the heart of things. They were hearty in their humour, and they enjoyed vigorous good health almost to the end of their days. But above all it was as the exemplar of ethical ideals, and as the supremely gifted musician who used his gifts in the service of God, and as the unfailing source of spiritual and intellectual refreshment that Bach personified certain truths important to Schweitzer and thus provided a locus to which Schweitzer could refer.

In a published tribute, a fellow musician recalled Schweitzer's performance on a sublime but dilapidated old Silbermann:

> One forgot everything for the moment, the awkward manipulation of the stops, the noise of shrunken mechanism, even the player himself. Only Bach was there. It was the complete relegation of all agencies of performance to a position of total unimportance, with a corresponding glorification of the music itself. Modern virtuosity of every type has too often created a barrier between the composer and the listener. Too often, indeed, is the music no more than a vehicle for the self-expression of the interpreter. Of all that there was nothing.[39]

On reading those words, Schweitzer wrote to their author in reply that he was more deeply touched than he could say by so sympathetic a grasp of his purpose and so clear a statement of 'what is fundamental, in my judgement, to the understanding and the interpretation of Bach's music.'[40]

Another witness to Schweitzer's art, this time at the recording sessions in St Aurelia's, writes:

> The organ stops. In the frame of the door that leads from the interior of the church into the sacristy Albert Schweitzer appears. I have surprised him in the midst of his work, in shirt sleeves. He has even taken off his vest here in the late autumn in the cold church. I see again the imposing head that reminds one of Nietzsche, the powerful form with the broad shoulders . . . .
> Before the organ over the church pews hangs the microphone; it carries the tones of the organ to the receiving apparatus in the sacristy. Here the wax disk turns, and here the needle scratches the organ tones in the surface of what looks like a thick, deep yellow honeycake. 'You are arriving just at one of the most difficult places,' said Albert Schweitzer to me, as he took me up to the choir loft with him. About half of the piece he is about to play is exclusively in the pedals. He supports himself on the organ bench with both hands, and plays with assurance and energy the difficult foot pedals once or twice through. Then he telephones the sacristy that he is ready. The man in charge of the reception there puts on a new disk and lowers the needle. Now a muffled bell beside the console gives the signal . . . a red light goes on . . . . The organ begins . . . .[41]

Notes and References

1. *Out of My Life and Thought*, p. 157.
2. Gavoty (1955), p. 28.
3. *Out of My Life and Thought*, p. 160.
4. Ibid., p. 83.
5. *J. S. Bach*, vol. I., p. 381.
6. Ibid., p. 210.
7. Ibid., p. 208. Johann Adolph Scheibe (1708–76), son of the organ builder, was a leading critic; Johann Nikolaus Forkel (1749–1818), who derived much of his information from Emanuel and Friedemann, published his biography of Bach in 1802.
8. Ibid., p. 297 and n.
9. *Out of My Life and Thought*, pp. 159–60.
10. *Johann Sebastian Bach: Complete Organ Works*, vol. IV, p. xvii.

11. Ibid.
12. Ibid.
13. *J. S. Bach*, vol. I., pp. 304–5.
14. Ibid., p. 304.
15. *Out of My Life and Thought*, p. 162. The first five volumes of *Johann Sebastian Bach: Complete Organ Works* were published by G. Schirmer in 1912–13 and contained the preludes, fugues, concertos, and sonatas; not until 1954 did a sixth volume, containing chorale arrangements, appear, and not until 1967 the final two volumes, containing the *Orgelbüchlein*, Catechism, Schübler, and Eighteen chorales, and the chorale variations. See below, Chapter 8.
16. *J. S. Bach*, vol. I., p. 315.
17. Ibid., pp. 312–13.
18. Amadou (1951), pp. 232–33.
19. *J. S. Bach*, vol. I., p. 298.
20. Ibid., p. 299n., and Joy, p. 165.
21. Joy, p. 165.
22. See Barzun (1969), vol. I., p. 380. A book by the musicologist André Pirro, dealing with Bach's esthetics, had appeared in 1895, but Schweitzer arrived independently at the conception of Bach as a synaesthetic artist. From Lambaréné on 4 January 1951 to Jacques Feschotte: 'I am interested to learn from you that according to the Revue de Musicologie of 12 July I needed to consult Pirro to write my Bach. I do not know what the person who expressed this opinion can base it on. I wrote my book in accordance with ideas I had arrived at by studying the relationships between Bach's music and the texts that it treated. Playing the organ in many performances of Bach's cantatas and Passions, at St William's in Strasbourg over a number of years, and knowing all the chorale and cantata texts thoroughly, I was brought to my view of the descriptive character of Bach's music which, to my great surprise, Spitta's great work on Bach ignored and wished to ignore, holding to the proposition that Bach was pure music . . . . I did not need to consult Pirro to develop my thesis, and did not do so . . . . I knew my Bach.'
    'Je suis intéressé d'apprendre par toi que d'après la Revue de Musicologie du 12 juillet, j'ai eu le besoin de consulter Pirro pour écrire mon Bach. Je ne sais sur quoi celui qui émet cette opinion peut se baser. J'ai écrit mon livre d'après les idées auxquelles je suis arrivé par l'étude des rapports existant entre la musique de Bach et les textes qu'elle traitait. Tenant l'orgue dans de nombreuses exécutions de cantates et de Passions de Bach à St Guillaume de Strasbourg durant une série d'années et connaissant à fond tous les textes de chorals et des cantates, j'ai été amené à ma notion du caractère descriptif de la musique de Bach qu'ignorait et voulait ignorer à mon grand étonnement le grand ouvrage de Spitta sur Bach, qui défendait la thèse que Bach était de la musique pure . . . . Je n'ai pas eu besoin de consulter Pirro pour développer ma thèse et ne l'ai pas fait . . . . Je connaissais mon Bach.'
23. *Jean-Sébastien Bach, le musicien-poète*, p. 216. See also *J. S. Bach*, vol. II., pp. 49–52.
24. *Jean-Sébastien Bach, le musicien-poète*, pp. 214–15. Schweitzer's proof is given in *J. S. Bach*, vol. II., pp. 56–122.
25 *J. S. Bach*, vol. II., p. 51.
26. Ibid.
27. Ibid., vol. I., p. 301.
28. Johann Gotthilf Ziegler in 1746. See David and Mendel, p. 237.

29. But the finished recordings left Schweitzer only 'tolerably' content, as he wrote from Lambaréné on 28 November 1942 to Gerhard Herz. 'I am still always looking for the organ and the church having the ideal acoustics that would be required to make satisfactory records. All Hallows in London, which gave me the most satisfaction, no longer exists.'
'De mes records [*sic*] de la musique d'orgue de Bach, je ne suis que médiocrement satisfait. Je cherche encore toujours l'orgue et l'église avec acoustique idéale qu'il faudrait pour faire des records satisfaisants. All Hallows à London, qui me donnait le plus de satisfaction, n'existe plus.' Joy tells us (pp. 245–46) that Schweitzer had had in 1936 the option of returning to All Hallows and preferred St Aurelia's, hence he may just have been unhappy with the engineering of the final disks. At the sessions, incidentally, he could only have heard the playback of a test, not of a take itself, since playing the wax masters destroyed them. The stoplist for the St Aurelia Silbermann, in whose restoration he had had a hand, is given in Appendix C. Some of the recordings were reissued as compact disks in 1992–93 (Pearl GEMM CD–9959 and CD–9992) by Pavilion Records, Ltd., East Sussex.
Schweitzer recorded for His Master's Voice (Queen's Hall, London, 1928); Columbia, England (All Hallow's, Barking-by-the-Tower, London, 1935, and St Aurelia's, Strasbourg, 1936); and Columbia, U.S.A. (Village Church, Günsbach, 1951–52). A Schweitzer discography may be found in Jacobi, *Musikwissenschaftliche Arbeiten*, pp. 581–85.
30. *Out of My Life and Thought*, p. 79.
31. The Widor quotation may be found in Schweitzer's organ-building essay of late 1905 (Joy, pp. 168–69); Boulanger's words are quoted from a taped conversation of 27 July 1969 with the author; Dupré's are from his preface to Florand, *Jean-Sébastien Bach*, p. 8.
32. *J. S. Bach*, vol. I., p. 166.
33. Ibid.
34. Ibid., p. 167.
35. Ibid.
36. Ibid.
37. Ibid., p. 169.
38. Ibid., pp. 169–70.
39. Archibald T. Davison, in Roback, pp. 204–5.
40. Lambaréné, 25 May 1946. 'Je lis et relis les pages que vous me consacrez dans le Jubilee Book et je suis touché, plus que je ne puis vous dire, de la sympathie et la compréhension que vous avez pour mon effort de rendre pour le mieux la musique de Bach . . . . Dans vos pages vous exprimez si clairement, ce qui est essentiel, selon mon avis, pour la compréhension et l'exécution de la musique de Bach.' See Appendix B, letter 14.
41. Louis-Edouard Schaeffer, quoted in Joy, pp. 243–44.

5   Organ Builder

Late on a midsummer evening in Strasbourg, Schweitzer sat in a sidewalk cafe taking pleasure at being outside beneath the trees and talking with a group of students from the United States. He and members of the Harvard Glee Club, which was on tour in that July of 1921, had just come from St Thomas's nearby, where they had spent a musical hour so memorable that Schweitzer would write of it nostalgically a quarter century later. In the mediaeval church, lighted only by a candle in the nave and by lamps in the organ loft, the musicians had made music for each other, the young men's anthems interposing between Schweitzer's solos. When, to crown the evening, Schweitzer had played the *Fantasia and Fugue in G Minor*, his listeners were carried in spirit to another St Thomas's, one of them was to say, by a performance they sensed was filled with the knowledge of Bach's own style and organ.[1]

If Schweitzer's understanding of classic styles grew from the Widorian tradition coupled with years of research and reflection, his understanding of classic organs grew from a zeal for the subject of organ building inherited by way of his mother's side of the family and from firsthand observation. Grandfather Schillinger was a pastor in Mühlbach, could improvise magnificently (though without great technical skill), and travelled far and wide to meet organ builders and watch them at work – indeed was scarcely more ardent about his own vocation than about theirs.[2] As for the grandson, a typical story tells how Schweitzer once came to Holland to preach a Christmas sermon and, arriving early, disappeared for several days only to be found covered with dust and sweat in the cathedral organ loft cleaning the pipes. At Christmas he gave a sermon in music as well as in words, playing the voluntaries for astonished parishioners who swore they had never heard their old organ sound so well.

Schweitzer grew up, moreover, in a corner of Europe abounding with organs that were unique in style. By its placement on the west bank of the Rhine, the Alsace region knew the tragedy but also the enrichment of centuries of Franco-German conflict. French under Louis XIV, taken by Germany in 1871, by France after the first World War and by Germany again during the second, Alsace incorporated both cultures into her architecture, language, and institutions. Happily, her mixture of the Mediterranean with the Nordic was embodied in the work of several organ builders of genius. To cite only two, Andreas Silbermann (1678–1734) immigrated to Alsace from Saxony and François Callinet (1754–1820) from Burgundy. In Alsace the art of each came to fruition, and they and lesser builders put up hundreds of organs in the seventeenth and eighteenth centuries – chiefly organs of modest size for village churches. Villages in fact sometimes competed with each other to have the largest or most costly instrument, and the ample revenues of forest and vineyard, thus placed at the service of music, gave builders the luxury of fine hardwoods for cases, alloys high in tin for pipes, and a leisurely pace for tonal finishing and woodworking.

Whether built by Silbermann or Callinet or others, the characteristically Alsatian organ contrasted or united classic German elements with classic French. It took from the north and east independent pedal divisions and principal choruses and from south and west third-sounding ranks and varieties of scales, among other features both numerous and subtle. Aided by its exquisite materials and workmanship, it produced a generally warm and mellow ensemble and a tutti whose power was smooth and of a different order from the penetrating 'bite' of northern instruments. Although Schweitzer was far from deprecating the genius of such northerners as Christian Müller and Arp Schnitger, taking special delight in Müller's masterpiece at St Bavo's in Haarlem and Schnitger's at St Jacobi's in Hamburg, he believed the sonority of the Alsatian organ approached perfection. And he especially favoured the Andreas Silbermann, because its tone was clear, refined, and brilliant in a way Schweitzer's ear told him was best for Bach's music and for later masters as well.

Throughout his life, the Silbermann tone and craftsmanship served Schweitzer as model for what a good organ should be. He liked the plenum, whose transparency let one discern the alto and tenor voices of even the most intricate Bach fugue, and he liked the delicacy of balance among individual timbres and the *forte* so innocent of stridor that one could listen for hours without fatigue. He liked the purely mechanical linkage of keys to pipes, considering tracker action ideal for all but the largest organs (for which, after his acquaintance with the Parisian builders, he deemed the Barker lever excellent), and he liked the slider windchest, whose design he thought contributed to the blend of tone by letting pipes of the same pitch in different ranks draw air from the same groove and hence resonate in sympathy. He liked the rückpositif division of pipes mounted in their own case on the gallery rail, asserting that the great and the positif were distinct personalities whose contrasts should be emphasized and that these personalities, together with the swell division of later instruments, ought to form a union analogous to that of the Trinity, in which three become one while yet remaining three.

From this analogue, furthermore, he argued against echo or antiphonal divisions and, adducing also the detrimental effect upon tone of masses of wood inside the case, more than one division enclosed.

It was as a student during the 1890s that Schweitzer began to get acquainted with organs of many kinds as he travelled at holidays to and from the universities of Strasbourg, Paris, and Berlin. In France he found that players and builders tended to remain conservative, holding to the slider windchest, mechanical action, and registration aids confined to the pedals devised by Cavaillé-Coll. But in Germany he encountered almost everywhere an enthusiasm bordering on mania for the advances lately brought about by electricity. Gone now the bellows pumped by hand and the limits thereby placed on the supply of air, hence stops could be voiced more powerfully than before and drawn in greater numbers, and the resultant heaviness of the key action could be overcome by using some of the limitless wind as a lever to open the pallets. Indispensable to the new voicing, quickly becoming a symbol of the new freedom to enlarge and louden, pneumatic action was thus the delight of progressive organists and builders. That their infatuation was inuring them to the sponginess of the action and the opacity of the tones became Schweitzer's conviction, the more firmly held as years went by.

In the autumn of 1896, on his way home after a first visit to Bayreuth, Schweitzer stopped in Stuttgart, he writes,

> in order to examine the new organ in the *Liederhalle* of that town, about which the newspapers had published enthusiastic reports. Herr Lang, the organist of the Stiftskirche, who both as musician and as man stood in the first rank, was kind enough to show it to me. When I heard the harsh tone of the much belauded instrument, and in the Bach fugue which Lang played to me perceived a chaos of sounds in which I could not distinguish the separate voices, my foreboding that the modern organ meant in that respect a step not forward but backward, suddenly became a certainty.[3]

Continuing to use his spare time in the next few years to get to know as many organs, old and new, as possible, and to discuss matters with all the organists and builders he met, he was mainly greeted with derision for saying that the old organs sounded better than the new. Nor would most of his colleagues agree with him that mechanical action conduced more than pneumatic to neatness and accuracy of touch.

By the same token, the unlimited supply of air was allowing consoles to be equipped with new devices for adding and withdrawing stops so that by the merest gesture a player could now instantly change timbre or go from *pianissimo* to *fortissimo* and back. But the crescendo pedal and combination piston were artistic drawbacks, Schweitzer believed, partly because the former, by which stops came into play successively from softest to loudest, was set by the builder once for all and could not be modified by the organist, and the latter was usually so made that stops could neither be added to an existing registration nor withdrawn therefrom. With these devices also, which were viewed as scientific marvels in an era that revered science, men whom Schweitzer knew to be otherwise perceptive were infatuated to the point of blindness.

For him, on the contrary, nothing could seem more reasonable than that the tone of an organ be considered at least as important as the mechanism, and that tone and mechanism together be made to serve the music. Thus Schweitzer, who could not abide cruelty in any form, least of all in his own words and actions, and who for this reason among others made it a lifelong principle never to engage in polemic that might injure reputations or feelings, now found himself facing a dilemma. To remain silent was to acquiesce in ideas he knew were corruptive; to speak out was to offend men whose emotions were, by the nature of art and artists, barely separable from those ideas – and who were his elders besides. Continuing to ponder the evidence from his travels and conversations, then, and persuaded that 'without stirring up arguments . . . one must nevertheless with restraint but with steadfastness speak the truth,'[4] he decided to write an essay on organ playing and building as practised divergently in France and Germany. In it, he could point out defects and propose remedies.

Published in 1906, his booklet is a masterpiece of scholarly exposition combined with common sense and tact.

> I take the floor [he states] as one who has had the advantage of both the German and the French schools, as one who by force of circumstances has felt for more than twelve years at home with both German and French organs, as one who defends the German art of organ playing in Paris and the French art of organ playing in Germany, and as one who is convinced that an agreement between the two types of organ and the two different conceptions must be reached.[5]

He then traces the disparities, always in the manner of the good historian who is both exact as to data and amiable as to presentation, noting that they began to appear 'about a generation ago. When old Hesse played upon the new organ of St Clotilde, he felt at once at home on it, and declared that it was his conception of the ideal organ.'[6] But nowadays the German who would play in France and the Frenchman who would play in Germany could do so only after long rehearsal and much 'intelligent assistance'[7] with the stops: the differences had grown to the point that Reger could not be performed on French or Widor on German organs without doing violence to the character of the instruments.

Schweitzer notes that a superficial difference in the placement of the registration aids, which in Germany were arranged chiefly for the hands as pistons but in France exclusively for the feet as pedals, accompanies a profound difference of principle – the artistic principle underlying the nature of that *crescendo* and *decrescendo* which are the essence of modern styles. In Germany the roller or cylinder determines how a composer will write a *crescendo*,

> as a glance at any new work for the organ makes sufficiently clear. In other words, we produce a *crescendo* by bringing all the stops into play one after the other without a break, so that they all operate in the same way . . .; we sacrifice in this *crescendo* the artistic individuality of the stops; we take it for granted that every increase means at the same time a change in tone colour; we reconcile ourselves to the monotony which necessarily results from the fact that the sequence of the stops is always the same; . . . we give up all our independence in the execution of the *crescendo*, at the very moment when freedom is so closely allied to artistry: and all this in order to be in a position to achieve a *crescendo* by the simple movement of a wheel or a pedal.[8]

So it was in Germany, but not in France. The French organist must indeed make several movements, but he is free to choose the progression of stops that is best suited to a given piece, a fact French composers naturally take into account.

> There is for each manual a ventil for reeds and mixtures, that is, a pedal by which the mixtures and reeds arranged for that manual are made to speak at the discretion of the player, so that the player has it in his hands – or rather in his feet – to introduce into the tone colour of the foundation stops the mixtures from the three manuals in any sequence he chooses, before, during, or after their coupling, or in alternation with it.[9]

This is in addition to the effect of the swell shutters, which enclose a group of stops ordinarily greater in power and variety than the German counterparts and indeed capable of dominating the whole coupled instrument. As a practical matter too, control by pedals is preferable because one can often count on having a foot free but seldom a hand.

Yet, Schweitzer continues, the German cylinder can produce unique effects unattainable with the French pedals, which have the disadvantage of controlling, besides the couplers, only the reeds and mixtures. It would thus be desirable to unite the systems by keeping both cylinder and pedals – the latter extended to control all the stops – and by making pedals and pistons correspond: 'One could, for instance, set a coupler with the hand, and then, since it would be set automatically at the same time in the feet, be in a position to shut it off either with the hand, or, if more convenient, with the foot.'[10] The utility of such resources, he notes, stands in inverse proportion to their simplicity.

Always concerned to promote good will, Schweitzer leavens his remarks with such disarming passages as these:

> I do not sit for five minutes beside Father Guilmant on the bench of his beautiful house organ at Meudon without his asking me, as if he had just remembered where we left off the last time: 'And in Germany do they still build pistons? That I can't understand. See how simple it is when one has everything under one's feet,' . . . and

the short, agile feet press couplers and combination pedals silently, then in a trice let them up again.

On another day Widor, for the twenty-fifth time, begins on the same subject. 'Tell my friend Professor Münch at Strasbourg that he must point out for me a single place in a Bach prelude or fugue when he has a hand free for a moment to reach for a piston! He must name someone for me who can play on the manual and at the same time press with his thumb the piston in the keyslip.'[11]

With comparable good humour mixed with seriousness Schweitzer turns to questions of touch and tone. Pneumatic actions, he asserts, offer a dead precision. Consisting as they do in the transmitting of power solely through wind pressure, they lack the vitality and elasticity of mechanical actions. Trackers alone, in Schweitzer's view, allow the player to have a really intimate relationship with the instrument and play clearly and accurately. With them, the finger feels a certain tension exactly when the tone comes, a kind of contact point. With pneumatics, there can be no such co-operation on the part of the keys, which moreover are often so badly regulated as to be without depth, or too deep, or without free play, or indeed with so much free play that the most careful finger substitution is hazardous because adjacent keys speak at the slightest touch. 'But the pneumatic organ operates so easily!' The man who threw in this comment, Schweitzer tells his readers cheerfully, was a giant who might have appeared as the strong man at any fair.[12]

Then: 'Are the advances in organ building beneficial to the tonal quality?' Schweitzer asks. Answering in the negative, he suggests that new organs are only more powerful than the old, not lovelier, and that even thoughtful builders were put onto a wrong track by the advent of unlimited wind made possible by electricity, and exchanged richness of tone for strength. The solution is to go back once more within the boundaries of art formerly imposed by the need to conserve wind, he writes; but to do so is easier in principle than in practice, for the century that gave birth to the railroad, steamship, and telegraph brought commercialization into the arts as well.

> Our organ builders found themselves in the embarrassing position of having to accept those inventions which made possible a reduction in prices, and therefore success in competition. Everything else, the purely artistic, was compelled to stand aside. The past forty years, the age of invention in organ building, will not appear some day on the pages of history as the great years of artistic progress, as many among us believe.[13]

Whether from necessity or by choice, builders in general followed the tendency of the times toward cheapness, failing to ask whether artistic work, which ignores the demands of time and money, was still possible. Only Cavaillé-Coll and a few others remained true to their convictions, and he accordingly ended his days in poverty. 'Yes, the old Cavaillé,' Schweitzer recalls a builder saying, 'when one of his men worked on something for three weeks and it did not please him entirely, he had him start again at the beginning; and if again it did not satisfy him, still another time. Who among us can do that? We should not last three months.'[14]

An introduction to Cavaillé-Coll and his works and to the artistic creation they inspired in Saint-Saëns, Franck, Guilmant, Widor, Vierne, and others makes up the second half of the essay. Schweitzer's purpose is as always to foster understanding among colleagues so that the 'partition' between the French art of organ playing and the German may be 'razed' and, each side learning from the other, new life arise in both.[15]

Cavaillé-Coll 'was more than a great builder: he was, like Silbermann, a genius . . . . I can never forget him; I can still see him today with his little cap, and with the good, true eyes in which so much of art and intelligence lay, sitting every Sunday beside Widor on the organ bench at St Sulpice.'[16] His main interest stands in just the opposite direction from that of the usual German builder, namely in perfecting timbre rather than in perfecting registration aids. With these he confines himself to couplers, ventils for reeds and mixtures, and in large organs a simple arrangement of blind combinations. He similarly prefers mechanical actions, assisted when necessary by the Barker lever, itself a kind of tracker device. His gambas, principals, and flutes are unsurpassed in tonal loveliness. They blend well. They evince in upper registers no trace of harshness. Even the mixtures, to which he devoted more and more thought during the last period of his work, are models of good blend and silvery tone – all of this according to Schweitzer. Cavaillé-Coll's well-blended tone may be attributed in part to his using slider windchests so divided that pressures of various intensities can be supplied to various ranks – and even to various pipes within the same rank – depending on the pressure needed to produce the best sound; in part to his using appropriately thick metal for the walls of pipes and appropriately large diameters; and in part to his using the best wood and the best tin. Above all he does not hurry the voicing.

Tonal finishing done on site by conscientious voicers, Schweitzer continues, takes four times longer than is customary in Germany and is proportionately expensive. He notes in passing that good voicers 'should occupy such a place in the rank of artists that one artistic voicer should be considered equal to six average *virtuosi*,'[17] since the latter are easier to find and soon forgotten but the work of a good voicer will outlive him, remaining to edify generation after generation.

Only two features of Cavaillé-Coll's designs give Schweitzer pause: the high-pressure reeds, whose tone he considers too dominant, and the placement of the positif division inside of the main case rather than in front. Because one of the triune persons of the ideal organ was thus eliminated, he thinks it mistaken that at St Sulpice the roomy positif case was left empty instead of being used for stops, and he confesses to having respectfully teased Widor about playing on a two-manual organ with five keyboards.

We may glance ahead to notice that Schweitzer always manifested deep feelings for the St Sulpice organ, quite apart from its association with a master whom he loved. As he writes in 1931 in his autobiography, it was the finest of all the organs he had known;[18] another thirty years later he calls it the most beautiful organ in the world.[19] The largest of Cavaillé-Coll's works, it was for Schweitzer in some ways, though not all, the archetype embodying his own ideal conceptions. For him the perfect organ consisted in a fusion of old and new: from the eighteenth century the slider chest, low wind pressures, reeds capable of blending, tracker action, and the rückpositif; from the nineteenth the fully-developed swell division, wind at various pressures, Barker lever when needed, a sufficient number of eight-foot stops, and such registration aids as best served the player and the music. This ideal organ he would call 'monumental,' perhaps less to denote size than to denote what is of enduring significance and value, for in all but the largest churches he believed it would need at most fifty or sixty stops and three manuals. It would be placed by preference in a west gallery above the entrance, so that sound might emerge unobstructed; if the church were especially long, the better placement would be at a certain height on a side wall midway down the nave, so that the echo might not destroy clearness in the music. The stops would exhibit much variety, excluding neither gamba and cello (though the string timbres would be so voiced as not to be conspicuous in the combined sounds of the whole instrument) nor clarinet and oboe – the clarinet staying more reliably in tune and having a mellower tone than its forerunner, the krummhorn, which was a stop he particularly disliked.[20] Even with reeds drawn, the sonority overall would be 'round, transparent, beautiful, rich.'[21]

The publication of his views brought Schweitzer about as much contumely as approbation, many readers taking it as an affront that he had criticized their taste for multitudes of accessories and for quantity rather than quality of stops. 'If an organ does not look like the central signal room of a great railway station,' he had written, 'it is from the very start worthless to a certain category of our organists.'[22] In vain did he reply to their displeasure: 'An organ is like a cow; one does not look at its horns so much as at its milk.'[23] But to many readers his position made sense. Among them was Guido Adler, the distinguished musical scholar and essayist, and hardly three years had passed when with Adler's endorsement he was invited to speak before a congress of the International Musical Society in Vienna. That august group had never sponsored a section on organ building, and to profit from what he saw as a unique opportunity Schweitzer devised by way of preparation a questionnaire to be sent to organists and builders in half a dozen countries and the results of which he could announce. He received some hundred and fifty replies, each one requiring hours of study and more than one being a veritable treatise, and in his address of May 1909 he was able to specify points of consensus and come close to defining 'the organ that Europe wants.'[24] For the first time organists and builders had been given the chance to 'discuss on an interconfessional and international basis the problems with which all friends of church music and organ playing are concerned.'[25]

Schweitzer then met with colleagues sharing his views to work out a list of 'International Regulations for Organ Building'[26] that countered the infatuation for purely technical achievements with a call for the production once more of carefully built instruments of fine tone. 'In the years that followed,' he recalls, 'it came to be perceived more and more clearly that the really good organ must combine the beautiful tone of the old organs with the technical advantages of the new. Twenty-two years after its first appearance it was possible for my pamphlet on organ building to be reprinted without alteration as the now accepted programme of reform.'[27] Yet even then his work was not finished, only well begun. Nor was it to proceed without obstacle, disappointment, the loss of friends, the occasional victory, and many defeats.

In the cause of the good organ, he writes, he sacrificed much time and much labour.

> Many a night have I spent over organ designs which had been sent to me for approval or revision. Many a journey have I undertaken in order to study on the spot the question of restoring or rebuilding an organ. Letters running into hundreds have I written . . ., but if I do not give it up, the reason is that the struggle for the good organ is to me a part of the struggle for truth.[28]

Notes and References

1. Archibald T. Davison, in Roback, pp. 202–3.
2. *Out of My Life and Thought*, pp. 12, 87.
3. Ibid., p. 87.
4. Letter to J. B. Jamison, Lambaréné, 17 December 1944. See Appendix B, letter 1.
5. Joy, p. 139.
6. Ibid., p. 140.
7. Ibid.
8. Ibid., pp. 140–41.
9. Ibid., pp. 141–42.
10. Ibid., p. 147.
11. Ibid., p. 144.
12. Ibid., p. 153.
13. Ibid., p. 156.
14. Ibid., p. 157.
15. Ibid., p. 176.
16. Ibid., p. 151.

17. Ibid., p. 166.
18. *Out of My Life and Thought*, p. 91.
19. In a letter to Marcel Dupré (Lambaréné, 15 March 1962), printed in the programme for the centennial of the installation. See below, Chapter 8.
20. Letter to A. J. Eckert, Lambaréné, 22 July 1945. See Appendix B, letter 8.
21. Letter to J. B. Jamison, Lambaréné, 17 December 1944. See Appendix B, letter 1.
22. Joy, p. 150.
23. Ibid., p. 137.
24. Ibid., pp. 253–54 and, for the responses to Schweitzer's questionnaire, pp. 255–89.
25. Ibid., p. 255.
26. Leipzig: Breitkopf and Härtel, 1909.
27. *Out of My Life and Thought*, p. 93.
28. Ibid., pp. 96, 101.

6 Reformer

Schweitzer was most often given the chance to examine organs and their manufacture in the years 1921–36, when he travelled as lecturer or recitalist to dozens of towns in Germany, France, England, Spain, Holland, Belgium, Sweden, Denmark, and Switzerland. Together with his writings and his growing celebrity as a humanitarian, his travels gave him a platform from which to influence the course of organ building in Europe and the New World alike. Indeed, although Emile Rupp and others preceded him in speaking and writing about the deficiencies of contemporary organs, and although organ reform movements began at different times in Germany, France, England, the United States, and elsewhere and had different aims, these movements worldwide owed much of their impetus to Schweitzer.

Sometimes his advice was sought directly, as in 1927 by the vestry of St Jacobi Church, Hamburg, who wished to repair a Schnitger that Bach himself had played. Its consummate sonorities were matched by its unique historical value, Schweitzer declared, after inspecting the organ, because the other instruments Bach knew, including those on which he carried out his duties in Arnstadt, Mulhouse, Weimar, Cöthen, and Leipzig, no longer existed. Only this Schnitger 'has come down to us as it was when its beauty enchanted the greatest organ master of all times,' and modern artists might learn from it in what way Bach played his music and with what timbres. 'It is a case of simple preservation. That which is damaged must be renovated, that which is missing replaced.'[1]

And yet Schweitzer's recommendations went beyond a restoration properly so called. 'The beauty and individuality of the organ is based on the pipes and windchests,' he writes.

As the foremost principle . . . pipes and chests must be preserved in their present state. Further, one must preserve the low wind pressure, for only thus will the pipes speak normally and in their full beauty.

The pipes that were requisitioned in the war should be replaced. In the rückpositif, the bärpfeife 8 should be reinstalled, and it may also be advisable to replace with the original schalmei 4 the trompete 8 that was added later. It goes without saying that the pneumatic voices that were added later to the oberwerk must be removed.

So much bespeaks a restoration pure. Not so, however, when Schweitzer adds:

> The completion of the short octaves on all four manuals is recommended, as well as the completion of the lower octave in the pedals. It would be interesting, of course, to preserve the imperfections of these old organs, such as incomplete and broken octaves, as a historical document. On the other hand, such imperfections, small as they may be, diminish the performance value of the instrument . . . .
>
> The question of whether the work should be tuned to normal pitch is difficult to decide. At the time of the restoration of the Silbermann organ in St Thomas in Strasbourg, I succeeded in having the work tuned to normal pitch, in view of the advantages of normal pitch at divine services. However, the pipes lost some of the original dimensions and proportions. For a unique work like St Jacobi, it may be preferable to keep the old tuning . . . . But if it were possible, merely by shifting the manuals and without great interference with the pipes, to achieve normal or near-normal pitch, there would be no objection. A careful study would be required to ascertain whether this is technically possible.
>
> As for adding a swell box to the oberwerk, this has also been done with old Dutch organs. During my inspection, it seemed to me there was sufficient space for the construction of swell shades, and if a thorough technical study should reveal that the addition of a swell is possible, I believe that this should not be rejected. The sound of the old organ will neither be harmed nor changed by adding a swell box. The expressiveness of the third manual will not be purchased by a disadvantage.
>
> The present tracker action has serious drawbacks. The keys are hard to depress and they drop low. On the other hand, it is due to the mechanism that the texture of the voices appears with such wonderful clarity . . . . Although it is possible to make the organ easier to play by using Barker levers and pneumatic tubes, it is to be feared that once one begins making changes one will not know when to stop. Replacing the tracker action with something else would be a serious interference with the work. Much of its historical value would in this way be lost. For this reason, I favour preserving the tracker action. It is to be restored with the best material available, by doing which a lighter touch can certainly be attained.
>
> Keeping the tracker action will limit the use of couplers. But this does not amount to much in a work such as that of St Jacobi. Each manual of the organ has its own complete individuality of sonority, and the full first manual has such richness that there is no need for coupling.
>
> Keeping the tracker action decides the question of whether the organ should have a console with modern aids for playing. It is certainly desirable to give the organist the ability in pulling and pushing the stops that he has on more recent instruments. But this would assume that the stops and the entire apparatus of registration be made pneumatic. Experience has shown that nothing is more difficult than to connect pneumatic systems with slider chests, especially when dealing with old chests . . . . I am not in favour of it . . . .
>
> Besides, not much changing of stops is necessary, since the richness of sonority at St Jacobi does not call for any frequent change of colour. If this organ is to be preserved as a historical monument, moreover, only Bach's music and music from the era before Bach would be in question, in which less is done with registration. The organ at St Jacobi will therefore be a teacher to the organ world concerning the correct interpretation of the old masters, by showing that they had simply for technical reasons to restrict the changing of stops.[2]

Thus, in this case and others, whether to rebuild or to restore was for Schweitzer determined not inflexibly by principle but by circumstances as well. At all events it was thanks in large measure to him that, as the organ builder Poul-Gerhard Andersen writes,

> an entire generation listened with open ears and was able to experience the tonal realm represented by the Jacobi organ. Generation after generation had used this organ without noticing anything unusual about it; it was generally considered to be an unimportant, antiquated, yet not worthless instrument; but now people began to listen in a completely different way, and a wealth of tonal resources was thrown open to contemplation, suggesting an entirely new trend.[3]

If at times Schweitzer's advice was sought directly, at other times his influence was exercised from afar, as in 1933 when Walter Holtkamp added a rückpositif division to the organ at the Cleveland Museum of Art – the first such installation in twentieth-century America – after having in part been inspired to do so by reading Schweitzer's autobiography.[4]

That Holtkamp in the early 1930s liked to sit at his desk with *Out of My Life and Thought* before him suggests the kind and degree of Schweitzer's influence, for more than one of the convictions on which Holtkamp's innovations were based – innovations of profound importance to the American reform movement – derived from Schweitzer or found reinforcement in Schweitzer's views: for example, Holtkamp's conviction that an organ ought to be so situated in a room as to speak directly to listeners and that an organ of modest size, so situated, ought to be thought preferable to a large organ installed in chambers; or again, that relatively low wind pressure contributed to good tone and blend, as did the slider chest; or again, that a well-developed chorus was the root of good tonal design; or again, that simplicity was both a governing principle to be embraced and an ideal toward which to strive.

It was in order to embody this ideal that the Holtkamp organ assumed – as the builder writes, describing an early example – 'a form which seemed to us best suited to its function and which expresses the function visually. In short, it is the simple solution. Simplicity marks the instrument in all its details, both structural and tonal.'[5] The functional look of his pipes and consoles was in fact to become the hallmark of his work, for Holtkamp was persuaded that the very sight of, say, a four-foot prestant made of copper, a sixteen-foot quintaten of wood, and a diapason of spotted metal, all reposing majestically in clear view, would evoke in the observer, he writes, 'an expectation of piquant variety' while presenting 'an appearance of dignity and ruggedness in keeping with the nature of the instrument.' He believed that the 'massive and virile effect' which he considered desirable in timbre would best be complemented in structure 'by exposing to the eye the pipes massed in strong architectural forms and by reducing the casework to a minimum consistent with good design.'[6] And though such conceptions differed from Schweitzer's experience with the old European case, and from his belief that voicing should in general tend less to the virile than to the mellow, they none the less took as starting point an ideal Schweitzer had espoused in print.

For his part, Schweitzer first learned of Holtkamp from an article in *The Diapason* and from correspondence with Arthur Quimby and Melville Smith, organists whose wish to perform the complete works of Bach at the Cleveland museum had been the impetus for Holtkamp's rückpositif there. 'Bravo for the first rückpositif in America,' Schweitzer wrote to Holtkamp on 22 May 1934. 'I congratulate you. This is work for truth.' And to the organists, on 26 November 1936: 'A thousand thanks for sending me your beautiful programmes. It interested me very much to learn that people are beginning to be interested in the rückpositif also in the U.S.A. Lovely! An organ that has a rückpositif is complete. All other organs, even if they have five manuals, are incomplete.'[7]

Holtkamp had first learned in detail about European reform by reading not only *Out of My Life and Thought* but also the pamphlet on organ building. So significant did he consider the pamphlet, in fact, that he wrote to Schweitzer to propose an English translation. From Lambaréné, Schweitzer replied on 4 June 1940 welcoming the idea, offering to undertake a few modifications and additions to complete the booklet, and congratulating Holtkamp once again for taking an interest in the rückpositif. The effect of the division would satisfy everyone, Schweitzer predicted, and he looked forward to visiting the United States someday and meeting Holtkamp.

World War Two intervened, confining Schweitzer to Africa, and nearly ten years were to pass before the encounter took place – years in which much pondering and experiment brought Holtkamp's artistic philosophy to its definitive form, a form that agreed with Schweitzer only in principle, not in practice. By 12 July 1949, when the two men met in Cleveland, Holtkamp had concluded, for example, that using tracker action in his instruments meant abandoning a foolproof electro-pneumatic system which had served him well and been well received by organists; that the slider chest could be adapted to accommodate such a system without detriment to tone; and that pipes sounded best when left unencased. Hence we may speculate that matters of key action, windchest, and casework made up much of the talk of the two men, as they spent the day together visiting Holtkamp's workshop and several of his organs, including those at the church of Our Lady of the Angels and the Cleveland Museum of Art. Doubtless each man carefully explained his views, and doubtless neither changed the other's mind. It is noteworthy that Holtkamp left no record of the conversations and said almost nothing about them to the son who succeeded him. As for Schweitzer, the attitude that seemingly underlay a conversation with Jacques Barzun a few days later is perhaps suggestive. 'He was a very (what shall I say?)

abstracted person,' Barzun reports. 'He didn't really converse . . . . He went on talking. He would listen very politely, but it made no impression.'[8]

What is certain is that during dinner together at the Oak Room restaurant in Terminal Tower, Schweitzer wrote out several sets of stoplists – mainly of two-manual instruments – for Holtkamp to peruse, perhaps again stating his ideas on the relationship of swell and positif, as he had done in a letter to Holtkamp on 2 February 1941:

> Thanks also for sending me the stoplist of the Barnes Memorial Organ. It interested me very much. I think the organ well designed. One remark, however: As a rule, it is better to put the trompette 8 and clarion 4 in the swell rather than in the choir. For the swell should be stronger than the choir: the choir remains an incomplete manual, and the swell should be complete. And César Franck, Widor, Gigout, Vierne, and all the great modern composers for the organ assume the trompette and the clarion (as well as the fagotto 16) always in the swell. See the registration indications in César Franck and Widor! So if the trompette 8 and clarion 4 are found in the choir, it is very complicated for the organist to render these works as they were conceived by the composer.[9]

Respect for the composer's intent was already implicit in Holtkamp's conviction – in accord with Schweitzer – that the musical works to be played on an organ provided the criteria by which it should be designed. Almost from the beginning, Holtkamp had been in reaction against a kind of instrument common in American churches and concert halls of the early twentieth century, the organ of large dimensions that was housed in chambers and voiced on high pressure and that contained too few stops of traditional chorus variety and too many imitative of orchestral timbres. 'I believe that we realize more and more,' he declared in 1935, 'that the modern organ is in a large measure a concession of tone to mechanism and location, and that actually it is not the perfected form of its predecessors, as we were once inclined to assume.'[10] Not least among its flaws, he believed, was its inability to supply the clarity needed by contrapuntal writing.

Although to him, as to Schweitzer, the music of Bach provided the test of an organ's quality, the ideal instrument, Holtkamp writes, 'will reproduce the worthwhile organ music of all ages.'[11] To realize that ideal, a 'new technic has had to be developed and this has often led us to the camps of the Silbermanns and Cavaillé-Colls. We have borrowed freely from these old masters, but always with an ear for our modern conditions. Stripping the instrument of inhibition and sophistication fulfills modern tenets and at the same time restores many of the most desirable of the primitive features.'[12]

By July 1949, when Schweitzer made his sole journey to the United States, reform had also long dominated the thought and activity of Holtkamp's distinguished competitor G. Donald Harrison, president of the Aeolian-Skinner Organ Company. Manifesting a similar conception of the ideal instrument, Harrison had stated in 1929: 'The organ has a wonderful literature, and every organ small or large should be designed so that both the classical and modern works from this literature can be played effectively upon it.'[13]

With this in mind, Harrison devised in about the same period as the Cleveland rückpositif a style of instrument later to be called 'American Classic' in which were united certain features from the modern organ with certain features from the old. In 1936 in Boston, for example, he built for the Church of the Advent a three-manual organ whose specification included not only the viole celeste, clarinet, and orchestral flute but also mixtures and mutations pitched higher and made more prominent than then usual, together with relatively low wind pressure overall and a positif installed at the front of the chamber and in effect unencased. So successful was this organ, and so widely did its reputation spread, that for the next quarter century his firm built almost nothing but organs similar in design, many of them at such renowned locations as the Mormon Tabernacle in Salt Lake City, the Cathedral of St John the Divine in New York, and Symphony Hall in Boston. 'The truly musical value of such voices as the French horn, English horn, strings, flute celestes and erzählers cannot be overrated,' Harrison had written, 'and, in fact, when added to the traditional scheme the instrument seems to reach the ideal and it is difficult to say in which direction further development is possible.'[14] Indeed, the very idea of an organ capable of rendering with appropriate colour the music of Bach and Franck alike was thought by some to symbolize America itself, the land where disparate cultures could magnificently coalesce.

The presence there of G. Donald Harrison was perhaps also symbolic, for he had been born in England and spent much of his career in organ building as an assistant to Henry Willis III. Not until 1927 did he move to the United States to join the Skinner firm, his preferences in tonal design having been shaped by his knowledge of English organs, Willis's above all.[15]

His preferences had been shaped as well by a particular love for polyphony and by his acquaintances among organists. 'About the year 1919,' he writes, 'Marcel Dupré came to England. I shall never forget the tremendous impression this great master's playing made upon me. It was after this that I made many trips to Paris and became deeply interested in the work of Cavaillé-Coll.'[16] A friendship and exchange of ideas ensued with Dupré, whose own comprehensive knowledge of organ building supported passionately held views as to what constituted the ideal organ, views that also helped to mould Harrison's thought. At the same time, Dupré's friendship with Willis and others led to some of Dupré's suggestions being incorporated into the design of the organ in Westminster Cathedral, an instrument many deemed Willis's masterpiece. Installed in the rear gallery of a vast and resonant nave, this organ boasted rich foundations, blazing reeds, and sparkling mixtures that together created massive sonorities of unusual transparency and grace. Its inauguration by Dupré, in 1924, followed by a series of recitals by other distinguished artists, marked a turning point for Harrison. That not only eighteenth-century repertories demand clarity but also, as he writes, 'the highly vivacious movements from the modern symphonies of the French composers'[17] was only one of the truths thus emphatically brought home to him.[18]

Although he had used some Silbermann pipe scales as early as 1935, it was not until after completing the organ in the Church of the Advent that Harrison heard the Silbermann and Schnitger timbres for himself. 'In 1936 I visited Germany complete with drawing equipment,' he writes. 'I soon gave up taking measurements and decided it was better to absorb the musical result[s] and then reproduce them in a modern way and in a manner that would be acceptable to modern ears and in our buildings.'[19] He had depended theretofore upon knowledgeable friends. 'Your description of the tone quality of the Silbermann Diapason is exactly as I imagined it,' he had written to Willis, for example, 'but I wished to have confirmation from a reliable source and from one who can use the words which mean something to an organ builder.'[20] He hastened to add that he was not attempting to imitate the Silbermann or any organ of the period, 'but am merely reintroducing some of the features of the older organ which have been lost in the modern organs, and using to some extent the principles utilized by the older builders in the general chorus; the sole object, of course, being to make the instrument a more nearly ideal one for the playing of the best literature written for this particular medium.'[21]

In what ways Schweitzer liked the American Classic organs he tried during his visit to Boston is uncertain. To the small group of admirers that accompanied him to the Church of the Advent and elsewhere he said little, according to one witness, E. Power Biggs, who adds that it was nevertheless almost impossible to get him to stop playing.[22] Although to our ears Harrison's voicing may seem a model of elegance and restraint, Schweitzer might well have judged it unfavourably by the full but mellow resonance of the Alsatian Silbermanns, finding the mixtures by comparison shrill, the diapasons thin, the reeds harsh. He would no doubt have liked the physical comfort of the consoles, the ease of manipulation of the stops, and the fine quality of the work and material in pipes and chests, all the while thinking it sad that Harrison, like Holtkamp, had rejected mechanical action and been often compelled to build organs in chancels rather than galleries. To have said as much, however, would have seemed to him a violation both of the canons of courtesy owed by guest to host and of a precept he had long obeyed: 'Never,' as he wrote on 28 January 1948 to a friend, 'deliberately destroy the illusions people wish to keep regarding the organ in their church. There speaks wisdom and good will.'[23] And in fact Schweitzer may have found the

American Classic organ a not-too-distant relative of organs he had known in England, a pleasant reminder of instruments he had thought lovely in their way.

In Boston, he was at all events mistakenly perceived by Harrison, and indeed by Biggs as well, as supporting their ideas, and by the public as affixing an imprimatur. Such perceptions were of course the more potent in their consequences for his being at the height of his fame as a man of principle, portrayed by the popular press as a saintly figure whose life and ideas were apt criteria by which other men and ideas might be judged. In any case, photographs of Schweitzer smiling and examining a pipe at the Aeolian-Skinner shop with Harrison at his side – a photograph that was to appear in the publicity of the firm for several years afterward – and of Schweitzer sitting at an Aeolian-Skinner console with Biggs at his side led many an organist to infer unqualified approval of Harrison's building, on the one hand, and Biggs's playing, on the other. That Schweitzer signed his name on a slip of wood in the organ being built for Symphony Hall was likewise viewed as something more than a friendly gesture. But the facts were otherwise.

Indeed, his influence on both men was slight. Harrison would probably not have read the pamphlet on organ building nor the pertinent chapters in *Out of My Life and Thought*: he was not fluent in German, and neither work was to be published in French or English until well after the direction of his reforms was fixed. That he would have had a translation made likewise seems improbable. Certainly Dupré would not have acquainted him with Schweitzer's ideas: though Dupré and Schweitzer had known each other since the turn of the century and alike revered their master, Widor, who had regarded each of them as a son, they held contradictory opinions about organ building; these they never discussed, preferring as they did to centre their friendship on matters conducing to agreement rather than to discord.[24] In fact, though Harrison knew something of Schweitzer's views, if only at second hand, those views would have seemed to him irrelevant to his own purposes – irrelevant, as a purely practical matter, to the kinds of organ needed by his clients. If nothing else, few of his organs could be installed in galleries, hence at this most elementary level began a necessary divergence from Schweitzer's theories.

Little more can thus be said than that Harrison's reforms took place in a climate of opinion that Schweitzer had helped to produce, indeed were enabled to take place thereby, and that in 1949, long after those reforms were conceived, Schweitzer unwittingly lent his prestige to a style of organ building only distantly echoing his own ideal.

By the same token, on E. Power Biggs, who was regarded by generations of organists as setting standards of authenticity for the building of organs and for the playing of Bach, Schweitzer had no effect whatever. We are told that Biggs was pleased to have found in Schweitzer's writings agreement with conclusions he had arrived at already, and that this was the extent of Schweitzer's influence.[25] Regarding Bach's music in particular, it seems unlikely, given the traditions Schweitzer respected, that he could have sanctioned Biggs's way of playing it: the rapid tempi, the choice of relatively small plenums in even the large preludes and fugues, the preference for stops only ostensibly appropriate to the period – some of which Schweitzer considered the epitome of ugliness (the krummhorn, for instance, that 'ghastly register [which] does not stay in tune'[26]) – and the phrasing and articulation which by comparison to the style of Lemmens and Widor could only have struck Schweitzer as arbitrary and idiosyncratic.

Still less could he sanction the turn soon to be taken by the American reform movement, in large measure because of Biggs's proselytizing, exclusively toward the baroque organ, though he would have been gratified to know that one of the future leaders of that movement, Charles Fisk, was to develop an interest in old organs thanks in part to having read Schweitzer while young, and was to esteem the Alsatian Silbermanns above all.[27]

Ironically, organs designed according to sixteenth- and seventeenth-century models were to gain in respectability from Schweitzer's own writings misunderstood and misapplied. As Schweitzer declared in a letter to J. B. Jamison, his ideal was 'a synthesis of the old organ and the modern, retaining from the old the rückpositif and enriching it with an expressive division, keeping the old windchest (Schleiflade), and avoiding too high wind-pressures. And above all I envisaged an organ in which the main concern was for the beauty and richness of the tone.'[28]

But the baroque organ was nevertheless soon to be lauded by many as the perfect instrument for the rendition not only of Bach and his predecessors but also Mendelssohn, Reger, Franck, Dupré, Messiaen. And as the 1950s and 1960s progressed, one was to hear more and more often, at recitals given in even the leading conservatories, where one would have supposed the knowledge of period and style to be most accurate and most revered, the music of late-romanticists performed in the timbres appropriate to Buxtehude and Böhm.

Notes and References

1. Letter of 19 January 1928. See Appendix B, letter 4.
2. Report of 19 January 1928 to the vestry and pastor. For the German text, see Appendix B, letter 4.
3. *Organ Building and Design*, p. 301.
4. See Ferguson, pp. 7, 19, 22. The rückpositif was inaugurated on 25 October 1933.
5. Holtkamp, p. 269.
6. Ibid., p. 270.

7. 'Bravo pour le premier Rückpositiv en Amérique. Je vous félicite. C'est le travail pour la vérité.' 'Tausend Dank für die Zusendung Ihrer schönen Programme. Es hat mich auch sehr interessiert zu erfahren, dass man sich in USA. Jetzt auch für Rückpositif zu interessieren beginnt! Wie schön! Eine Orgel, die ein Rückpositif hat ist vollständig! Alle anderen Orgeln, auch wenn sie 5 Claviaturen haben, sind unvollständig.'

8. Conversation with the author, 16 October 1979.

9. See Appendix B, letter 2. Whether writing in French or German, Schweitzer often uses English terms, for instance 'swell' and 'choir,' in his letters to English-speaking correspondents. Both the context and his stated views make it clear that by 'choir' he means 'positif.' He understood English well, though he rarely spoke it.

10. Holtkamp, p. 272.

11. See Ferguson, pp. 45–47.

12. Holtkamp, p. 272. The demonstration of his theories was perhaps most notably seen in such organs as those for St Paul's Episcopal Church in Cleveland, Crouse Hall at Syracuse University, and Battell Chapel at Yale.

13. Harrison, p. 32.

14. Ibid. In fact Harrison's organ at the Groton School was the first of his 'American Classic' instruments properly so called, but the school was distant enough from Boston to be a less convenient showcase, for visiting organists, than the Church of the Advent.

15. The Skinner Organ Company, founded by Ernest M. Skinner, was merged on 2 January 1932 with the pipe-organ division of the Aeolian Company, Skinner himself eventually leaving, amid controversy and bad feeling, to found in 1936 the Ernest M. Skinner and Son Company, Inc. Harrison was named technical director of the Aeolian-Skinner company in 1933, president in 1940. See Holden, pp. 138–45, 156–75; Callahan, pp. 194–95 and passim; and Ambrosino, 'A History of the Skinner Company,' pp. 266–67.

    Ernest M. Skinner is regarded by many thoughtful critics as the greatest of twentieth-century American builders. Though his esthetic convictions were not directly affected by Schweitzer's, the two men long carried on a friendly correspondence, as Dorothy J. Holden tells us (pp. 224–25), and they met in Boston in 1949, the year of Skinner's retirement. See Appendix B, letter 11.

16. Buhrman, pp. 48–49.

17. Harrison, p. 32.

18. Nicolas Kynaston, who was for ten years organist at Westminster Cathedral, states that the most important of Dupré's suggestions about the design of the instrument had to do with its placement in a back gallery, rather than in the transcepts as originally planned, and with the choir mutations, which differed from what Willis usually devised. (Conversation with the author, 27 January 1990).

19. Callahan, p. 277.

20. Ibid., p. 144.

21. Ibid.

22. Mrs E. Power Biggs, conversation with the author, 5 February 1990. See also E. Power Biggs, 'The Organs in the Germanic Museum of Cambridge, Massachusetts,' in Pape, p. 11.

23. From Lambaréné, to Jean Daniel Weber. 'Donc ne jamais détruire délibérément les illusions que les gens voudraient garder sur l'orgue de leur église: ainsi parlent la sagesse et la bonté.'

24. Mme Marcel Dupré, conversation with the author, 23 April 1975. For Dupré's

views, see Murray (1985), pp. 129–34, 138, and below, Chapter 8. For the same reason they never discussed the interpretation of Bach.

25. Mrs E. Power Biggs, conversation with the author, 5 February 1990.

26. Lambaréné, 22 July 1945, letter to A. J. Eckert. See Appendix B, letter 8.

27. Barbara Owen, conversation with the author, 4 January 1990. Fisk writes: 'One of the original reasons, I suppose [for building tracker-action organs], was that I admired Schweitzer and took him at his word with regard to the total scope of the organ reform. There are, of course, all of the musical reasons ordinarily put forth with regard to traditional voicing, slider chests, and mechanical action, which I largely agree with. Certainly I would not now wish to build any other kind of organ, and I suspect that I would say this even if tracker organs were still as unpopular as they were when we began building them . . . . Essentially, I believe that we should try to pick up where the classical builders left off and go forward from there . . . .' (Douglass et al., vol. II., p. 168.) Fisk likewise recalls (ibid., p. 42): 'I must say that . . . although our organs in the past have appeared eclectic, they have all sprung from the *Klangideal* of the Alsatian builder Andreas Silbermann, whose work I have never been able to get out of my head. If our organs have shown unusual ability to bring to life both French and German music, I suppose it is because the chosen model itself stands on the border between the two countries. Frankly, I do not ever expect to escape the Alsatian ideal, and perhaps that is good, because the sound is beautiful beyond recall.'

28. Lambaréné, 17 December 1944. Reprinted, with Schweitzer's consent, in *The Diapason*, 36 (March 1, 1945), p. 4. See Appendix B, letter 1.

7   Recitalist

Neither as a student in Europe in 1893–1913 nor afterward as a doctor in Africa did Schweitzer give music the central place in his activity. Notwithstanding his passion for organ playing and building, he kept them as avocations in order to undertake tasks he deemed greater and imposed by duty. His accomplishment in music is thus the more praiseworthy for having been, as it were, incidental. Indeed, the two books on Bach, the pamphlets on organ building, the letters of counsel and exhortation, the journeys, the concerts, and the editions might well have made up many a man's life-work entire. And the books on Bach might have been its crown, given their insight, logic of organization, scrutiny of sources, and elegance of diction: in a word, their consummate scholarship. Yet while writing them Schweitzer was preaching weekly at St Nicholas in Strasbourg or at his father's church in Günsbach, or giving university lectures about the Pauline epistles and doing research for a book about the saint, or finishing a treatise on the historical Jesus, or commencing a near-decade of studies to earn a doctorate in medicine – this last by attending courses in anatomy, physiology, chemistry, physics, zoology, botany, bacteriology, pathology, and pharmacology, as he recalls, and by mastering laboratory and surgical techniques, preparing a dissertation, and serving in hospital as intern and resident. We can well believe him when he says that he experienced in those years such a crisis of fatigue as he had never known. But the works remain, and, whether treating the philosophy or the practice of music, they show the disciplined authority of a powerful intellect.

Not the least of their contributions to the world of organists and organ builders, one may add, consists in Schweitzer's having regarded that world, and treated it in his writings, as part of the intellectual world at large: not alone the broad musical world from which the organ has long been so unhappily separated – the realm of divas and impresarios and chamber players and orchestras – but the world of common talk among the educated.

Schweitzer was meantime accompanying choral performances, travelling to play with orchestras led by Widor, and giving recitals. His earliest appearance had taken place on 7 November 1894, when at the Deutsche

Reformierte Kirche in Mulhouse the Evangelische Kirchenchor and an orchestra performed under Eugène Münch's direction an arrangement of the chorale 'Ein feste Burg ist unser Gott' of Bach, *Ein deutsches Requiem* of Brahms, and 'The Flight into Egypt' from *L'Enfance du Christ* of Berlioz, Schweitzer playing the organ part in the Bach and the Brahms. With the same choir in the same city he was to accompany Handel's *Judas Maccabeus* (25 October 1899) and Mendelssohn's *St Paul* (14 March 1900).

With the choir and orchestra of St William Church in Strasbourg, led by Ernest Münch – a brother of Eugène, it will be recalled, and the father of Charles, the future conductor of the Boston Symphony Orchestra – Schweitzer accompanied most notably Bach's *St Matthew Passion* (30 and 31 March 1899), some cantatas (21 June 1900), *Mass in B Minor* (15 January 1905), and *St John Passion* (29 March 1907); Handel's *Messiah* (12 and 13 December 1903); and Mozart's *Requiem* (17 January 1904). With the Paris Bach Society (29 January 1908) and the Orfeó Català of Barcelona (26 October 1908) he gave the Bach *Magnificat*, in Barcelona performing also as soloist in a Handel concerto.

He did similar duty as a soloist in Strasbourg (27 March 1905), when Widor conducted his own *Symphony for Organ and Orchestra* – Schweitzer closing the programme, under Ernest Münch, with the Rheinberger *Concerto in F Major* – and in Munich (20 September 1910), when Widor conducted his own *Sinfonia Sacra*.

> I delight in letting the organ unite its music to that of the orchestra in a concert hall [Schweitzer was to state]. But if I find myself in the position of having to play it in such a hall as a solo instrument, I avoid as well as I can treating it as a secular concert instrument. By my choice of the pieces played and my way of playing them I try to turn the concert hall into a church. But best of all I like, in a church as in a concert hall, to introduce a choir and thus change the concert into a kind of service . . . . By its even tone which can be maintained as long as desired the organ has in it an element, so to speak, of eternity. Even in the secular room it cannot become a secular instrument.[1]

Such was his attitude when at the Salle Gaveau with the Paris Bach Society (22 December 1911) he accompanied the motet *Jesu meine Freude*, an Advent cantata, the cantata for the first Sunday after Epiphany, and excerpts from the *Christmas Oratorio*; and such was his attitude when a few months later (25 April 1912) he and the Society gave in the same hall a benefit concert to raise funds for his first sojourn in Africa, the programme a mix of organ solos and choral works and arranged in sections according to the liturgical seasons of Advent, Christmas, Epiphany, Passiontide, and Pentecost; the audience was asked not to applaud.

He had played regularly for the Society since 1905, when, with Widor, d'Indy, Dukas, Guilmant, Fauré, and its conductor Gustave Bret, he helped to found it as a way to bring Bach's cantatas and Passions before the French public. To fulfill his duties, Schweitzer was compelled, during the very years of his medical studies, to travel several times each winter to Paris. 'Although I only had to attend the final practice,' he writes, 'and could travel back to Strasbourg during the night following each performance, every concert took at least three days of my time. Many a sermon for St Nicholas did I sketch out in the train between Paris and Strasbourg.'[2] Many a time he stepped off that morning train and hurried to attend a medical lecture or to do hospital rounds without having been to bed at all.

Made up largely of professional singers and players, the Bach Society exhibited a high degree of technical competence but not of spiritual involvement, according to one listener, who thought Schweitzer's work far more distinguished than theirs:

> I was struck, first of all, by Schweitzer's indifference to any 'effectiveness' in registration or manner of playing, the entire process being concentrated in the presentation of the music in its proper setting without the slightest effort to make it 'telling' of itself. And it must be remembered that the question was not of the great organ compositions; it was solely of the organ background to, let us say, one of the cantatas . . . . The unpretentious accompanimental parts must always be a pretty routine affair to the organist who loves his playing better than the music he plays. Schweitzer, however, never once obtruding himself, lavished upon them all the scrupulous attention they deserve but all too seldom receive.[3]

It was Schweitzer's view that Bach's recitatives and solos were meant to be accompanied by the organ, Bach having used the harpsichord only for rehearsals.[4]

Our witness continues:

> As far as I can remember, Schweitzer, in spite of his authoritative knowledge, was never consulted – publicly, at least – regarding any of the questions involved in the performance of Bach's music. In fact, the only occasion upon which I remember his forsaking the near-anonymity of the organ bench was at a rehearsal when the conductor, wishing to judge an effect from the rear of the hall, put his baton in Schweitzer's hand, and asked him to direct the chorus and orchestra. At that time, at least, Albert Schweitzer was in no sense a conductor, and it is significant . . . that he made no pretense of being one. Turning his back squarely upon both orchestra and chorus, one hand thrust in his trousers pocket, his head back, staring up into the dark of the Salle Gaveau, his arm moving in awkward sweeps and unorthodox directions, it was quite obvious that if he gave himself a thought – which I doubt – it was only to consider himself the agent who should bring the music to life. Beyond that he had no responsibility. It was for the conductor to judge whether the balance of tone or the seating of the participants was satisfactory. Above all, there was complete detachment; entire absorption in the sound of the music. To this day I can remember the intense admiration I felt for Schweitzer's indifference to externals.[5]

The members of the Paris Bach Society must likewise have thought highly of Schweitzer, judging by the extravagance of their gift to him when he left for Africa: a piano equipped with organ pedals that was specially lined with zinc to resist the insects and humidity of the tropics.

But friendly relations and some memorable performances over nearly a decade did not weaken his belief that a chorus made up of paid singers was in important ways inferior to one made up of volunteers, and without criticizing the Bach Society by name he published in 1927 an article deploring the state of choral music in Paris. Only professional choruses long survived there, he wrote, because the task of assembling a mixed chorus of amateurs was made impracticable by French life itself: on the one hand, no young girl of good family might think of going out unescorted, nor could matrons easily attend rehearsals at night; on the other hand, few men could regularly take time from work to attend rehearsals of an afternoon. That professionals must be paid, however, necessarily limited the number and length of rehearsals and hence any deep study of the music. The routine work of paid singers 'is of course superficially good; gross mistakes seldom occur even after the hastiest study. But dynamic and depth are lacking.'[6] Discipline he thought likely to be lax, the singers needing to watch their scores from beginning to end and the director thus needing to make concessions; morale, too, was shallow – the sense of unity produced by a common goal and by the 'deep emotion and inspiration that spring from the long and devoted study of a work and give warmth and fire to it.'[7] In contrast, the chorus of amateurs benefits from the principle that in art, 'as in all places where the realm of the spirit begins, there are things which only the free man is able to accomplish.'[8] Schweitzer adds that one must not underestimate the joy and the pride that sometimes raise even an average chorus to artistic heights.

The choir of St William's in Strasbourg, another focus of Schweitzer's musical activity for a decade, was indeed far above average, its volunteers having been carefully trained by an expert leader and their attitudes shaped by the old German tradition of community singing. Founded by Ernest Münch in 1884, the choir had grown from forty members to more than one hundred around the turn of the century and had performed oratorios by Handel and Mendelssohn, psalms by Schütz, and the requiems of Mozart and Brahms besides no fewer than sixty of the two hundred cantatas by Bach, one of whose Passions it presented each year during the week before Palm Sunday. Schweitzer was beginning his university days when in 1893–94 he became accompanist at rehearsals. He was soon accompanying the four or five annual concerts as well.

Ernest Münch, who exerted on him an influence nearly as profound as Widor's, was skilled as orchestral conductor, teacher of singing, and organist no less than in that art of combining persuasion with discipline which is essential for leaders of amateur ensembles. His powers of persuasion and discipline he owed – Schweitzer recalls – to 'his simplicity, his naturalness, his cordiality . . . . What marvellous musical ardour prevailed at these rehearsals! . . . He conducted the rehearsals with much care and sensitiveness, and never wearied the performers. It was evident that he had prepared these rehearsals down to the last detail. He never lost time with secondary matters, but devoted all his efforts to the essential thing. This is the reason the attention of the performers never faltered, however long the rehearsals lasted.'[9]

During his years as accompanist, Schweitzer adds, the choir

> began to realize the plan of its director to interpret, not only the few cantatas of Bach which were already pretty well known, but also to give . . . those that were not known. At that period the enterprise was a bold one, for it was necessary first of all to train the public just to understand Bach . . . . It is probable that we produced in the course of those years a good many cantatas that had not been played since [his] death . . . . Little by little our auditors arrived at the point where we were able to demand of them some comprehension of the serious and less accessible compositions.[10]

Organist and director would spend evening after evening together studying the scores and 'regretting our inability to play them all at the same time! Before we separated for our vacations at the end of the summer we had chosen the four cantatas which were to be given in the concert on Reformation Sunday. It was often necessary to copy the parts, for we could not yet procure them in print.'[11]

It was in these same years that Schweitzer began his career as a solo recitalist. Though his technique, as we have seen, was excellent and even brilliant, he was not a virtuoso as the term is commonly understood: he did not play from memory, and his style, for all its warmth of expression, was strict to the point of austerity not only in Bach but in the four other composers for whom he had a predilection, Franck, Widor, Mendelssohn, and Reger. Yet there was in Schweitzer's performances a quality that many listeners found gripping. It may have had to do with his choice of pieces (chorales fitting the liturgical season, for example) suitable for turning concert halls into churches; or with physical aspect – his big frame and leonine head, his dignified deportment at the console; or later, when most of his concerts benefited the African hospital, with his renown as a humanitarian. But the impression seems to have been heightened by a perceptible spirituality in the interpretations themselves, filled as they were with respect for the music and its makers' intentions and with the painstaking thought that we have already noticed. 'Certainly he does not play brilliantly – perhaps would not if he could,' observed a London critic after a recital at St Paul's Cathedral, 'but there is a sense of a certain privilege in hearing Schweitzer.'[12] Indeed, one may assert that the self-transcending attitude he held in common with many great interpreters is communicated in a thousand subtle ways to sensitive hearers and compels attentiveness.

Of his chosen repertory the following programmes are suggestive. For a Lenten recital at Westminster Abbey on 7 March 1922 he played Bach's

'Cathedral' *Prelude and Fugue in E Minor*, the chorales 'O Mensch, bewein dein' Sünde gross' and 'Herzlich tut mich verlangen,' the *Canzona* (a work for which he had special fondness), the *Adagio* from *Toccata, Adagio and Fugue in C Major*, and the hymn 'Jesus, Lover of My Soul.' A few days earlier, on 25 February 1922 at Carrs Lane Congregational Church in Birmingham, he had begun with Bach – the same prelude and fugue, three Epiphany chorales, 'In Dir ist Freude,' and the *Canzona* – then played three sonata movements by Mendelssohn, then Bach again (*Fugue in G Major*) to end. In Dortmund, Germany, on 11 November 1928 he gave a Bach recital to which he added Franck's *Prière*; in Munich on 7 July 1932 Franck's *Chorale in E Major* followed Bach's *Prelude and Fugue in C Minor*, three Catechism chorales, the 'little' *Fugue in G Minor*, 'Vater unser im Himmelreich,' 'Gottes Sohn ist kommen,' 'Komm, Gott, Schöpfer, Heiliger Geist,' and the *Prelude and Fugue in G Major* – the chorales sung by a choir.

The choir of the Bach Cantata Club of London assisted Schweitzer more than once in a concert at St Margaret's, Westminster, for instance a programme on 29 October 1935 at which he played the *Prelude and Fugue in F Minor*, 'In Dich hab ich gehoffet, Herr,' 'Wer nur den lieben Gott lässt walten,' the accompaniment for 'Singet dem Herrn ein neues Lied' and for the Doxology, 'Lobt Gott, ihr Christen, allzugleich,' 'Helft mir Gotts Güte preisen,' and the 'Wedge' *Prelude and Fugue in E Minor*.

Choirs assisted in like fashion at several of his Alsatian and Swiss programmes in the spring of 1936 – programmes chiefly made up of works by Bach but including, from Widor's *Symphony No. 6*, either the *Cantabile* or the *Adagio* or both, and either the first or second of Franck's *Three Chorales*. A recital at St Paul's in Strasbourg on 20 April offered the *Prelude and Fugue in D Major*, 'Vater unser im Himmelreich,' 'Ich ruf zu Dir, Herr Jesu Christ,' 'Jesu, meine Freude,' 'Komm, Gott, Schöpfer, Heiliger Geist,' the *Canzona*, and the *Prelude and Fugue in G Major* of Bach; both Widor movements; and the Franck *Chorale in E Major*. Although such programmes may seem to us unbalanced, since we would nowadays hesitate to play an hour of Bach and a mere quarter hour of someone else, they seem so only on paper, the works being inwardly akin. Take for example a Passiontide concert given on 13 March 1949 in Königsfeld, when Schweitzer concluded with the Franck *Chorale in A Minor* after having played Bach's *Prelude in B Minor*, 'O Lamm Gottes unschuldig,' 'Herzlich tut mich verlangen,' 'O Mensch, bewein dein' Sünde gross,' 'Wenn wir in höchsten Nöten sein,' and *Canzona* – again with the chorales sung by a choir. Here the contemplative spirit of the Franck, present even in the masterly development sections and triumphal close, could not have been a more fitting counterpart to the spirit of the earlier works.

It may be added that well into old age Schweitzer recalled how profoundly Franck had surprised most contemporaries by writing such sublime music. 'I still remember what a stir the Three Chorales . . . made,' Schweitzer declared more than seventy years later. 'Franck was a wonderful improviser, but no one expected from him a great work like the Three Chorales. They were published soon after his death. My friends in Paris sent me one of the first copies. I spent a whole night reading and rereading them.'[13] They were to figure in many a Schweitzer programme.

But Bach remained at the centre of his attention. When he played in the Ulm Münster on 11 July 1932, ending with the *Sonata No. 4 in B-flat Major* of Mendelssohn, he had begun with the *Prelude and Fugue in G Major*; *Canzona*; *Toccata, Adagio and Fugue in C Major*; and six chorales of Bach. On the same fund-raising tour for his hospital, he had played nearly the same programme at New College, Oxford (15 June), and at the cathedrals of Manchester (20 June), Edinburgh (23 June), and Glasgow (27 June), substituting for the G Major prelude and fugue the *Fantasia and Fugue in G Minor*.

It was long his cherished practice to commemorate Bach's death with a concert given at St Thomas in Strasbourg on the anniversary. On 28 July 1909 he played Bach's *Prelude and Fugue in F Minor*, 'Mit Fried und Freud ich fahr dahin,' 'Herr Gott, nun schleuss den Himmel auf,' *Prelude and Fugue in G Minor*, 'In Dir ist Freude,' and *Prelude and Fugue in G Major*. On 28 July 1910 he played the *Fugue in G Major*, 'Wer nur den lieben Gott lässt walten,' *Toccata, Adagio and Fugue in C Major*, 'Gelobet seist Du, Jesu Christ,' *Toccata in D Minor*, 'Ach wie nichtig, ach wie flüchtig,' 'Alle Menschen müssen sterben,' 'Jesu, meine Zuversicht,' and *Prelude in B Minor*. On 28 July 1911 he played the *Prelude in C Minor*, 'Erbarm dich, Herr,' *Fugue in C Minor*, *Adagio in A Minor*, *Prelude and Fugue in E Minor*, *Prelude in G Major*, 'Gottes Sohn ist kommen,' *Fugue in G Major*, 'Nun freut euch,' and 'In Dir ist Freude.' Other such commemorations took place in 1928, 1932, 1934, 1936, 1951, and 1954.

The last of these was particularly moving. The musicologist Erwin R. Jacobi recalls:

> The concert, given by the eighty-year-old master organist, accompanied by a choir that sang the chorale after each prelude (a performance practice which, based on a tradition from Bach's times, was requested by Schweitzer whenever a choir was available), had to be repeated the following evening because of the enormous crowd which had gathered from near and far, and because Schweitzer did not want any concert-goers to have to stand. The proceeds from the collection at these two concerts were not intended for his hospital in Lambaréné as usual, but following Schweitzer's wishes were to go toward completing the restoration of the Silbermann at St Thomas's, which had been begun by him nearly fifty years before.[14]

He played in public for the last time on 18 September 1955 in the village church at Wihr-au-Val, near Günsbach, sharing the programme with Edouard Nies-Berger. Bach's *Prelude and Fugue in E Minor*, 'Liebster Jesu, wir sind hier,' 'Ich ruf zu Dir, Herr Jesu Christ,' and *Adagio* from *Toccata, Adagio and Fugue in C Major*; the *Andante* from Mendelssohn's *Sonata No. 1 in F Minor*; and the *Cantabile* from Widor's *Symphony No. 6* made up – as is noted in his handwriting on a copy of the programme – 'the final concert of Albert Schweitzer.'

Notes and References

1. *Out of My Life and Thought*, pp. 100–101.
2. Ibid., p. 120.
3. Archibald T. Davison, in Roback, pp. 200–201.
4. See *J. S. Bach*, vol. II., pp. 447–59.
5. Davison, op. cit., p. 201.
6. Joy, p. 49.
7. Ibid.
8. Ibid., pp. 49–50.
9. Ibid., pp. 39,44. Ernest Münch was born in Niederbronn on 31 December 1859 and died in Strasbourg on 1 April 1928. He was appointed organist at St William Church in 1882.
10. Ibid., pp. 35–36. It was helpful that the texts were printed in the programmes.
11. Ibid., p. 36.
12. Richard Capell (1885–1954), music critic for the *Daily Mail* and, after 1933, the *Daily Telegraph*. Schweitzer played at St Paul's in June 1932.
13. Letter to Melville Smith, Lambaréné, 11 February 1962.
    'Je me souviens encore du grand évènement qui étaitent le Trois Chorals de César Franck. Franck était un admirable improvisateur mais personne n'attendait de lui une grande oeuvre comme le sont les Trois Chorals! On a publiés ceux-ci aussitôt après sa mort. Mes amis de Paris m'ont envoyé un des premiers exemplaires. J'ai passé toute une nuit à les lire et les relire.'
14. *Albert Schweitzers nachgelassene Manuskripte über die Verzierungen bei Johann Sebastian Bach*, p. 8.

8 Editor

Although in his last years Schweitzer became more and more preoccupied with running his hospital and finishing his *Philosophy of Civilization*, music was rarely absent from his daily life.

In Günsbach he was visited by musicians of every variety, would listen to them perform, and would then repair to the village church to play for them in turn. He had supervised the renovation of its organ, and he liked to show what music could be drawn from an instrument of modest size if its stops were lovingly made.[1] On Sundays he would seldom preach, but he would play for services in this sanctuary where as a boy he had listened to an organ for the first time.

In Africa he would refresh himself with half an hour at the pedal-piano, memorizing for pleasure and enrichment repertory learned long ago – the chorales of Bach, the sonatas of Mendelssohn, the symphonies of Widor. After dinner with his doctors and nurses, he would accompany their singing of a hymn, having introduced it with a few moments of improvisation. During the meal, in a dining room open to the jungle breezes, he delighted in hearing as background the rustle of palm leaves and the myriad other sounds of the equatorial night, themselves a kind of music.

He could occasionally be induced to listen to a phonograph record, perhaps an excerpt from Wagner, whose music he continued to revere, or Mozart, whose music he respected, or Schubert, whose piano impromptus his wife had liked to play. He had in fact begun to write a book on Schubert, only to be forced to abandon it for want of time, eventually giving to another biographer the materials collected in preparation. He had written on Wagner, directly in *J. S. Bach* and elsewhere, and indirectly, when in 1933 he published an account of his meetings with the composer's wife and son.[2] To Schweitzer this music remained 'so great, so elemental, that it makes Wagner the equal of Bach and Beethoven. Such assurance in composition, such grandiose musical architecture, such richness in his themes, such consummate knowledge of the natural resources of each instrument, such poetry, dramatic life, power of suggestion. It is unique; unfathomable in its greatness, a miracle of creative power!'[3]

He would turn to music even while travelling. When the jolting of trains prevented him from writing, in particular from answering the multitude of letters his fame now brought him, he would practise his repertory, his fingers tapping his knees, his feet the floor. Or he might read articles about organs and organists, though he would more often read articles that kept him abreast of developments in medicine, above all pharmacology.[4]

His correspondence had become a time-consuming distraction from other work, and when travelling he would take with him a canvas bag full of letters to be answered. Some asked for information or counsel. Some were required by the government regulations to which his hospital was now subject and which necessitated, as he once stated, no fewer than twenty-seven letters merely to engage a new nurse or doctor.[5] Some, having to do with world peace, were exchanged with scientists and political leaders and discussed the relations of states or the testing of atomic weapons. But some dozens among the hundreds he received and wrote each year had to do with music. And these, like the moments spent at his pedal-piano, he seems to have found refreshing.

To E. S. Ochs: 'I entirely agree with you about [excessive] tempi in the works of Bach, and also in classical works generally. People no longer have a natural feeling for this. It is the same with organists.'[6]

To Isidore Philipp: 'I am able to maintain my hospital . . . thanks to the aid of devoted friends in England and . . . the U.S.A., above all in the world of organists. I am moved at the thought of all these unknown persons who are helping me so.'[7]

To E. M. Skinner: 'You can be sure that I will not do the tour in a hurry . . . . I allow ten or twelve hours to prepare the registration for a recital.'[8]

To Jean Daniel Weber: 'Always write down the fingering in the organ works you are studying. One must play them with a set fingering that leaves nothing to chance . . . . One can never practise the organ too conscientiously: this I had from Widor.'[9]

To Edouard Nies-Berger: 'What irritates me about these baroque organs (the authentic ones and the copies) is that the two manuals have absolutely the same value and the same personality. The idea that the organ is an instrument in which different personalities form a unity is still absent.'[10]

To Wanda Landowska: 'It was in 1899 in Paris. I no longer know just how our first meeting took place. I believe you had learned that I was a pupil of Widor and that I had had some talks about Bach with him. He asked me to give a lecture, on this master and his works, for his students at the Conservatoire. You yourself were associated with the Schola Cantorum. There was accordingly between us the gulf that existed between the Conservatoire and the Schola Cantorum. We crossed it . . . . I spoke to you of Bach and of the nature of his work; through you I came to know the French masters of the clavecin .... We can both consider ourselves privileged, because we have been able to complete the work we have undertaken. And we shall continue in a spiritual relation during the years we are still on earth, you in America, I in Africa.'[11]

Indeed, the chief musical work undertaken by Schweitzer late in his life was the completing, after a hiatus of forty years, of his edition of the organ works of Bach.

The New York publishing house of G. Schirmer had in 1910 commissioned Schweitzer and Widor to edit Bach, as we have seen. But of the planned eight volumes only five, containing the preludes, fugues, sonatas, and concertos, had appeared before the interruption of World War One.

In a letter written in December 1919 to Theodore Baker, his friend and editor at Schirmer, Schweitzer takes up the story:

> In the summer of 1914 the three volumes of the Organ Chorales were ready. I had only to wait for some material on the origin of some of the chorale melodies which was to come from experts in the field and for the opinions of some organ professors who had read my notes. At the end of the summer you were to receive everything. And in the spring of 1915, again on holiday in Europe, I would have read the proofs. But the war came. I could not dare to send the manuscript on account of the submarines — and the war would have made publication impossible.

When in 1917 Schweitzer, a German in French territory, was arrested as an enemy alien and sent to prisoner-of-war camps in Europe, he

> left the ledgers with the manuscript in Africa — first because of the submarine danger (I did not want you to have to lament my death in the ocean together with the loss of the manuscript!) and secondly, because I was an internee whom any sergeant could have deprived of anything written. After I had left, everything was seized. The manuscripts were in a large box, tin-lined to protect them in some measure from the termites.

On regaining his freedom,

> I petitioned from Alsace (it is now more than a year) for the release of my seized properties to get hold of the manuscript as soon as possible and to deliver it to you. M. Widor, too, tried his best. Result: promises — and nothing else. One of my friends who arrived from Africa recently and had planned to bring the manuscript with him arrived empty handed.

Schweitzer then decided to reconstruct the work from sketches recovered in Europe.

> I promised my dear master Widor to begin and I will keep my word. On the first of January you will receive the music for the first volume of the chorales, soon afterward the remaining sections. On February 1 the introductory notes for the first volume will be completed, and by March the rest. I hope my strength will hold. Afterwards, I'll sleep for three weeks![12]

But by January 1920 a new director who was neither keen about the project nor tactful as a correspondent had taken charge at Schirmer, and Schweitzer was peremptorily informed that the three volumes would 'have to be deferred and delayed until business conditions have become normal again.'[13] Vexed, he turned to other work, and upon retrieving the African manuscripts set them aside.

Years passed, the maladroit director left the scene, and Schweitzer was again asked to finish the edition – sales of the first volumes having increased and a company memo having noted in 1927 that 'Dr Schweitzer evidently is peeved and that makes the situation very embarrassing.'[14] It did not help matters that the firm had proposed to pay royalties at a pre-war rate in German marks which were rendered nearly worthless by inflation.[15]

Even so, when in 1934 Robert Schirmer visited Schweitzer in Günsbach, offering fairer terms and proposing to release the last volumes in 1935 to commemorate the 250th anniversary of Bach's birth, Schweitzer agreed in principle, no doubt glad to resume amicable relations. But he declined to set dates. His time was wholly committed to other tasks, and Widor, moreover, was now ninety years old and in poor health and could no longer help as collaborator.

The meeting was thus followed only by friendly letters, not a manuscript. In 1937: 'I am at present fully occupied with philosophy . . . . It is now three years since you visited me in Günsbach. How much sadder has the state of the world since become.'[16] In 1939 war erupted once more, and Schweitzer, labouring to ensure the very survival of his hospital, remained in Lambaréné for the duration, almost entirely cut off from the world outside.

Nor could he soon return to Europe after the war ended. To Schirmer in 1945: 'Now that the friendly rapport between the house and myself has been restored I should finish the three volumes. But I cannot. All my energy and time has to go to my work on philosophy which I hope to finish before I die. And all this has to be done in addition to my work in my hospital.' And again, in 1946: 'My life is so full and I have so much to do. Ah, if this could have been arranged after the first war, when I was not yet engaged in other work.'[17]

Not until his journey to the United States, in 1949, did Schweitzer visit the Schirmer office in New York and settle the matter. A witness recalls that although a

> music publishing house is accustomed to visits of celebrities and the coming and going of the great and famous . . . this was different. There was a hushed presence of people near the elevator, in the hall, looking out of doors. In the big conference room we were seated around the tall, erect figure, groping for the right word and never sure we had found it . . . . A detailed working plan was designed at the meeting. The pre-World War One notes, spared by the termites, needed careful revision in the light of present-day Bach research. Most important was a new approach to the ornaments – an extended treatise on the trills, mordents,

ascending and descending appoggiaturas and their interpretation was to be added. Again it was a formidable task. Again, the years passed.[18]

Accompanying Schweitzer to the meeting as translator was the distinguished recitalist Edouard Nies-Berger, son of an old Alsatian friend and now resident in the United States as organist for the New York Philharmonic and teacher at the Peabody Conservatory, and it was he whom Schweitzer proposed for collaborator, succeeding Widor. So it was that during the following year work commenced in earnest.

Nies-Berger was to recall the summer of 1950 as the first of several summers spent in Günsbach, most of it given to sorting the manuscripts. These had survived World War Two sealed once more in a metal box and hidden this time in the cellar of Schweitzer's Alsatian home, only too near the shelling that almost levelled the town of Münster. Nies-Berger's assigned task was to prepare for Schweitzer outlines of the hymnology relative to the organ chorales and of post-1900 musicological discoveries relative to the ornaments. The needed research was therefore vast in scope, and the overall assignment was made the more arduous by Schweitzer's indomitable determination to control every detail of the finished books.[19]

At length, however, in 1954, the sixth volume appeared, no fewer than sixty-three of its large pages offering disquisitions on ornamentation, history, and style, and, in 1967, posthumously, the seventh and the eighth volumes followed. The work was done at last, the promise to Widor fulfilled.[20]

Always in his final years, whenever he visited Paris, Schweitzer would return to St Sulpice to listen at mass or vespers to its Cavaillé-Coll, 'which, apart from a few deficiencies, I consider to be the finest of all the organs I know,'[21] and to remember Widor, who had died in 1937. He had been *titulaire* of the instrument for sixty-four years. 'You will want to know,' his widow had written Schweitzer, 'that he reposes in the burial vaults of St Sulpice and that he will remain permanently in this church which he loved so much.'[22] The five manuals and hundred stops of its organ were now presided over by Marcel Dupré, whom Widor had chosen as successor and whose veneration for the instrument and its maker equalled Schweitzer's own.[23]

Dupré had become Widor's sub-organist in 1906. In 1914, while Widor's pupil in composition, he won the Premier Grand Prix de Rome. In 1920 he began his concert career by performing the complete organ works of Bach from memory. Then with ten tours of North America, dozens of tours throughout the United Kingdom and the continent, and in 1939 a world tour that included Australia and New Zealand, he won renown not only as virtuoso but as composer and improviser. Such of his works as *Variations on a Noël* and *Prelude and Fugue in G Minor* became widely known, and for his improvised fugues and sonatas he was likened in his mastery of form to such forebears in the extempore art as Handel and Mozart. Thus when Schweitzer would visit St Sulpice, and Dupré hasten to invite him to play, Schweitzer would invariably decline: 'No, no, Dupré. You play for me . . . . Improvise. Improvise in the contrapuntal styles. That is what interests me most.'[24]

Dupré recalls in his memoirs that he first met Schweitzer at the home of the Comtesse de Behague during a soirée at which Widor's *Sinfonia Sacra* was performed, and, regarding the sinfonia, that when Widor had been named a member of the Berlin Royal Academy of Fine Arts, it was Schweitzer who suggested he compose by way of thanks a work for organ and orchestra dedicated to the academy.

> In co-operation with him, Widor chose as theme the melody of Bach's chorale 'Nun komm, der Heiden Heiland.'
> From time to time Schweitzer came to have lunch with Widor at the Restaurant Foyot, and I was present on the day he announced to our master his decision to leave for Gabon and found a hospital . . . . Widor tried to dissuade him from it by pointing out that he would be obliged to interrupt the great works he had undertaken, in particular on Bach and his times.

('I remember this conversation very well,' Schweitzer tells us. 'It took place on a Sunday in 1905.'[25])

> Full of deference, head bowed, Schweitzer replied to each argument: 'Yes, *Maître*, but God calls me.' The next day I asked Widor if he had managed to convince him. He replied: 'My poor Dupré, what can you do when a man answers you with "God calls me"?'
> Schweitzer left for Gabon, and we corresponded. He returned to Paris about every two years and never failed to come to St Sulpice, where seated beside me on the organ bench, as he had done in Widor's time, he listened to that favourite instrument.[26]

When in 1962 a concert was being planned to mark the centennial of the organ, and Dupré asked him for a reminiscence that could be published in the programme booklet, Schweitzer offered the following:

> It was in October 1893 that, for the first time, I went up to the organ loft at St Sulpice to hear Charles-Marie Widor, whose pupil I had become, play upon the marvellous organ of that church.
> The hours which I subsequently spent in that loft, over the course of many years, figure among the most beautiful of my life.
> I hoped to find myself there again, for the celebration of the centenary of the organ. Alas, it is impossible for me to make my way to Europe for the 3rd of May. But on that Thursday afternoon I shall be in thought at St Sulpice, and in my imagination I shall hear once more the sounds of the most beautiful organ in the world.[27]

On me too,' he added privately to Dupré, 'Cavaillé-Coll made a profound impression. I saw him several times in the organ loft at St Sulpice in 1893. I also saw the firm in the Avenue du Maine. I have never understood how the Cavaillé-Coll firm could have collapsed. It had orders . . . . I always wondered why Widor and the great organists of Paris did nothing to save the firm.'[28]

And again: 'Thanks for your letter of 23 March 1962 giving me some particulars about the programme for the celebration on 3 May. How delightful!: you will be 76 years old on the day that the 100 years of your organ are celebrated! I congratulate you both . . . . I was very interested to learn from you that César Franck, Saint-Saëns, and Guilmant inaugurated the organ of St Sulpice. Guilmant I heard when he was still playing at Trinity Church, which he was obliged to leave later. He was always very kind to me.'[29]

The day after the concert, Dupré replied:

> I received your very affectionate letter yesterday morning . . . . You thought of me, as I thought of you. The concert went very well. It seemed to me that the organ was more splendid than ever. I was delighted to see the church absolutely filled to capacity, and the audience listened in a moving silence.
>
> I am sending you a programme that I kept for you. You will see that your beautiful letter was reproduced with perfect clarity. I thank you again for it with all my heart. You have helped me mightily, in the opinion of many, in affirming the glory, so greatly unappreciated, of Monsieur Cavaillé-Coll.
>
> While playing, I thought constantly about our private conversation in front of the choir screen . . . . Those minutes were among the most precious of my entire life.[30]

He relates part of the conversation in his memoirs. It took place in 1959, during Schweitzer's last visit to St Sulpice, and demonstrates the particular union of formality and warmth that characterized this friendship between the two most eminent of Widor's pupils:

> It was a feast of All Saints. After services, Schweitzer wanted to go down to the crypt with me and meditate before Widor's grave. It was decided that we would meet at 2 o'clock . . . . Abbé Lesourd accompanied us to the crypt and recited the Lord's Prayer. Then we went back upstairs into the church, and, when we were alone, Schweitzer headed for the nave, stopped, turned toward the organ, and said to me: 'We are among the last representatives of an era in which Guilmant and Widor, those two great organists, opened for the organ a glorious path.' Then, unexpectedly: 'I am going to ask you [thee] for something. I should like you to address me as *tu*.' Taken aback, I answered: 'From you to me, with joy. But from me to you, I could never!' 'Yes, you can, since I beg it of you.' I made every effort to do so, until the end of our conversation. We parted on the Place St Sulpice. I was not to see him again.[31]

Their correspondence continued, however, and the following spring Schweitzer sent Dupré a copy of *Out of My Life and Thought*, which had just been published in French, together with a touching inscription. Dupré responded: 'I did not want to convey my thanks to you before having finished a first reading of your marvellous book . . . . Your recollections, many of which coincide with mine, the unceasing effort of your admirable existence, and the exposition of your thought – I would like to say: of your truth – have deeply moved, enlightened, and nourished me.'[32]

The book in fact propounded many an idea with which he heartily disagreed, since love for a shared tradition and master had not kept the two men from drawing disparate conclusions about Bach and about organs.

But one may well pause briefly here to suggest that within the profession of organist, where polemics have so often damaged lives and repertories and instruments, it is exemplary to note that never was there exchanged between Schweitzer and Dupré the least reproach for difference of opinion, even though a lifetime of reflection and experience had led each master to views passionately held and mutually irreconcilable.

Dupré with some exceptions disliked tracker action, preferring electro-pneumatics and considering specious the argument that trackers were more responsive to the player's touch; Schweitzer thought trackers ideal and electro-pneumatics unreliable. Dupré favoured solo divisions and high-pressure reeds; Schweitzer advocated one enclosed division only and reeds that could blend with foundations. Dupré insisted that a positif division belonged in the case, Schweitzer that no organ was complete without a positif mounted separately.

As interpreter of Bach, Dupré held to the legato taught by Widor, Schweitzer to the conviction that legato must be enlivened by respirations throughout; Dupré to minimal changes of stops within a prelude or fugue, Schweitzer to frequent drawing and retracting of reeds; Dupré to mathematical exactitude of repeated notes and phrasings, Schweitzer to plasticity.

As editor, Dupré placed within Bach's scores all of the phrasings, fingerings, and tempo and dynamic marks he thought needed by the students for whom his edition was intended; Schweitzer remained convinced that editorial suggestions should appear in prefaces only.

But Dupré and Schweitzer would have been quick to agree that truth takes many seemingly contradictory forms and is still truth; that there is thus more than one right way to build an organ or edit a score or play a piece by Bach; and, assuming discipline, knowledge, and a right intention by builder or editor or player, that each way is part of a larger truth in which contradiction is only felt, not real.

Hence not friendship alone made them refrain from argument: 'If you speak of music,' Dupré writes, expressing Schweitzer's view as well,

> the phrase 'heritage of the past' is thoroughly misleading. At the least you must perceive that heritage as a living force in our midst, like a lovely garden we have inherited from our forebears and which we now cultivate ourselves, and not like a wilted flower pressed to dry between the pages of a book. It is always the same garden, yet with variations in the strength of its foliage and in the cycle of its seasons.[33]

Notes and References

1.   Partly as demonstration, he chose this instrument for the recordings he made in

1951–52 (for which he himself wrote extensive programme notes). He lauds it as follows: 'Two manuals and pedal, twenty-seven stops in all, with which one can play Bach as well as Widor, Franck, and Reger . . . . The organ of the future should allow us to perform, in appropriate sonority, the works of all the masters of the organ – Bach's predecessors, Bach himself, Mendelssohn, Reger, and the French.'

'Deux claviers, un pédalier, vingt-sept jeux en tout, avec lesquels on peut jouer Bach aussi bien que Widor, Franck et Reger . . . . L'orgue de l'avenir devra nous permettre d'interpréter en sonorité caractéristique les oeuvres de tous les maîtres de l'orgue, les prédécesseurs de Bach, J. S. Bach lui-même, Mendelssohn, Reger et les Français.' Quoted in Jacobi, *Albert Schweitzer und die Musik*, pp. 9–10. For the stoplist, see Appendix C. Among the musicians whose visits brought Schweitzer special delight was the violinist Georges Frey, who in 1949 showed him how tellingly Bach's solo works could be rendered with a curved bow. Schweitzer had long had an interest in such a bow and had described it in articles and in *J. S. Bach* (vol. I., pp. 388–91). Not everyone shared his views. See Robert Donington (1977), *The Interpretation of Early Music*, London: Faber and Faber, pp. 541–44.

2. Joy, pp. 58–62.
3. Ibid., pp. 57–58. Other kinds of music interested him too. His daughter recalls his liking for *Porgy and Bess* and for certain popular music (conversation with the author, 8 March 1991), and Jacques Barzun remembers him seated at the piano improvising jazz, after dinner at the home of J. S. Bixler, the president of Colby College, and after having 'played Bach for us beautifully' (conversation with the author, 16 October 1979).
4. Dr David Miller, conversation with the author, 8 March 1991.
5. Cousins, p. 59.
6. Lambaréné, 21 November 1944. 'Je suis tout à fait de votre avis au sujet des mouvements dans les Oeuvres de Bach et aussi dans la musique classique en général. Les gens n'ont plus le sentiment naturel dans ce domaine. C'est le même cas chez les organistes.' While in New York City, Schweitzer visited a friend who lived in a building equipped with an old-fashioned hydraulic elevator. As it crept upwards, he turned to his escort and said: 'That is how slowly one should play Bach!'
7. Lambaréné, 26 February 1944. 'Je puis maintenir mon hôpital pendant la guerre grâce à l'aide d'amis dévoués en Angleterre et au secours que me portent des amis d'USA, surtout dans le monde des organistes. Je suis ému de penser à tous ces inconnus qui m'aident ainsi.'
8. Lambaréné, 6 November 1945. See Appendix B, letter 11.
9. Lambaréné, 28 January 1948. 'Ecrivez toujours les doigtés dans les oeuvres d'orgue que vous étudiez. Il faut les jouer avec un doigté établi qui ne laisse rien au hasard . . . . . Man kann nicht gewissenhaft genug Orgel üben: das habe ich von Widor.' The shift from French to German, and the fifth ellipsis dot are in the original.
10. Lambaréné, 29 October 1945. 'Ce qui m'énerve sur ces instruments du baroque – les authentiques et les imités – c'est que les deux claviers ont absolument la même valeur et la même personnalité. L'idée que l'orgue est un instrument où différentes personnalités forment une unité est encore absente.' See Appendix B, letter 6.
11. Lambaréné, 30 May 1959. 'C'était en 1899 à Paris. Je ne sais plus au juste comment notre rencontre s'est faite. Je crois que vous aviez apprise, que j'étais

élève de Widor et que j'avais des entretiens sur Bach avec lui. Il m'avait demandé de faire une conférence sur ce maître et ses oeuvres à ses élèves du Conservatoire. Vous vous étiez en relation avec la Schola Cantorum. Il y avait donc entre nous l'abîme qui existait entre le Conservatoire et la Schola Cantorum. Nous l'avons franchi . . . . Je vous parlais de Bach et de la nature de son oeuvre. Par vous j'ai fait connaissance avec les maîtres français du clavecin . . . . Les deux nous pouvons nous estimer privilégiés parce que nous avons pu accomplir l'oeuvre que nous avons entrepris. Et nous continuous à rester en relations spirituelles dans les années que nous passerons encore sur terre, vous en Amérique moi en Afrique.'

12. Quoted in Heinsheimer, p. 30.
13. Ibid.
14. Ibid.
15. Rhena Schweitzer Miller, conversation with the author, 8 March 1991.
16. Heinsheimer, p. 31.
17. Ibid.
18. Ibid.
19. Nies-Berger (1985), pp. 20–21.
20. In 1954–56 Schweitzer undertook as well a revision of the sections on ornamentation in his biography of Bach. For an account of his revised views about the ornaments, views that thus supersede those published in volume 6 of the Schirmer edition, see Jacobi, *Albert Schweitzers nachgelassene Manuskripte über die Verzierungen bei Johann Sebastian Bach*, pp. 7–11, 35–52. Although as late as 1962 Schweitzer was corresponding with his London publisher about the revisions, they were not to be completed.
21. *Out of My Life and Thought*, p. 91. The stoplist may be found in Appendix C.
22. Widor had married, in April 1920, Mathilde Marie Anne Elisabeth de Montesquiou Fezensac (1883–1960), daughter of one of the noble houses of France. See Arnaud de Montesquiou Fezensac, *La Maison de Montesquiou Fezensac* (Paris, 1962).
23. In Widor's honour upon his retirement, a principal 16 and a principal 8 were added to the pedal division of the organ of St Sulpice, bringing the instrument to 102 stops. The stoplist may be found in Appendix C.
24. Marcel Dupré, conversation with the author, 26 July 1969. 'I never heard him play,' Dupré added, 'but he was a pupil of Widor, a beloved pupil of Widor. He gave concerts, recitals . . . . Widor told me he played well.'
25. Dupré had related the anecdote to Ewald B. Lawson, the president of Upsala College in East Orange, New Jersey, who published it in *The Diapason* for January 1942. Schweitzer made a longhand copy of the article, in German, and appended to it the statement here quoted.
26. Dupré (1972), p. 71.
27. Lambaréné, 15 March 1962. 'C'est en octobre 1893 que je suis pour la première fois monté à la tribune de Saint Sulpice, pour entendre Charles Marie Widor, dont j'étais devenu l'élève, jouer sur l'orgue admirable de cette église. Les heures que dans la suite, au cours d'une longue série d'années, j'ai passées sur cette tribune comptent parmi les plus belles de ma vie. J'espèrais m'y trouver à nouveau pour la fête du centenaire de l'orgue. Hélas, il m'est impossible de me rendre en Europe pour le trois mai. Mais dans l'après-midi de ce jeudi-là je serai en pensée à Saint Sulpice et je réentendrai en imagination les sons du plus bel orgue du monde.'
28. Lambaréné, 25 March 1962. 'A moi aussi Cavaillé-Coll a fait une profonde

impression. Je l'ai vu plusieurs fois à la tribune de Saint-Sulpice en 1893. J'ai aussi vu la maison de l'avenue du Maine. Je n'ai jamais compris que la maison Cavaillé-Coll ait pu crouler. Elle avait des commandes . . . . Je me suis toujours demandé pourquoi Widor et les grands organistes de Paris n'ont rien fait pour sauver la maison.'

29. Lambaréné, 24 April 1962. 'Merci de ta lettre du 23 mars 1962 qui me donne des renseignements du programme de la fête du 3 mai. Que c'est charmant: tu auras 76 ans le jour où l'on fêtera les 100 ans de ton orgue! Je vous félicite les deux . . . . J'ai été très intéressé d'apprendre par toi, que César Franck, Saint-Saëns et Guilmant ont inauguré l'orgue de Saint-Sulpice. Guilmant je l'ai encore entendu jouer à l'église de la Trinité qu'il a dû quitter plus tard. Il a toujours été très gentil pour moi.' Guilmant's widow presented his watch to Schweitzer, who framed it in a place of honour on a wall of the house in Günsbach.

30. Meudon, 4 May 1962. As themes for the improvisation with which he ended the concert, Dupré used the *Salve Regina* and the Pascal *Alleluia*. The resulting work reflected both the ebullience and the solemnity of the occasion and was published as *Choral et Fugue*, Op. 57.

31. Dupré (1972), p. 74.

32. Meudon, 23 April 1960.

33. Dupré (1965), p. 133.

9   Writer

In the near-century that his books on Bach, on philosophy, and on theology have been the object of study and debate, hardly anyone has remarked upon Schweitzer as a literary artist. Perhaps the variety and degree of his other attainments has seemed so astonishing, and the example of his life so powerful, that the fact has simply been overlooked that he was, in addition to everything else, a splendid writer.

It is not surprising that great musicians are sometimes great writers, for literary merit demands many of the faculties requisite to high accomplishment in music. Whether composer or interpreter, the able musician communicates what may be called, for want of a precise term, insights. These may be intuitive glimpses of transcendent reality, or emotion more poignant than is commonly felt, or the perceived essence of shape and hue and texture, or any or none of a dozen other things. For what the insights consist of, indeed what music is and how it affects us, have never been conclusively explained.

We may pause briefly to notice that each conception of music has its partisans, often brilliant ones indeed. The pianist Lorin Hollander, for example, refers to the sublimest music as

> more than high art. It is an inseparable connection between certain truths . . . . I think it interesting that those who are best in a position to understand reality – namely the particle physicists, astrophysicists, and researchers into states of consciousness and transpersonal psychology – that they all look toward music. Music, after all, is the art of the vibration: the bottom line of existence as we understand it. And whether we speak of electromagnetism or the relationship between light seen as a wave mechanism or light seen as a particle, somehow it points to the vibration, and to understanding life in terms of cycles. And all of this is so close to music and musical systems that we have to re-examine Pythagoras and Newton and others who saw music as something more than just a manifestation that man brought forth. They see it more that man, in his highest moments, *tapped into* something.[1]

In contrast, Jacques Barzun finds music to be entirely humanist because centred upon feelings. It is not the less transcendental for that, but the transcendence has nothing to do with the non-human; it comes instead from music's ability to arouse emotion so keen that we seem to be liberated for a time from our earthbound selves. Indeed, Barzun shares Mendelssohn's conviction – astonishing at first glance – that music conveys feelings that are not too vague for words but too precise. Music is adjective, so to speak, and adjective razor sharp: 'The names we use – joy, love, fear – fool us into thinking each is one thing. Each is a hundred different things, with no names to tell them apart. That's where music comes in: it distinguishes – and we respond.'[2]

At all events, the able musician communicates insights. These, in turn, spring from a cultivated sense of order. Inborn, mysterious, sovereign, Order dictates how things must be placed – things tangible or intangible – so as to be in ideal relation to one another. The sense of order lets the musician discern balance among sections and movements, discriminate among the nuances of sounds, and apprehend that sequence of components which accents the essential and downplays the subsidiary – be they component notes in a phrase, phrases in a period, or periods in a movement.

That sense of order is shared by the able writer, together with communicative and perceptive talents that differ from the musician's only in application. The feeling for order allows the writer to discern balance among paragraphs and chapters, discriminate among the nuances of words, and apprehend that sequence of components which accents the essential and downplays the subsidiary words in a phrase, phrases in a sentence, or sentences in a paragraph. The insights conveyed are likewise kindred, secret, and acute.

Mystery aside, certain readily identifiable gifts are shared as well. Both kinds of artist must have an ear for euphony, and the good writer can no more tolerate a sentence full of sibilants than a musician a sequence of raucous timbres – unless sibilance and stridor are deliberate, of course; that is another matter. Both kinds of artist must have a feel for rhythm, since the cadences of writing or of music are its heartbeat. And both kinds of artist must possess that taste for the seemly which in the one deplores unintended rhyme or alliteration and in the other parallel fifths. What is deplored is perhaps less the inadvertence than the use of any device that calls attention to itself, since art cannot be lofty that is self-conscious.

Then too, the able practitioner of notes or of words strives to eliminate everything superfluous. For the needless motion of a player's wrist conduces to inaccuracy, and the needless tone in a composer's score to an agglomeration of sounds that lacks clarity; by the same token, the needless adjective in a sentence diminishes eloquence and force, and the needless digression in a drama impedes narrative flow. Not that clarity, flow, eloquence, and force are desirable at all times and in all places, for many an artist has tellingly employed their opposites. But in general the artist worthy of the name is the implacable enemy of clutter. As the good painter abides no unnecessary brush-stroke and the good poet no unnecessary comma, the adroit maker of music or of prose relentlessly searches for superfluity and relentlessly culls every flaw.

Not only do literary and musical accomplishment demand certain collateral talents, but all of the various arts are, in some sense, one. Bach was a poet and painter in tone, as we have heard Schweitzer declare, and in words Goethe sketched and Nietzsche made music.

Schweitzer explains why this is true:

> Every artistic idea is complex in quality until the moment when it finds definite expression. Neither in painting, nor in music, nor in poetry is there such a thing as an absolute art that can be regarded as the norm, enabling us to brand all others as false, for in every artist there dwells another, who wishes to have his own say in the matter, the difference being that in the one case his activity is obtrusive, and in the other hardly noticeable. Herein resides the whole distinction. Art in itself is neither painting nor poetry nor music, but an act of creation in which all three co-operate.[3]

Hence to classify the arts according to the material they use is a purely external division. 'In reality,' Schweitzer concludes, 'the material in which the artist expresses himself is a secondary matter. He is not only a painter, or only a poet, or only a musician, but all in one.'[4]

Measured by all of the foregoing criteria, then, and judged not only by the examples to follow but by every passage quoted in the chapters above, Schweitzer himself was master musician and master of prose. And though he preferred objective demonstration for persuading people to his views, and disapproved of argument won by an appeal to sentiment, he was at times a poet as well. Whenever his feelings are stirred, when for example he writes of his discovery of the principle of Reverence for Life, his diction becomes evocative and indeed springs from his heart:

> Slowly we crept upstream, laboriously feeling – it was the dry season – for the channels between the sandbanks. Lost in thought I sat on the deck of the barge, struggling to find the elementary and universal conception of the ethical which I had not discovered in any philosophy. Sheet after sheet I covered with disconnected sentences, merely to keep myself concentrated on the problem. Late on the third day, at the very moment when, at sunset, we were making our way through a herd of hippopotamuses, there flashed upon my mind, unforeseen and unsought, the phrase, 'Reverence for Life.' The iron door had yielded: the path in the thicket had become visible. Now I had found my way to the idea in which world- and life-affirmation and ethics are contained side by side! Now I knew that the world-view of ethical world- and life-affirmation, together with its ideals of civilization, is founded in thought.[5]

Clearly, Schweitzer knows how to choose words that evoke in us something of the emotion that events evoked in him.

Clearly, he knows how to set a scene. Intuitively or by design, he makes the laborious physical threading of a path among hazardous channels and unfriendly beasts a parallel to the laborious mental threading of a path toward his philosophical goal. He knows how to weave a narrative whose inherent drama compels our interest. That the narrative relates facts does not diminish the expertise of its construction or the praise due its author. He could easily have told his story with less grace.

Other skills too are evident, whether one reads this passage in the original German, in the French version that Schweitzer himself edited, or in the English translation. Like every good writer, for example, he knows how to use rhythmic flow to convey subtleties, how to give that gentle emphasis here and stronger emphasis there – now delaying the beat, now anticipating it – with which a pianist shapes the melody in a nocturne.

Or again, deeming it imperative that his philosophy be grounded in the rational, so that any thinking person can reach like conclusions without recourse to feeling, he naturally considers the word 'thought' crucial; he therefore places it where it receives the greatest possible emphasis: at the end.[6]

The born writer learns to be ceaselessly aware of words as words – their nuances, their look, their tone – and this trait as well Schweitzer displays. He does so in an obvious way when he playfully calls the cantatas of Bach not only children of the muse but of leisure ('sind nicht nur Kinder der Muse, sondern auch Kinder der Musse'[7]); he does so subtly and movingly when he gives this account of Bach's death:

> At the end he was attacked by a painful malady of the eyes . . . . He appears to have passed his last days wholly in a darkened room. When he felt death drawing nigh, he dictated to Altnikol a chorale fantasia on the melody 'When in the Hour of Utmost Need' but told him to head it with the beginning of the hymn 'Before Thy Throne I Now Appear' that is sung to the same melody. In the manuscript we can see all the pauses that the sick man had to permit himself; the drying ink becomes more watery from day to day; the notes written in the twilight, with the windows closely curtained, can hardly be deciphered.
>
> In the dark chamber, with the shades of death already falling round him, the master made this work, that is unique even among his creations. The contrapuntal art that it reveals is so perfect that no description can give any idea of it. Each segment of the melody is treated in a fugue, in which the inversion of the subject figures each time as the counter-subject. Moreover the flow of the parts is so easy that after the second line we are no longer conscious of the art, but are wholly enthralled by the spirit that finds voice in these G Major harmonies. The tumult of the world no longer penetrated through the curtained windows. The harmonies of the spheres were already echoing round the dying master. So there is no sorrow in the music; the tranquil quavers move along on the other side of all human passion . . . .[8]

With consummate ease Schweitzer thus moves from narrative to technical idiom and back to narrative, all the while choosing words eloquent in their simplicity and perfectly apt in tone.

Like many a great writer, Schweitzer perfected his skill by experience, reflection, acquaintance with great literature, and advice from editors. Witness this anecdote about his first encounter with the most influential of these: the profoundly intellectual – and lovely – young activist who was to become his wife.

In 1898 it happened that he was invited to a dinner at which Helene Bresslau, the daughter of a celebrated historian, was seated nearby. Throughout the meal, Helene listened quietly as Albert dominated the table talk. But she noticed that the more passionately he expressed his views, the more pronounced and rough-hewn became his Alsatian dialect. When at length he turned to her and asked some question, she dumfounded him by responding: 'Well, Dr Schweitzer, your ideas are interesting, but they would be more so if expressed in good German!'

A moment passed before he replied, earnestly: 'Perhaps, Miss Bresslau, you would be kind enough to let me call upon you for assistance?'

Assist him she did, with both the spoken language and the written. She was to collaborate in his every article and book from *J. S. Bach* to *Out of My Life and Thought*, and, fluent alike in French and English, help him as well to emend the translations.

Hence his seemingly effortless ability to embody the relations of thought in equivalent relations of syntax may have been one of the talents she helped him to foster. Certainly the gift is evident whether he is positing philosophical abstractions or narrating commonplace events. Consider this passage from his autobiography, a passage at first glance unremarkable, in which he recalls the charitable work he and fellow students had undertaken and for which they had sought contributions:

> In our youthful inexperience we no doubt often failed, in spite of the best intentions, to use all the money entrusted to us in the wisest way, but the purpose of the givers was nevertheless fully carried out in that it pledged young men to take an interest in the poor. For that reason I think with deep gratitude of those who met with so much understanding and liberality our efforts to be wisely helpful, and hope that many students may have the privilege of working, commissioned in this way by the charitable, as recruits in the struggle against poverty.[9]

So effortlessly does meaning flow from his mind into ours that we are hardly aware of the deft equipoise of ideas. Nor, without that balance, could we easily accept the pace of his sentences, whose leisure and length are more common in nineteenth-century prose than in twentieth.

Not to be overlooked in the passage just cited, or indeed in anything Schweitzer wrote, is his simplicity and directness. And no matter how intricate the thought he means to express, he shows to the reader that exquisite courtesy which tries to make the task of comprehension as easy as possible. This accounts in part for Schweitzer's amicably forthright tone. Never, of course, does he talk down to the reader. And never does vast knowledge convey any trace of conceit. The reader discerns, rather, a healthy modesty that recognizes self-worth and subordinates it to duty.

It is further characteristic of Schweitzer's style that friendliness and tact concur with a certain decorum, a decorum whose chief effect is to remind us of the difference in manners between his day and our own. In fact by his own lights, and in contrast to the usual convolutions of Germanic scholarly prose, he writes in a most relaxed and unceremonious way. Indeed, as Jacques Barzun once remarked of John Jay Chapman, he never deviates from perfect informality – the rarest of all literary gifts.

Balance, cadence, and concision were among the virtues that Schweitzer discovered early on. When he first undertook *J. S. Bach*, the difficulty of writing in French while also lecturing and preaching in German led him to reflect on the nature of language:

> I profited much in my work on Bach by the remarks made to me on the style of my manuscript by Hubert Gillot, at that time a lecturer in French in Strasbourg University. He tried with special emphasis to impress upon me that the French sentence needs rhythm in far stronger measure than does the German . . . . Always accustomed in French to be careful about the rhythmical arrangement of the sentence, and to strive for simplicity of expression, [I found] these things became equally a necessity to me in German. And now through my work on the French *Bach* it became clear to me what literary style corresponded to my nature.[10]

And when writing *On the Edge of the Primeval Forest*, whose publisher imposed limits of length, he discovered that 'the fact that I was compelled to count my words was, after all, advantageous for the book, and since then I have held myself down – even in the exposition of my Philosophy of Civilization – to the greatest possible conciseness in the expression of my ideas.'[11]

Because the Alsatian dialect that was his native language is Germanic, one may add, Schweitzer, though bilingual, considered German his mother tongue. He writes:

> The difference between the two languages, as I feel it, I can best describe by saying that in French I seem to be strolling along the well-kept paths in a fine park, but in German to be wandering at will in a magnificent forest. Into literary German there flows continually new life from the dialects with which it has kept in touch. French has lost this ever-fresh contact with the soil. It is rooted in its literature, becoming thereby, in the favourable, as in the unfavourable sense of the word, something finished, while German in the same sense remains something unfinished. The perfection of French consists in being able to express a thought in the clearest and most concise way; that of German in being able to present it in its manifold aspects.[12]

If good writing is first of all clear, and if clarity of utterance depends on clarity of thought, Schweitzer, whose thought and expression are crystalline, is a very good writer indeed. And though he is continually aware of his ideas, he never loses sight of what must happen in the reader's mind in order for them to be grasped. It is noteworthy that when dealing with abstraction he recurs whenever possible to the concrete. As George Seaver has pointed out, readers of Schweitzer's *Quest for the Historical Jesus* may well forget his argument for eschatology derived from a multitude of minutiae in the sacred text, but they can never forget his 'majestic image of the Man who lays hold of the Wheel of the World to set it moving to its final revolution, and then throws Himself upon it to be crushed.'[13] Or again, readers of *The Philosophy of Civilization* may forget Schweitzer's account of the causes that led to the bankruptcy of discursive reason in the history of rationalism, but they can never forget his 'picture of the master-mariner, Hegel, on the bridge of his ocean liner, proudly explaining to passengers the marvels of its machinery and the mysteries of its log, whilst the fires in the boiler are burning out, and the vessel, no longer responsive to the helm, is becoming a plaything of storms.'[14]

If, then, the chief beauty of Schweitzer's prose lies in the contrast between density of thought and transparency of medium, let chapter and book come to an end with a statement of that conviction which informed not only his literary art but his musical, not only his art but his life:

> With the spirit of the age I am in complete disagreement, because it is filled with disdain for thinking. That such is its attitude is to some extent explicable by the fact that thought has never yet reached the goal which it must set before itself. Time after time it was convinced that it had clearly established a world-view which was in accordance with knowledge and ethically satisfactory. But time after time the truth came out that it had not succeeded.
>
> Doubts, therefore, could well arise as to whether thinking would ever be capable of answering current questions about the world and our relation to it in such a way that we could give a meaning and a content to our lives.
>
> But today in addition to that neglect of thought there is also prevalent a mistrust of it. The organized political, social, and religious organizations of our time are at work to induce the individual man not to arrive at his convictions by his own thinking but to make his own such convictions as they keep ready made for him. Any man who thinks for himself and at the same time is spiritually free, is to them something inconvenient and even uncanny. He does not offer sufficient guarantee that he will merge himself in their organization in the way they wish . . . .
>
> Thus, his whole life long, the man of today is exposed to influences which are bent on robbing him of all confidence in his own thinking. The spirit of spiritual dependence to which he is called on to surrender is in everything that he hears or reads; it is in the people whom he meets every day; it is in the parties and associations which have claimed him as their own; it pervades all the circumstances of his life.
>
> From every side and in the most varied ways it is dinned into him that the truths and convictions which he needs for life must be taken by him from the associations which have rights over him. The spirit of the age never lets him come to himself. Over and over again convictions are forced upon him in the same way as, by means of the electric advertisements which flare in the streets of every large town, any

company which has sufficient capital to get itself securely established, exercises pressure on him at every step he takes to induce him to buy their boot polish or their soup tablets.

By the spirit of the age, then, the man of today is forced into skepticism about his own thinking, in order to make him receptive to truth which comes to him from authority . . . .

In a period which regards as absurd and of little worth, as antiquated and long ago left far behind, whatever it feels to be in any way akin to rationalism or free thought, and which even mocks at the vindication of inalienable human rights which was secured in the eighteenth century, I acknowledge myself to be one who places all his confidence in rational thinking . . . .

Because I have this certainty I oppose the spirit of the age, and take upon myself with confidence the responsibility of taking my part in the rekindling of the fire of thought.[15]

Notes and References

1. Conversation with the author, 4 November 1980.
2. Jacques Barzun, 'Overheard at Glimmerglass,' in *Berlioz Studies*, Peter Bloom, ed. (1992), Cambridge: Cambridge University Press, p. 255. See also Barzun's essay on 'The Meaning of Meaning in Music,' in *Critical Questions*, Bea Friedland, ed. (1982), Chicago: University of Chicago Press, pp. 75–98.
3. *J. S. Bach*, vol. II, p. 13. 'Bis zum Momente, wo er durch eine bestimmte Sprache in die Erscheinung tritt, ist jeder künstlerische Gedanke komplex. Weder in der Malerei, noch in der Musik, noch in der Dichtung gibt es eine absolute Kunst, die man zur Norm erheben kann, um alles andere darufhin als falsche Kunst stempeln, weil eben in jedem Künstler noch ein anderer wohnt, der mitreden will, nur dass er es bei dem einen aufdringlich, bei dem andern kaum merklich tut. Darin liegt der ganze Unterschied. Die Kunst an sich ist weder Malerei noch Dichtung noch Musik, sondern ein Dichten, in welchem sie noch alle vereint sind.'
4. Ibid., p. 8. 'In Wirklichkeit ist das Material, in welchem sich der Künstler ausdrückt, etwas Sekundäres. Er ist nicht nur Maler, oder nur Dichter, oder nur Musiker, sondern alles zusammen.'
5. *Out of My Life and Thought*, pp. 185–86. 'Langsam krochen wir den Strom hinauf, uns mühsam zwischen den Sandbänken – es war trockene Jahreszeit – hindurchtastend. Geistesabwesend sass ich auf dem Deck des Schleppkahnes, um den elementaren und universellen Begriff des Ethischen ringend, den ich in keiner Philosophie gefunden hatte. Blatt um Blatt beschrieb ich mit unzusammenhängenden Sätzen, nur um auf das Problem konzentriert zu bleiben. Am Abend des dritten Tages, als wir bei Sonnenuntergang gerade durch eine Herde Nilpferde hindurchfuhren, stand urplötzlich, von mir nicht geahnt und nicht gesucht, das Wort "Ehrfurcht vor dem Leben" vor mir. Das eiserne Tor hatte nachgegeben; der Pfad im Dickicht war sichtbar geworden. Nun war ich zu der Idee vorgedrungen, in der Welt- und Lebensbejahung und Ethik miteinander enthalten sind! Nun wusste ich, dass die Weltanschauung ethischer Welt- und Lebensbejahung samt ihren Kulturidealen im Denken begründet ist.'

   'Nous naviguions lentement à contre-courant, cherchant notre voie, non sans peine, parmi les bancs de sable. C'était la saison sèche. Assis sur le pont d'une des remorques, indifférent à ce qui m'entourait, je faisais effort pour saisir cette notion élémentaire et universelle de l'éthique que ne nous livre aucune philosophie. Noircissant page après page, je n'avais d'autre dessein que de fixer mon esprit sur ce problème qui toujours se dérobait. Deux jours passèrent. Au soir du troisième, alors que nous avancions dans la lumière du soleil couchant, en dispersant au passage une bande d'hippopotames, soudain m'apparurent, sans que je les eusse pressentis ou cherchés, les mots "Respect de la vie." La port d'airain avait cédé. La piste s'était montrée à travers le fourré. Enfin je m'étais ouvert une voie vers le centre où l'affirmation du monde et de la vie se rejoignent dans l'éthique.

'Je tenais la racine du problème. Je savais que cet ensemble qui détermine une civilisation digne de ce nom, trouve son fondement dans la pensée.'

6. That the beginning and end of a sentence or paragraph are places of natural accent is a truth which appears to apply only sometimes to German and to French, but to English invariably. Nor is the accent on a word necessarily weakened if one or two monosyllables follow.

7. *J. S. Bach*, vol. I., p. 166.

8. Ibid., pp. 223–24. 'Die letzte Zeit scheint er ganz im verdunkelten Zimmer zugebracht zu haben. Als er den Tod nahen fühlte, diktierte er Altnikol eine Choralphantasie über die Melodie "Wenn wir in höchsten Nöten sein," hiess ihn jedoch als überschrift den Anfang des Liedes "Vor deinen Thron tret ich allhier," das nach derselben Weise gesungen wird, zu setzen. In der Schrift sind alle Ruhepunkte, die sich der Kranke gönnen musste, abzulesen; die versiegende Tinte wird von Tag zu Tag wässriger; die in Dämmerlicht bei dicht verhangenen Fenstern geschriebenen Noten sind kaum zu entziffern.

'Im dunkeln Zimmer, schon von Todesschatten umspielt, schuf der Meister dieses Werk, das selbst unter den seinen einzig dasteht. Die kontrapunktische Kunst, die sich darin offenbart, ist so vollendet, dass keine Schilderung mehr einen Begriff von ihr geben kann. Jeder Melodieabschnitt wird in einer Fuge behandelt, in welcher die Umkehrung des Themas jedesmal als Gegenthema figuriert. Dabei fliessen die Stimmen so natürlich einher, dass man schon nach der zweiten Zeile die Kunst nicht mehr gewahr wird, sondern ganz unter dem Banne des Geistes steht, der aus diesen G dur-Harmonien redet. Das Weltgetümmel drang durch die verhängten Fenster nicht mehr hindurch. Den sterbenden Meister umtönten bereits Sphärenharmonien. Darum klingt kein Leid mehr in seiner Musik nach; die ruhigen Achtel bewegen sich schon jenseits jeglicher Menschenleidenschaft.'

9. *Out of My Life and Thought*, p. 105. 'Sicherlich haben wir in unserer jugendlichen Unerfahrenheit trotz besten Wollens nicht alles uns anvertraute Geld in der zweckmässigsten Weise verwandt. Aber seine Bestimmung hat es dennoch vollauf dadurch erfüllt, dass es junge Menschen verpflichtete, sich um Arme zu bekümmern. Darum gedenke ich derer, die für unser Streben nach solcher Betätigung Verständnis und offene Hand hatten, in tiefer Dankbarkeit und wünsche, dass es vielen Studenten verliehen sein möge, in solcher Art, als Beauftragte von Gebern, Rekrutendienste im Kampfe gegen die Not zu tun.'

'Sans doute dans notre inexpérience de jeunes, et malgré la meilleure volonté, n'avons-nous pas toujours employé l'argent qui nous était donné de la manière la plus appropriée. L'entreprise avait néanmoins pleinement atteint son but en ce sens qu'elle obligeait des jeunes gens à s'occuper de malheureux. C'est pourquoi je garde une profonde reconnaissance à ceux qui se sont montrés compréhensifs et généreux envers notre oeuvre, et je souhaite qu'il soit possible à beaucoup d'étudiants d'être aidés par des donateurs.'

10. Ibid., pp. 78–79. 'Grossen Nutzen hatte ich bei der Arbeit an dem Buch über

Bach von den Bemerkungen, die Hubert Gillot, damals Lektor des Französischen an der Strassburger Universität, mir über den Stil meines Manuskriptes machte. Besonders eindringlich wies er mich darauf hin, dass der französische Satz in viel stärkerem Masse das Bedürfnis nach Rhythmus in sich trägt als der deutsche . . . . Vom Französischen her gewohnt, auf die rhythmische Gestaltung des Satzes bedacht zu sein und Einfachheit des Ausdrucks zu erstreben, ist mir dies auch im Deutschen zum Bedürfnis geworden. Über der Arbeit an dem französischen Bach kam ich zur Klarheit über die meiner Natur entsprechende Schreibweise.'

'Au cours de la rédaction de ce livre, je tirai grand profit des remarques stylistiques qui m'étaient faites par Hubert Gillot, alors lecteur de français à l'Université de Strasbourg. Il insistait particulièrement sur le rythme qu'exige la phrase française beaucoup plus que la phrase allemande . . . . Habitué par le français à m'appliquer à la cadence rythmique de la phrase et à viser à la simplicité de l'expression, cela m'est devenu indispensable aussi en allemand. C'est en travaillant à mon livre français que j'ai reconnu clairement le style correspondant à ma nature.'

11. Ibid. p. 221. 'Dass ich gezwungen war, mit Worten zu rechnen, ist dem Buche zum Vorteil geraten. Seither habe ich mich selber – auch in der Ausarbeitung der *Kulturphilosophie* – zu höchster Sparsamkeit im Ausdruck angehalten.'

'Toutefois, le fait d'être contraint de compter les mots d'un livre m'est apparu comme un avantage. Depuis, je me suis appliqué – notamment dans *La Philosophie de la civilisation* – à la plus stricte économie d'expression.'

12. Ibid., pp. 78–79. 'Den Unterschied zwischen den beiden Sprachen empfinde ich in der Art, als ob ich mich in der französischen auf den wohlgepflegten Wegen eines schönen Parkes erginge, in der deutschen aber mich in einem herrlichen Wald herumtriebe. Aus den Dialekten, mit denen sie Fühlung behalten hat, fliesst der deutschen Schriftsprache ständig neues Leben zu. Die französische hat diese Bodenständigkeit verloren. Sie wurzelt in ihrer Literatur. Dadurch ist sie im günstigen wie im ungünstigen Sinne des Wortes etwas Fertiges geworden, während die deutsche in demselben Sinne etwas Unfertiges bleibt. Die Vollkommenheit des Französischen besteht darin, einen Gedanken auf die klarste und kürzeste Weise ausdrücken zu können, die des Deutschen darin, ihn in seiner Viegestaltigkeit hinzustellen.'

'Je ressens la différence entre les deux langues comme si, en français, je suivais les allées bien soignées d'un beau parc, et en allemand, comme si je me promenais dans une magnifique forêt. Les dialectes avec lesquels l'allemand littéraire a gardé le contact, lui infusent sans cesse une vie nouvelle. La langue française prend racine dans sa littérature. C'est pourquoi elle est devenue, au sens favorable comme au sens péjoratif du mot, quelque chose d'achevé, tandis que la langue allemande reste dans les deux sens quelque chose d'inachevé. La perfection du français consiste à pouvoir exprimer une pensée de la manière la plus claire et la plus concise, celle de la langue allemande à présenter cette pensée sous ses multiples aspects.'

13. *Albert Schweitzer: The Man and his Mind*, p. 243.

14. Ibid.

15. *Out of My Life and Thought*, pp. 254–260. 'Mit dem Geiste der Zeit befinde ich mich in vollständigem Widerspruch, weil er von Missachtung des Denkens erfüllt ist. Dass er so gesinnt ist, ist bis zu einem gewissen Grade daraus verständlich, dass das Denken das Ziel, das es sich stecken muss, bisher nicht erreicht hat. Soundso oft war es überzeugt, eine erkenntnismässig und ethisch

befriedigende Weltanschauung in einleuchtender Weise begründet zu haben. Nachher aber stellte sich immer wieder heraus, dass ihm dies nicht gelungen war.

'So konnten Zweifel daran aufkommen, ob das Denken jemals imstande sein würde, uns die auf die Welt und unser Verhältnis zu ihr gehenden Fragen in der Art zu beantworten, dass wir unserem Leben Sinn und Inhalt zu geben vermöchten.

'Bei der heutigen Missachtung des Denkens ist aber noch Misstrauen gegen es mit im Spiele. Die organisierten staatlichen, sozialen und religiösen Gemeinschaften unserer Zeit sind darauf aus, den Einzelnen dahin zu bringen, dass er seine Überzeugungen nicht aus eigenem Denken gewinnt, sondern sich diejenigen zu eigen macht, die sie für ihn bereit halten. Ein Mensch, der eigenes Denken hat und damit geistig ein Freier ist, ist ihnen etwas Unbequemes und Unheimliches. Er bietet nicht genügende Gewähr, dass er in der Organisation in der gewünschten Weise aufgeht . . . .

'Sein ganzes Leben hindurch ist der heutige Mensch also der Einwirkung von Einflüssen ausgesetzt, die ihm das Vertrauen in das eigene Denken nehmen wollen. Der Geist der geistigen Unselbständigkeit, dem er sich ergeben soll, ist in allem, was er hört und liest; er ist in den Menschen, mit denen er zusammen kommt; er ist in den Parteien und Vereinen, die ihn mit Beschlag belegt haben; er ist in den Verhältnissen, in denen er lebt. Von allen Seiten und auf die mannigfachste Weise wird auf ihn eingewirkt, dass er die Wahrheiten und Überzeugungen, deren er zum Leben bedarf, von den Genossenschaften, die Rechte auf ihn haben, entgegennehme. Der Geist der Zeit lässt ihn nicht zu sich selber kommen. Wie durch die Lichtreklamen, die in den Strassen der Grossstadt aufflammen, eine Gesellschaft, die kapitalkräftig genug ist um sich durchzusetzen, auf Schritt und Tritt Zwang auf ihn ausübt, dass er sich für ihre Schuhwichse oder ihre Suppenwürfel entscheide, so werden ihm fort und fort Überzeugungen aufgedrängt.

'Durch den Geist der Zeit wird der heutige Mensch also zum Skeptizismus in bezug auf das eigene Denken angehalten, damit er für autoritative Wahrheit empfänglich werde . . . .

'In einer Zeit, die alles, was sie irgendwie als rationalistisch und freisinnig empfindet, als lächerlich, minderwertig, veraltet und schon längst überwunden ansieht und sogar über die im 18. Jahrhundert erfolgte Aufstellung von unverlierbaren Menschenrechten spottet, bekenne ich mich als einen, der sein Vertrauen in das vernunftgemässe Denken setzt . . . .

'Weil ich diese Gewissheit habe, lehne ich mich gegen den Geist der Zeit auf und nehme mit Zuversicht die Verantwortung auf mich, an der Wiederanfachung des Feuers des Denkens beteiligt zu sein.'

'Je suis en désaccord avec l'esprit de ce temps, parce qu'il est plein de mépris pour la pensée.

'On a pu douter que la pensée fût jamais capable de répondre aux questions sur l'univers et sur notre relation avec lui, de sorte que nous puissions donner un sens et un contenu à notre existence.

'Dans le mépris actuel de la pensée entre aussi de la méfiance. Les collectivités organisées, politiques, sociales et religieuses de notre temps s'efforcent d'amener l'individu à ne pas forger lui-même ses convictions, mais à s'assimiler seulement celles qu'elles tiennent toutes prêtes pour lui.

'L'homme qui pense par lui-même, et qui en même temps est libre sur le plan spirituel, leur est un être incommode et mystérieux. Il n'offre pas la garantie qu'il se fondra à leur gré dans l'organisation . . . .

'Sa vie durant, l'homme d'aujourd'hui est donc exposé à des influences qui cherchent à lui ôter toute confiance en sa propre pensée. La suggestion de dépendance spirituelle à laquelle il doit se soumettre se manifeste dans tout ce qu'il entend dire ou lit. Il la trouve chez les gens qu'il rencontre, dans les partis et les associations qui l'ont annexé. Des manières les plus diverses, on fait pression sur lui, afin qu'il reçoive les vérités, dont il a besoin pour vivre, des associations qui ont des droits sur lui. L'esprit de notre temps ne laisse pas l'individu faire un retour sur lui-même. Sans cesse on s'efforce de lui imposer des convictions, comme dans les grandes villes on fait flamboyer les enseignes lumineuses d'une compagnie assez riche pour s'installer solidement et pour nous enjoindre à chaque pas de donner la préférence à tel cirage ou à tel potage en poudre.

'L'esprit de notre temps contraint donc l'homme à douter de sa propre pensée, afin de l'amener à recevoir ses vérités du dehors . . . .

'A une époque qui juge ridicule, sans valeur, vieilli et dépassé depuis longtemps tout ce qui lui semble être rationnel ou indépendant, qui raille même les inaliénables droits de l'homme proclamés au XVIIIème siècle, je déclare que je mets ma confiance dans la pensée rationnelle . . . .

'Ayant cette certitude, je proteste contre l'esprit de notre temps et assume avec une entière confiance la responsabilité de ranimer, pour ma part, la flamme de la pensée.'

Appendix A Biographical Sketch

Born on 14 January 1875 in Kaysersberg, Upper Alsace, Albert Schweitzer was the second child of the Reverend Ludwig Schweitzer and his wife, Adèle, née Schillinger. When the boy was six months old the family moved to Günsbach, where his father had been called as pastor, and in that village in the Münster valley Albert Schweitzer grew up, together with three sisters and a brother, enjoying a childhood uncommonly happy and free of care.

At age five, he began to take lessons on the piano. At seven, he surprised his schoolmistress by picking out hymn-tunes to which he supplied his own harmonies. At eight, though his legs were hardly long enough to reach the pedals, he began to play the organ, and at nine he played for the first time at a service in church. At ten he began to study the piano, and five years later the organ, under Eugène Münch.

His schooling, meantime, had not begun brilliantly. He had trouble learning to read and write, and although he satisfactorily completed his early years at the village school in Günsbach and at the *Realschule* in Münster, he was a poor pupil in the months just after he entered, in 1885, the *Gymnasium* in Mulhouse. Not even the discipline imposed upon him by the aunt and uncle with whom he was to board for the next eight years – discipline as relentless as it was well-intentioned – made up at first for his lack of a good grounding in Latin, still less for his dreaminess, and a full term was to pass before he learned to study properly and to take pride in mastering subjects in which he felt no interest. Mathematics and languages stirred him little, natural history and science much. But he applied himself as diligently to each and, at eighteen, left the *Gymnasium* with a respectable, if undistinguished, record of accomplishment.

From the autumn of 1893 to the spring of 1898 he studied theology and philosophy at the University of Strasbourg. His studies were impeded only slightly during a year of obligatory military service (1894–95), for he was allowed to attend lectures even while on duty. Musical activity centred on organ lessons with Widor in Paris and on accompanying the Bach Passions and cantatas performed in Strasbourg by the choir of St William Church under Ernest Münch.

In October 1898 Schweitzer enrolled at the Sorbonne to begin work on a doctorate in philosophy, attending lectures as well at the Protestant Theological Faculty and studying the organ with Widor and the piano with Marie Jaëll, who had been a pupil of Liszt, and with Isidore Philipp. He took his degree at Strasbourg in July 1899 and a few months later saw his dissertation, on the religious philosophy of Kant, into print.

In December 1899, having the previous year passed a first examination in theology, he took a post as deacon, later curate, at St Nicholas Church in Strasbourg, preaching being to him an inner necessity. For the next five years he delighted in giving the Sunday-afternoon sermons and teaching the weekly confirmation classes. At holidays he would travel to Paris to study with Widor and occasionally to give in German before the Foreign Language Society lectures on German writers and philosophers. He undertook at the same time research into the life of Jesus, in 1900 obtaining the Licentiate in Theology with a dissertation on the Last Supper, and in 1902 a post as *Privat-dozent* at the University of Strasbourg with a treatise on Jesus' messiahship and Passion. Research into the music of Bach and into the comparative history of German and French organ building likewise occupied those years, together with the duties associated with an appointment (October 1903) as Principal of the Protestant Theological Seminary.

Troubled, however, by the contrast between his own happiness and the suffering he saw around him, he had concluded as early as the mid 1890s that he must give back something in return for the familial contentment, robust health, and satisfying intellectual and artistic life which he had been granted. Until his thirtieth birthday he would pursue philosophy and music, he decided, but would thereafter devote himself to some vocation of direct service to humanity, letting circumstances determine the form his service should take.

Cherishing his independence, he had hoped for an activity free of supervision. But when in 1904 he learned that the Paris Missionary Society needed workers in the Congo, this need seemed to him perfectly matched with his own, and he resolved to volunteer. He moreover resolved to become a doctor of medicine, wishing to serve without having to talk, as he later explained, so as to demonstrate by deeds rather than words the Christian religion of love.

Although his friends and family thought him mad to consider embarking at age thirty upon so arduous a course of study, not to mention becoming once more a student at the very university where he was now a dean, he knew his decision to be right and was determined to proceed.

In the event, Schweitzer laboured for eight long years to earn his doctorate in medicine (1905–13) – completing as well his *Quest of the Historical Jesus, Paul and His Interpreters*, two biographies of Bach, five volumes (with Widor) of an edition of Bach's organ music, and as thesis for his degree *The*

Psychiatric Study of Jesus – and was then accepted by the Paris Missionary Society, but with reservations. To some of its directors his theological views seemed unorthodox to the point of heresy, hence likely to corrupt the native Africans, and he was accepted only on condition that he solemnly promise to refrain from preaching. He vowed to stay mute as a carp.

Having collected sufficient funds for the venture by giving concerts and begging from friends, he accordingly set off on Good Friday of 1913, accompanied by his wife, Helene Bresslau, whom he had married on 18 June 1912, to establish at his own expense a clinic in equatorial Africa.

Once there, he found the need was even more urgent than he had supposed. Hardly had he begun to unpack his seventy crates of instruments and drugs when patients began to line up at his door. Physical misery among the natives was greater overall, and malaria, leprosy, elephantiasis, sleeping sickness, and heart and lung diseases were more widespread, than anticipated, and he was glad that in defiance of all objections he had carried out his plan of going to the Congo as a doctor. He was delighted as well with his choice of Lambaréné for the site of his hospital (a choice made merely on the strength of a map and incomplete data), because the sick from two hundred miles around could be easily brought to him in canoes on the Ogowe River.

His wife, who had helped him with completing and proofreading his literary projects before the departure for Africa, now proved to be an invaluable help with running his hospital. Trained as a nurse, she took charge of linen, bandages, instruments, and dispensary, prepared patients for surgery, administered anaesthesia, and managed the household besides. In future years, however, her health was to prove unequal to such demands and to the tropical climate, and for much of the marriage she was to remain in Europe.

Schweitzer was warmly welcomed by his fellow missionaries, not only as doctor but eventually as theologian. Unlike the board of the Paris Missionary Society, they were less concerned with dogma than with the Gospel, and to the natives they necessarily taught a simple Christianity whose emphasis was upon the ethical. Soon they invited Schweitzer to take his turn at preaching, and he found particular satisfaction in bringing the message of Jesus to persons who heard it for the first time.

The hospital flourished for about a year, accommodating besides the outpatient queue as many as forty resident patients per day, together with the companions who travelled with them. But when in August 1914 war broke out in Europe, Schweitzer and his wife, as Germans in French territory, were deemed enemy aliens, placed under house arrest, and forbidden contact with anyone. The hospital was thus closed and would open only intermittently until 1924; though they were released in November and allowed to resume work, they were absent in 1915–16 during intervals of rest required by Helene Schweitzer's failing health, and in September 1917 were again interned, this time to be sent to a succession of prisoner-of-war camps in France.

It was in caring for the sick that Schweitzer spent many an hour of his captivity; he was sometimes the only doctor for hundreds of prisoners. Other hours he spent practising the organ, using as keyboards a tabletop and as pedals the floor, or pacing to and fro in the camp yard, or talking to the specialists imprisoned with him – scholars, artists, hotel managers, bank directors, merchants, architects, waiters, engineers, seamen – learning about their occupations much that he found fascinating. On Sundays he would play the harmonium at the Catholic service, then take the rostrum at the Protestant to preach. And he was preoccupied throughout with planning a book on what he feared was the decline of civilization itself, a decline by then manifest for all to see, in the cataclysm destroying Europe, but which he had noticed long before.

Contrary to the then prevailing optimism, he had believed as early as 1899 that civilization was not advancing but regressing. He was convinced that mankind was losing its sense of those spiritual and ethical qualities in which true civilization is rooted, and that the idea of mankind's inexorable progress toward perfection was therefore illusory.

As he pondered the matter, his *Philosophy of Civilization* grew to be not only an exposition of the problems but a proposal for their solution, and in the first two volumes (1923) he argued that a world-view based on respect for life, together with an ethic founded on that respect, could alone bring mankind to a civilized state. The book was to be regarded by many as his magnum opus, and to be particularly praised because its arguments embraced not just human life but non-human as well. The ethic of Reverence for Life was ever after to dominate his thought and guide his activity.

In July 1918 he and Helene were released from prison. Although his wife's health had improved as soon as the Congo was left behind, his own had been undermined by recurrent dysentery whose aftereffects of chronic fatigue, fever, and pain did not soon abate. These, reinforcing a pessimism made the more profound by the war's devastation, the death of loved ones, and the abandonment of his African mission, led him to wonder gloomily what course his future should take and how indeed he should make a living. Having returned to Strasbourg, however, he felt his black mood begin to lift when he was offered posts as doctor at the municipal hospital and as curate once more at St Nicholas; when by the kindness of the Chapter of St Thomas he was given a parsonage in which to live; when surgical operations relieved his physical symptoms; and when on 14 January 1919, his own birthday, his daughter, Rhena, was born.

In the spring of 1920, Schweitzer gave a series of lectures at the University of Uppsala, choosing as topic world- and life-affirmation and ethics in philosophy and the world religions, and expressing publicly for the first time conclusions he had reached while writing *The Philosophy of Civilization*. So well received were these talks that he stayed in Sweden until July, giving organ recitals and lecturing on his work in Africa and by that means gathering enough money to pay back much of the debt he had incurred to found his hospital. Encouraged by this success, he decided not only to go back to Lambaréné but also to resign his posts in Strasbourg and thereafter to earn his keep solely by giving concerts, lecturing, and writing. He was no doubt further led to this decision by the success of *On the Edge of the Primeval Forest* (1921), which appeared first in Swedish and German and soon afterwards in Dutch, French, Danish, and Finnish.

In 1921–24 he worked on *The Philosophy of Civilization* and gave lectures and concerts in England, Switzerland, Denmark, Sweden, and Czechoslovakia. In 1923 a series of lectures on *Christianity and the World Religions* appeared in print and in 1924 *Memoirs of Childhood and Youth*.

Finally, after an absence of seven years, Schweitzer returned to Lambaréné at Eastertide of 1924. The jungle had reclaimed nearly every scrap of the hospital buildings, and the construction of new ones, first on the old site and later on a site two miles up-river, so exhausted his time and strength that his planned return to Europe was repeatedly postponed and his idea abandoned of completing while in Africa a book on *The Mysticism of St Paul the Apostle*. Far from being able to spend his leisure moments on intellectual work, he was instead required to learn the skills of carpenter, mason, and farmer. Not the least ambitious of his projects, undertaken to help feed his community, was the planting of fruit trees in jungle lands laboriously reclaimed. But *More from the Primeval Forest* (1924–27) at length appeared in print.

Word of his mission – now independent from Parisian control – having spread in Europe, both friends and strangers were regularly volunteering so much time and money that he was soon able to send for doctors and nurses to help with the ever growing number of patients – by 1927 about one hundred and sixty in hospital, not counting outpatients – and to entrust some of his duties to assistants.

Schweitzer was thus able to begin to divide his time between Lambaréné and Europe. In 1927–29 he gave lectures and recitals in Holland, Sweden, England, Germany, Switzerland, Denmark, and Czechoslovakia, finished his book on St Paul, and, at Queen's Hall in London, made his first phonograph records. In Africa in 1929–31 he added new buildings to the hospital and treated the sick by day; by night he worked on the third volume of his *Philosophy of Civilization*, on *Out of My Life and Thought* (1933), and on a lecture that would commemorate in 1932 the centenary of Goethe, with whom he had always felt a special affinity. Particularly in the mixing of mental work with physical was he delighted to take Goethe as exemplar.

More recitals and lectures followed in Europe in 1932–33 and 1934–35, and in 1933–34 a fourth stay in Africa. In 1936 *Indian Thought and its*

Development appeared in print, and he made in London and Strasbourg more phonograph records. The years 1937–39 saw him back in Africa.

War was imminent when in February 1939 he arrived again in Europe. Fearing that hostilities might break out at any moment and prevent his return, he re-embarked after only ten days. With that abrupt change of plan commenced one of the most difficult periods of his life. He was sixty-four. Deprived of many of his staff, compelled to do alone much of the work of his hospital, cut off for months on end from the world outside and hence from shipments of food and medicine, he was for most of a decade to labour without pause, sometimes despairing of being able to feed and care for his patients and of being strong enough himself to go on. More than once essential supplies were on the point of giving out when aid would arrive – in 1941 and 1943 medicines and surgical tools sent from the United States, where funds had been raised on his behalf by, among other groups, the Unitarian Service Committee, the Episcopal Church, and the American Guild of Organists. Nor was the fighting always far away: the Vichy French and the Free French attacked each other within sight and hearing of Lambaréné, terrifying the patients, disrupting the routine of the hospital, and once by mistake firing at Schweitzer himself.

With the peace came political changes in Africa and the world that were to cause him new worries: the movement by Africans toward independence and by the world toward atomic annihilation. To the first he responded that the hospital was sited on land granted by the government, which could of course revoke the grant when his services were no longer desired. To the second he responded that nothing could more profoundly contravene the ethic of Reverence for Life than atomic weapons of mass destruction, the testing of which was poisoning air and land and ocean for generations to come. Together with three subsequent broadcast appeals and his private letters to world leaders, such public statements as his 'Declaration of Conscience,' which was read to a broadcast audience worldwide and published by magazine and newspaper in almost every country, helped bring about treaties to end nuclear tests in the atmosphere.

He visited Europe at intervals in the years 1948–59, in 1951–53 making in Günsbach his last recordings and in 1954 speaking in Oslo on 'The Problem of Peace in the World of Today.' On 1 June 1957 Helene Schweitzer died in Switzerland. He returned to Europe to bring her ashes back to Lambaréné.

Among the honours he received in his last years were membership in the French Legion of Honour (1950), the French Institute (1951), the American Academy of Arts and Sciences (1954), the British Order of Merit (1955), and the West German Order of Merit (1955). He had received honorary degrees from, among others, the universities of Cambridge, Oxford, Edinburgh, Prague, and Chicago – this last in 1949 while visiting Chicago during his sole journey to the United States. In 1952 he was awarded the Nobel Peace Prize.

At the age of ninety, on 4 September 1965, in Lambaréné, having continued to work until only days before the end, Albert Schweitzer died.

His ethical convictions and the example of his life, however, have not ceased to influence and to inspire. His writings appear in new editions and translations. In various countries societies bearing his name sponsor publications and conferences to disseminate his thought. He has been the subject of a dozen biographies and scores of articles.

His hospital continues to treat hundreds of patients each year. Indeed, it was reported in 1988 by the *New York Times* that patients prefer the Schweitzer hospital to the excellent state-run hospital nearby, though the latter is free and the Schweitzer imposes a nominal charge.

Perhaps most indicative of all, an Albert Schweitzer Institute for the Humanities was formed in 1990 as a non-profit, non-governmental organization associated with the United Nations. Among its activities, it holds a symposium every two years at which experts from many countries gather to discuss the urgent questions confronting humankind at the beginning of the new millennium. Questions of nuclear danger, disregard for human rights, the deterioration of the environment, and unacceptable ill-health are posed and answers sought in the light of Schweitzer's life-affirming ethic, with the conviction that the philosophy of Reverence for Life can inspire action that will lead to a more harmonious world.

Appendix B Letters

Most of the hundreds of letters Schweitzer wrote about music remain unpublished. Among the exceptions are 161 letters to the organ builders Fritz Haerpfer and Alfred Kern, edited by Bernhard Billeter in 'Albert Schweitzer und sein Orgelbauer'; letters to Pablo Casals, Marcel Dupré, and others, selected and edited by Harald Schützeichel in *Albert Schweitzer: Briefe und Erinnerungen an Musiker* or quoted in *Die Orgel im Leben und Denken Albert Schweitzers*; and letters about the Bach biographies and edition, edited by Erwin R. Jacobi in *Albert Schweitzers nachgelassene Manuskripte über die Verzierungen bei Johann Sebastian Bach*. Otherwise, only the occasional letter on music has appeared in print: for example a letter, celebrated by Norman Cousins in *Dr Schweitzer of Lambaréné*, to a fifteen-year-old American boy who hoped to save the organ in his church, and letters to Romain Rolland and to Donald Francis Tovey. The sampling below, in addition to presenting Schweitzer's views in his own words, may accordingly suggest what treasure remains to be published, and what substance.

1) To J. B. Jamison, organist, Los Gatos, California, from Lambaréné, 17 December 1944

Dear Mr Jamison,

You are very nice to divulge nothing in public of what I write in letters, without asking me. I am profoundly distressed when people act otherwise. Thank you for your thoughtfulness.

Here is my opinion about baroque organs. You may use these lines as you see fit.

The idea of turning back from the modern (in the bad sense of the word) organ toward the true organ was promoted by me in my little booklet 'German and French Organ-Building and Organ-Playing' (Breitkopf and Härtel 1906). I had come to have misgivings about the modern organs that the big German and Swiss firms were building (I did not yet know the English organs), because I had in my ears the round, transparent, beautiful, rich sonority of the old organs by Silbermann, maintained and restored by Alsatian organ builders who had remained in their tradition. In making the acquaintance of the organs of Cavaillé-Coll, I found that they were closer to this tradition (except for the reeds) than those of modern builders. I saw that people were now seeking to perfect, in very debatable ways, the connection from key to pipe and the means of changing stops, while neglecting what was essential: the sonority. I also noticed that none of the modernized windchests (Windladen) could produce the round and full sonority of the old windchest (Schleiflade) which Cavaillé-Coll had held to. Although I could not tell why physically this was so, I knew it to be true, as an old inebriate knows one wine is better than another without bothering to analyse the fact.

Another finding: I perceived the importance of the rückpositif – that is, of a division whose pipes project into the nave. This I understood from noticing the quite special effect of old Alsatian organs with rückpositifs, small and imperfect though these were in some instruments.

When I left for Africa in 1913, I felt certain that this movement back to the organ of beautiful tone was underway. But I did not go further back than to the organ of Bach's time, to the *monumental* organ that suited his organ works. And I pictured this organ as enriched with a large division under expression. The organ is a likeness of the Trinity, containing three very distinct personalities and making of them one: great – rückpositif – expressive manual (swell).

I was amazed that Cavaillé-Coll had purposely given up the rückpositif, and that Guilmant and Widor and Gigout had not observed the acoustical importance of the rückpositif. I had many a discussion with Widor on this subject, but it was only later, when listening with me one day to the organ at St Eustache, where Merklin (who was a worthy competitor of Cavaillé-Coll, which people too often forget!) had, in his fine restoration, kept the rückpositif, that Widor recognized the importance of this division. It was at St Eustache, moreover, while hearing this organ for the first time – in the traditional religious concert for St Cecilia's Day (the Prelude and Fugue in E-flat was played) – in 1899, that I was deeply impressed by hearing the effect of a rückpositif which was large, having known until then only the old, rather skimpy rückpositifs which nevertheless made so striking an impression.

Therefore, my ideal was a synthesis of the old organ and the modern, retaining from the old the rückpositif and enriching it with an expressive division, keeping the old windchest (Schleiflade), and avoiding too high wind-pressures. And above all I envisaged an organ in which the main concern was for the beauty and richness of the tone, and not for the purely outward improvements (console, registration aids).

In travelling about Europe after the war I noticed the curious tendency among certain organists interested in organ building, mainly in Germany but also in Switzerland, to go further back than to the monumental organs of the

Silbermanns and others, and to recreate the non-monumental organ of the time before Bach, in which the two keyboards are of equal importance. I also noticed that people were after the sonorities of these organs, with their surly reeds. At first I attached little importance to this archaistic tendency, cultivated chiefly by professors of music history at various universities.

But during my sojourns in Europe between 1920 and 1932, I had to admit that this non-monumental and archaic organ was beginning to be considered the true ideal organ in many circles. I saw many organists whom I knew to be men of sound judgement infected by this false ideal that called itself *baroque organ* (though the baroque period, properly so called, is chiefly marked in architecture). It was then that I was affected by this movement and that I voiced my opinion frankly when people wanted to make me play Bach on these non-monumental organs.

And what weighed on me most heavily was that certain representatives of this movement were using me as a reference, saying that they were only carrying out my ideas. However, I did not wish to enter into a polemic, because many times I recognized that these sectarians of archaism were driven by the best intentions, and that to their credit they usually thought the rückpositif important and believed they were carrying out my ideas. Above all, I did not want to hurt well-meaning organ builders who were incurring expenses to build these organs.

One must not stir up polemics. This principle has always seemed to me right. But one must, with restraint but with firmness, state the truth. The truth is that the monumental organ – such as the preludes and fugues of Bach require and such as the great builders of his day, and after him, created – is an acquisition that must at all costs be preserved.

The works of Bach are the measure of this organ. The monumental organ includes a great division (representing God in the Trinity), dominating the other divisions but demanding them as its complement.

When I play the monumental organ I feel as if I am riding a fine horse; when I play the so-called baroque organ I feel I am mounting a pony. That is why, in my moments of ill humour and sadness at the thought that people are straying from the ideal Bach organ, I call these organs pony organs. I regret not finding in these organs the beautiful roundness of sonority that only a sufficient number of eight-foot stops can produce.

What I judge to be most mistaken about these organs is not only their structure, but also the return to primitive reeds of unsteady tone. The question of reeds is of prime importance. They must have stable pitch and stay in tune well. To get these qualities, Cavaillé-Coll made them too loud. They then dominate the ensemble. This is not greatly evident in the very large organs and vast naves, but mainly in organs of small and medium size. To his more modest organs Cavaillé-Coll gave too little attention, yet it is these that people build in greatest numbers. I can still hear the reeds of German and

Swiss builders from between 1860 and 1885, which were stable, round, and which merged ideally into the ensemble of foundations and mixtures. What keeps us from managing to make such reeds? The tongues? One thing is sure: people no longer worry about voicing (Intonation) as they used to. They no longer sacrifice the time that is needed, they no longer train master voicers. This art has been lost, or is being lost.

Competition forces organ builders to provide at a set price the greatest number of stops. They sacrifice quality to number, the essential to the subordinate. It is for organists to support organ builders in such a way as to let them create organs of quality and to maintain prices that make artistic work possible – as in the good old days, whose last glimmers I knew in Alsace. There lies the problem for all countries, those of the old world and those of the new. I have been close to many organ builders, and I have seen how much they suffered from circumstances that kept them from being the master artisans they could have been and wanted to be.

This declaration is incomplete and cut short. My fatigue and my work do not permit me to go into detail. I am giving up part of the night for you to write these pages. Thanks for the information you give me about the Tabernacle organ. I shall write soon to Mr Skinner, whose friendly letter I have received.

I think, while writing you, about the beautiful Dutch organs I loved so much that have been destroyed by the war (the great organ in Rotterdam!) and about the organs whose loss I shall have to lament when I go back to Alsace.

> With best wishes,
> Your devoted . . . .

[Cher M. Jamison,

Vous êtes bien gentil de ne rien divulguer en public de ce que j'écris dans des lettres, sans me demander. Je suis peiné profondément quand des gens agissent autrement. Je vous remercie de votre délicatesse.

Voici mon Opinion au sujet des orgues baroques. Vous pouvez faire l'usage de ces lignes que vous voudrez.

L'idée d'un retour de l'orgue moderne (dans le mauvais sens du mot) au vrai orgue a été lancée par moi dans ma petite brochure 'Deutsche und französische Orgelbaukunst und Orgelkunst' (Breitkopf und Härtel 1906). J'étais arrivé à douter des orgues modernes que construisaient alors les grandes firmes allemandes et suisses (je ne connaissais pas encore les orgues anglaises) parce que j'avais dans l'oreille la sonorité ronde, diaphane, belle, riche des orgues anciennes de Silbermann, entretenus et restaurés par des facteurs d'orgue Alsaciens qui étaient restés dans leur tradition. En faisant connaissance des orgues de Cavaillé-Coll j'ai constaté qu'ils étaient plus dans cette tradition (sauf les reeds) que les facteurs modernes. Je me rendais compte qu'on cherchait maintenant des perfections techniques et très discutables de la transmission de la touche au tuyau sonore et des ressources pour les changements de registres, en négligeant l'essentiel, la sonorité. J'ai aussi constaté que tous les sommiers (Windladen) modernisés ne pouvaient produire la sonorité ronde et pleine de l'ancien sommier (Schleiflade) que Cavaillé-Coll avait maintenu. Je ne pouvais pas m'expliquer le fait dans ses origines physiques, mais je constatais comme un vieil ivrogne constate qu'un vin est supérieur à l'autre, sans prendre soin d'analyser le fait.

Autre constatation: je me rendis compte de l'importance du Rückpositif, c'est à dire d'un clavier dont les tuyaux avancent dans la nef. Ceci je l'ai constaté en me rendant compte de l'effet tout particulier des anciennes orgues d'Alsace avec des Rückpositifs, si petits et si défectueux qu'ils pouvaient être sur certains instruments. En partant pour l'Afrique en 1913 j'avais la certitude que ce mouvement tendant à revenir vers l'orgue à belle sonorité était en marche. Mais je ne retournais pas plus en arrière qu'à l'orgue de Bach, à l'orgue *monumental* qui correspond à ses oeuvres d'orgue. Et je me figurais cet orgue enrichi d'un important clavier expressif. L'orgue est une image de la Trinité comprenant en elle trois personnalités bien distinctes et se fondant en une seule. Grand Orgue – Rückpositif – Clavier expressif (Récit). J'étais étonné que Cavaillé-Coll ait délibérément sacrifié le Rückpositif et que Guilmant et Widor et Gigout n'aient pas remarqué l'importance acoustique du Rückpositif. J'ai eu bien des entretiens avec Widor à ce sujet et ce n'est que tard, en écoutant un jour avec moi l'orgue de St Eustache, où Merklin (qui était un digne concurrent de Cavaillé, ce qu'on oublie trop souvent!) dans son admirable restauration avait maintenu le Rückpositif, qu'il a reconnu l'importance de ce clavier. Du reste c'est à St Eustache, en entendant cet orgue pour la première fois dans le concert religieux traditionnel du jour de la St Cécile (on jouait prélude et fugue en mi bémol) en 1899 que j'ai été profondément impressionné en entendant l'effet d'un Rückpositif important, après n'avoir connu jusque là que les anciens Rückpositifs un peu étriqués et cependant se faisant valoir si fortement. Donc mon idéal c'était une synthèse de l'orgue ancien et moderne, gardant de l'orgue ancien le Rückpositif et s'enrichissant du clavier expressif, gardant l'ancien sommier (Schleiflade), évitant les pressions du vent trop élevées, et surtout un orgue où le premier souci c'est la beauté et la richesse de la sonorité et non les perfectionnements purement extérieurs (Console, ressources de la registration) que j'envisageais. En voyageant en Europe après la guerre j'ai constaté la tendance curieuse chez certains organistes s'intéressant à la construction d'orgue, surtout en Allemagne, mais aussi en Suisse, de remonter plus en arrière de l'orgue monumental des Silbermann et des autres et de réaliser l'orgue non-monumental du temps avant Bach, où les deux claviers sont de même importance; j'ai aussi constaté qu'on recherchait les sonorités de ces orgues avec leurs reeds grincheuses. Je n'attachais d'abord pas grande importance à cette tendance archaïque cultivée surtout par les professeurs d'histoire de la musique à différentes Universités. Mais dans mes séjours en Europe entre 1920 et 1932 j'ai dû constater que cet orgue non-monumental et archaïque commençait à être considéré comme le véritable idéal de l'orgue dans bien des milieux. Je vis bien des organistes que je connaissais comme hommes sensés, être contaminés par ce faux idéal qui s'intitulait Barockorgel (quoique la période dite du Barock est surtout marquée dans l'architecture).

C'est alors que je me suis ému de ce mouvement, et que je disais carrément mon opinion quand on voulait me faire jouer du Bach sur ces orgues non-monumentaux. Et ce qui me pesait le plus, c'est que certains représentants de ce mouvement se recommandaient de moi en disant qu'ils ne faisaient que réaliser mes idées . . . . Cependant je ne voulais pas entrer en polémique parce que bien des fois je reconnaissais que ces sectaires archaïsants étaient animés des meilleures intentions et qu'ils avaient ordinairement le mérite d'attacher de l'importance au Rückpositif et croyaient réaliser mes idées. Surtout je ne voulais pas blesser des facteurs d'orgue qui faisaient des dépenses pour construire ces orgues, dans la meilleure intention. Il ne faut pas déchaîner de polémique: ce principe m'a toujours semblé le bon. Cependant il faut, avec modération, mais avec fermeté dire la vérité. La vérité est que l'orgue monumental tel que l'exigent les préludes et fugues de Bach et tel que les grands facteurs d'orgue de son époque et après lui l'ont créé est une acquisition qu'il faut absolument maintenir. C'est les oeuvres de Bach le critérium de cet orgue. L'orgue monumental comprend un grand clavier (représentant Dieu dans la Trinité), dominant les autres mais les demandant comme son complément. Quand je joue l'orgue monumental j'ai le sentiment de chevaucher sur un beau cheval; si je joue le soit disant orgue baroque j'ai l'impression de monter un poney. Et c'est pour cela que dans mes instants de mauvaise humeur et de tristesse de constater qu'on s'égare de l'idéal de l'orgue de Bach, j'appelle ces orgues des orgues poney.

Ce que je juge surtout erroné dans ces orgues ce n'est pas seulement leur structure, mais aussi le retour aux reeds primitifs, avec la sonorité vacillante. Je regrette de ne pas y trouver la belle rondeur de la sonorité que peuvent seuls produire les 8' en quantité suffisante.

La question des reeds est de première importance. Il faut qu'ils aient un ton stable, qu'ils tiennent pour le mieux l'accord. Pour avoir ces qualités Cavaillé-Coll les a fait trop forts. Ils dominent alors dans l'ensemble. Ceci ne se manifeste pas tellement dans les tout grands orgues et dans les vastes nefs, mais surtout dans les orgues moyens et petits. Aux orgues moyens Cavaillé-Coll a accordé trop peu d'attention, et ceux-ci sont cependant ceux qu'on construit dans le plus grand nombre. J'ai dans mes oreilles des reeds de facteurs allemands et suisses entre 1860 et 1885 qui étaient stables, ronds et qui se [mélangeaient] idéalement dans l'ensemble des fonds et mixtures. A quoi cela tient-il qu'on n'arrive pas à faire ces reeds? Aux langues? Un facteur est certain: c'est qu'on ne se préoccupe plus de l'harmonisation (*Intonation*) comme autrefois. On ne sacrifie pas le temps nécessaire, on ne forme plus des maîtres d'harmonisation. C'est un art qui s'est perdu ou qui est en train de se perdre. La concurrence force les facteurs d'orgue de donner pour un prix déterminé le plus grand nombre de jeux. On sacrifie le nombre à la qualité, l'essentiel à l'accessoire. C'est aux organistes de soutenir les facteurs d'orgue pour leur permettre de créer des orgues de qualité et de maintenir des prix où un travail artistique, comme dans le bon vieux temps (dont j'ai encore connu en Alsace les dernières lueurs) est possible. C'est là le problème pour tous les pays, ceux du vieux et ceux du nouveau monde. J'ai vécu dans l'intimité de bien des facteurs d'orgue et j'ai vu combien ils souffraient des circonstances qui leur défendaient d'être les maîtres artisans qu'ils auraient pu être et qu'ils voulaient être.

Voici une confession, incomplète et écourtée. Ma fatigue et mon travail ne me permettent pas d'entrer dans les détails. Je sacrifie une partie de la nuit pour vous écrire ces pages. Merci des indications sur l'orgue du Tabernacle que vous me donnez. J'écrirai prochainement à Mons. Skinner dont j'ai reçu l'aimable lettre.

Je pense en vous écrivant aux belles orgues hollandaises que j'aimais tant qui ont été détruit dans la guerre (le grand orgue de Rotterdam!) et aux orgues dont j'aurai à déplorer la perte en rentrant en Alsace.

Avec mes bonnes pensées
votre dévoué . . . .]

2) To Walter Holtkamp, organ builder, Cleveland, from Lambaréné, 2 February 1941

Dear Sir,

Thanks for informing me of your correspondence with Breitkopf. After the war I hope to complete this work on organ building, and then publish it. I will then be in touch with you.

But there is nothing to prevent an American organist who is a writer from expressing now, in a brochure or an article, the basic ideas on organ building that are found in my brochure. Ah, when will I have the pleasure of showing you some organs built in Alsace according to my ideas!

I thank you also for wanting to donate to my work the proceeds from the publication of my brochure.

Thanks also for sending me the stoplist of the Barnes Memorial Organ. It interested me very much. I think the organ well designed. One remark, however: As a rule, it is better to put the trompette 8 and clarion 4 in the swell rather than in the choir. For the swell should be stronger than the choir: the choir remains an incomplete manual, and the swell should be complete. And

César Franck, Widor, Gigout, Vierne, and all the great modern composers for the organ assume the trompette and the clarion (as well as the fagotto 16) always in the swell. See the registration indications in César Franck and Widor! So if the trompette 8 and clarion 4 are found in the choir, it is very complicated for the organist to render these works as they were conceived by the composer . . . .

Another question. It is a pity that the Barnes Memorial Organ should be free only at the front, and not on both sides. The success of this beautiful instrument is thus reduced by two fifths. The sound cannot emerge freely. Notice that the old organs are always situated in such a way as not to be obstructed at the sides. But modern architects provide only a niche for the organ. They imprison it. Hence one of the first things to do is to struggle to persuade architects to give the organ a suitable location from which its sound can freely develop. This will be a great struggle, because architects are unconcerned about giving a suitable place to the organ. I have this struggle as well in Europe. The Silbermann organs not only sound so beautiful because they are well built, but also because they are placed in high galleries from which their sound can develop in all directions. Why do architects commit this heresy? Organists ought to take an interest in the plans for churches under construction and insist that the place intended for the organ be suitable. For this is the prime condition for the effectiveness of the sacred instrument . . . .

[Cher Monsieur,

Merci de m'avoir mis au courant de votre correspondance avec Breitkopf. Après la guerre j'espère compléter cet ouvrage sur la construction d'orgue, et alors on le publiera. Je m'adresserai alors à vous.

Mais rien n'empêche qu'un organiste américain, qui est écrivain n'expose dès maintenant dans une brochure ou un article les idées fondamentales sur la construction d'orgue qui se trouvent dans ma brochure. Ah, quand aurai-je le plaisir de vous montrer quelques orgues construits d'après mes idées en Alsace!

Je vous remercie aussi d'avoir voulu consacrer à mon oeuvre ce que rapporterait la publication de ma brochure.

Merci aussi de m'avoir envoyé la composition des claviers du Barnes Memorial Organ. Cela m'a bien intéressé. Je trouve l'orgue bien composé. Une remarque cependant: En principe il vaut mieux de mettre Trumpet 8' et Clarion 4' dans le Swell au lieu dans le Choir. Car le Swell doit être plus fort que le Choir: Le Choir reste un Clavier incomplet et le Swell doit être complet. Et César Franck, Widor, Gigout, Vierne et tous les grands modernes compositeurs d'orgue, supposent la trompette et le Clarion 4' (ainsi que Fagotto 16') toujours dans le Swell. Voyez les indications de registration chez César Franck et Widor! Alors si la trompette 8 et le Clarion 4 se trouvent sur le Choir, c'est très compliqué pour l'organiste de rendre ces oeuvres comme elles sont pensées par l'auteur . . . .

Encore une question: C'est dommage que le Barnes Memorial Organ soit seulement libre devant, mais pas des deux côtés! Le rendement de ce bel instrument est ainsi diminué de deux cinquième. Le ton ne peut pas sortir librement. Voyez les anciennes orgues sont toujours placées de façon à ne pas être enfermées de côté. Mais les architectes modernes n'offrent pour la place de l'orgue qu'un trou. Ils l'emprisonnent. Ainsi une des premières choses à faire, c'est de lutter pour décider les architectes de donner une place convenable à l'orgue où son son puisse s'épanouir librement. Ce sera une grande lutte, car les architectes ne se soucient pas de donner une place convenable à l'orgue. J'ai cette lutte aussi en Europe. Les orgues de Silbermann ne sonnent pas seulement si belles, parce qu'elles sont bien construites, mais aussi parce qu'elles sont placées sur des tribunes hautes, où leur son peut s'épanouir de tous les côtés. Pourquoi les architectes commettent-ils cette hérésie? Les organistes devraient s'occuper des plans des églises qu'on construit et insister que la place destinée à l'orgue soit convenable. Car ceci c'est la première condition de l'effet de l'instrument sacré . . . .]

3) To Frank Holcomb Shaw, Director, Oberlin Conservatory of Music, Oberlin, Ohio, from Strasbourg, n. d. [*c.* 1928]

Sir,

I learn from Mr [Maurice] Kessler that Oberlin College wishes to build a large concert hall with an organ. As an Alsatian, and as an expert in organ building, I take the liberty of addressing an opinion to the conservatory of music at this college which bears an Alsatian name.

You are aware that a renaissance in organ building is underway which began nearly twenty-five years ago in Alsace. We have marvelled at the beautiful sonority of the organs of Silbermann, the great Alsatian organ builder of the eighteenth century, the contemporary of Bach. We have studied his organs; we have studied all the old organs, the beautiful eighteenth-century instruments that are still found in Europe, and we have tried to find out why they have a much more beautiful, much rounder, much more transparent sonority than organs being built now. And we have found the reasons.

These are: 1) the old organs have much lower wind pressure than modern organs; 2) the pipe scales and the evolution of the scales throughout the compass are governed by traditions that have great value; 3) the old-style windchests are much more resonant than modern ones.

Starting from these observations, we set ourselves to building in accordance with the old way, while perfecting it, naturally, from a purely technical point of view. Thus we are managing to build organs that have all the advantages of the old organs and at the same time the advantages of modern organs. A new future is opening up for organ construction. Already these organs are being built in Switzerland, Denmark, Germany.

This prompts me to ask if perhaps you would not like to build at Oberlin an organ in the style of the organs of the great Alsatian builder Silbermann, and be first in America to have an organ embodying the principles of the renaissance in organ building.

You would render a great service to organ building in America, I believe, by acquainting it with an organ that unites the characteristics and sonorities of the old organ and of the modern organ. I believe that my reputation as an expert in organ building assures you that this is a matter of some interest. You could also send your organ professor to Europe to experience this beautiful sonority for himself.

The simplest thing would naturally be for an Alsatian organ builder to construct this organ for you. I offer, quite impartially, to collaborate in the designs. Or perhaps the Alsatian builder could construct the organ in collaboration with an American builder.

But an essential question: will your organ be well placed in the concert hall, so as to speak freely? Modern architects have the unhappy idea of placing concert-hall organs in corners where they are closed in on all sides and where, from the start, they are doomed to failure in producing their full sonority. If your organ is destined to be located in a corner, it is pointless to fashion it after the principles of the renaissance in organ building. For the first of these principles is that the organ must be located on the platform, free in front and on both sides, so as to be able to project its tones directly into the room.

On these organs that unite the characteristics of the old organ and the modern organ, one can play the works of Bach in the sonorities in which he himself played them. On a modern organ, Bach's music cannot be rendered as he himself conceived it. The future certainly belongs to the organ that unites the characteristics of old and modern organs. Because of this, I am bold enough, as biographer of Bach and as interpreter of his works, and above all as an Alsatian, to ask the directors of the Oberlin Conservatory whether there might not be an interest in equipping the concert hall at Oberlin with an organ that derives from the great Alsatian traditions of organ building of the eighteenth century: a Silbermann organ at Oberlin!

Kindly forgive the liberty I am taking . . . .

[Monsieur.

J'apprends par M. M[aurice] Kessler que l'Université d'Oberlin veut construire une grande salle de concert avec un grand orgue. En ma qualité d'Alsacien et de connaisseur en facture d'orgue je me permets d'adresser un avis au Conservatoire de Musique de l'Université qui porte un nom alsacien.

Vous savez qu'il se prépare une Renaissance de la Construction d'orgue, qui prend son départ, depuis près de 25 ans, d'Alsace. Nous avons été émerveillés par la belle sonorité des orgues de Silbermann, le grand constructeur d'orgue Alsacien au XVIIIème siècle, le contemporain de Bach. Nous avons étudié ses orgues; nous avons étudié toutes les anciennes orgues, les beaux instruments du XVIIIème siècle qui se trouvent encore en Europe, et nous avons cherché les raisons pourquoi ils ont une sonorité beaucoup plus belle, beaucoup plus ronde, beaucoup plus diaphane que les orgues qu'on construit actuellement. Et nous avons trouvé les causes. Les voici: 1) les anciennes orgues ont une pression de vent beaucoup plus faible que les modernes. 2) les mesures et les progressions dans les tuyaux sont réglées par des traditions qui ont une grande valeur. 3) les layes (Windladen) du système ancien sont beaucoup plus sonores que les layes modernes.

Partant de ces constatations nous nous sommes mis à construire d'après cette façon ancienne, en la perfectionnant naturellement sous le point de vue purement technique. Avec cela nous sommes arrivés à construire des orgues qui ont tous les avantages des orgues anciens et en même temps les avantages des orgues modernes. Un nouvel avenir s'ouvre pour la construction d'orgue. Déjà on construit de ces orgues en Suisse, au Danemark, en Allemagne.

Ceci me donne l'idée de vous demander si peut-être vous ne voulez pas construire un orgue dans le style des orgues du grand Facteur d'Orgue Alsacien Silbermann à Oberlin et avoir les premiers en Amérique un orgue d'après les principes de la Renaissance de la Construction d'Orgue. Vous rendriez, je crois, un grand service à la construction d'orgue en Amérique en lui faisant faire la connaissance d'un orgue qui réunit les qualités et les sonorités de l'ancien orgue et de l'orgue moderne. Je crois que mon nom comme expert en construction d'orgue vous donne la certitude qu'il s'agit d'une chose qui a de l'intérêt. Vous pouvez aussi envoyer votre professeur d'orgue en Europe pour se rendre compte lui-même de cette belle sonorité.

Le plus simple serait naturellement si un facteur d'orgue Alsacien vous construisait cet orgue. Je m'offre d'une façon tout à fait désintéressée pour collaborer aux plans. Ou peut-être le facteur alsacien pourrait construire l'orgue en collaboration avec un facteur américain.

Mais une question essentielle: Est-ce que votre orgue sera bien placé dans la salle de concert, de façon de sonner librement? Les architectes modernes ont la malheureuse idée de mettre les orgues des salles de concert dans des coins où ils sont enfermés de tous les côtés et où ils sont condamnés d'avance à ne pas pouvoir donner leur pleine sonorité. Si votre orgue est destiné à être placé dans un coin, alors il est inutile de le créer d'après les principes de la Renaissance de la Construction d'orgue. Car le premier de ces principes est que l'orgue doit être placé sur la tribune, libre de devant et des deux côtés de façon à pouvoir envoyer ses sons directement dans la salle.

Sur ces orgues qui unissent les qualités de l'orgue ancien et de l'orgue moderne on peut jouer la musique de Bach dans les sonorités, dans lesquelles il les jouait lui-même. Sur un orgue moderne la musique de Bach ne peut pas être rendue telle qu'il se la représentait lui-même. L'avenir est certainement à l'orgue qui unit les qualités de l'ancien orgue et de l'orgue moderne. C'est pour cela que je prends le courage, comme biographe de Bach et comme interprète de ses oeuvres, et surtout comme Alsacien, de demander aux dirigeants du Conservatoire de l'Université d'Oberlin, s'il n'y aurait pas intérêt de doter la salle de concert d'Oberlin d'un orgue qui est né des grandes traditions de la construction d'orgue en Alsace au dix-huitième siècle . . . . un orgue Silbermann à Oberlin!

Veuillez excuser la liberté que je prends . . . .]

4) To the vestry of St Jacobi Church, Hamburg, from Königsfeld, 19 January 1928 (For the translation, see Chapter 6. See also Schweitzer [1930], 'Gutachten über die Orgel zu St Jacobi in Hamburg.')

Einzig die Orgel zu St Jacobi in Hamburg, nach der seine Sehnsucht stand, ist uns so überkommen, wie sie war, als ihre Schönheit den grössten Orgelmeister aller Zeiten bezauberte. Auf ihr können sich die Künstler der Jetztzeit vergegenwärtigen, auf welche Art Bach seine Werke ausführte und welche Klangmöglichkeiten er voraussetzte . . . .

Es handelt sich um eine einfache Erhaltung. Was schadhaft ist, muss renoviert, was fehlt, muss ersetzt werden . . . .

Die Schönheit und Eigenart des Klanges der Orgel zu St Jacobi beruht auf den Pfeifen und den Windladen. Als erstes Prinzip bei der Erhaltung der Orgel ist also aufzustellen, dass Pfeifen und Laden so erhalten werden, wie sie sind. Weiter ist festzulegen, dass der niedrige Winddruck, unter dem allein diese Pfeifen normal und in voller Schönheit aussprechen, beibehalten werde.

Die im Krieg abgelieferten Pfeifen sind zu ersetzen. Im Rückpositiv ist Barpfeife 8 wieder einzusetzen. Auch dürfte es sich empfehlen die hier später eingebaute Trompete 8 wieder durch die ursprüngliche Schalmey 4 zu ersetzen. Dass die später ins Oberwerk eingebauten pneumatischen Stimmen in Wegfall kommen müssen ist selbstverständlich.

Der Ausbau der kurzen Oktaven in allen vier Clavieren empfiehlt sich, ebenso der Ausbau der unteren Oktave im Pedal.

Natürlich wäre es interessant in den unvollständigen und gebrochenen Oktaven auch die Unvollkommenheiten der alten Orgeln in einem historischen Dokument zu erhalten. Andererseits aber beeinträchtigen diese Unvollkommenheiten, so gering sie an sich sein mögen, den Spielwert des Instrumentes . . . .

Die Frage ob das Werk auf Normalstimmung zu bringen sei, ist schwierig zu entscheiden. Ich selber habe seiner Zeit bei der Erhaltung der Silbermannorgel in St Thomas zu Strassburg es durchgesetzt, dass jenes Werk auf Normalstimmung gebracht wurde, im Interesse des Vorteils den die Normalstimmung für den gottesdienstlichen Gebrauch mit sich bringt. Durch den Eingriff haben die Pfeifen aber in etwas ihre originalen Masse und Proportionen verloren. Für ein so einzigartiges Werk wie das zu St Jacobi aber, wäre es wohl eher zu empfehlen, die alte Stimmung beizubehalten, in der das Werk in seiner vollen Schönheit erklingt.

Sollte es aber technisch möglich sein, rein durch Verrückung der Claviaturen, ohne nennenswerte Eingriffe an den Pfeifen, die Orgel auf Normalstimmung – oder ungefähr auf Normalstimmung – zu bringen, so wäre nichts einzuwenden. Ob dies technisch durchführbar ist, müsste eingehend studiert werden.

Was den Einbau eines Schwellkastens für das Oberwerk (Recit) betrifft, so ist dieses auch in alten holländischen Orgeln durchgeführt worden. Bei der Besichtigung erschien mir, dass genügend Platz zur Anbringung der Jalousien vorhanden sei. Ergibt sich bei eingehendem technischem Studium, dass die Anbringung von Jalousien möglich ist, so glaube ich dass dies nicht zu verwerfen sei. Durch die Anbringung des Schwellkastens wird der Klang der alten Orgel weder beeinträchtigt noch verändert. Die Ausdrucksfähigkeit des dritten Claviers wird durch keine Nachteile erkauft.

Die gegenwärtige mechanische Traktur hat ernsthafte Nachteile. Die Tasten geben schwer und fallen tief. Andererseits aber ist der mechanischen Spielart zu verdanken, dass auf der Orgel zu St Jacobi das Gewebe der Stimmen in so wunderbarer Klarheit herauskommt. Denkbar wäre in irgend einer Weise durch Anwendung von Barckerhebel oder Zwischeneinschaltung von Röhrenpneumatik, der Orgel eine leichtere Spielart zu geben. Andererseits aber ist zu befürchten, dass wenn man einmal mit Änderungen anfängt, man nicht weiss, wo man Halt machen kann. Die Ersetzung der mechanischen Traktur durch etwas anderes, wäre ein erheblicher Eingriff in das Werk. Es würde dadurch viel von seinem historischen Werte verlieren. Darum trete ich für die Erhaltung der mechanischen Traktur ein. Sie ist mit bestem Material zu erneuern, wobei sich wohl eine leichtere Spielbarkeit erreichen lässt.

Bei Beibehaltung der mechanischen Traktur ist die Benutzung der Coppeln eingeschränkt. Dies hat aber bei einem Werke wie dem zu St Jacobi nicht soviel zu besagen. Jedes Clavier der Orgel ist ja hier eine vollendete Klangpersönlichkeit und das volle Werk des ersten Claviers weist eine solche Fülle auf, dass die Ankoppelung der anderen Claviere keine Notwendigkeit ist.

Mit der Beibehaltung der mechanischen Traktur entscheidet sich die Frage, ob die Orgel einen Spieltisch und moderne Spielhilfen erhalten soll. An sich wäre es ja sicherlich wünschenswert, dass dem Organisten die Möglichkeit des Zuziehens und Abstossens von Registern gegeben würden, die er auf neueren Instrumenten vorfindet. Dieses aber würde voraussetzen, dass die Registerzüge und der ganze Registrierapparat pneumatisch angelegt würden. Nun ist erfahrungsgemäss nichts schwieriger als Pneumatik mit Schleiflade zu verbinden, besonders wenn es sich um alte Laden handelt. Zu St Thomas in Strassburg hat man es in meiner Abwesenheit getan. Nun ist zwar das Registrieren viel leichter, aber das Zuziehen oder Abstossen des Registers braucht eine gewisse Zeit bis es in Kraft tritt. Dies ist ein grosser Nachteil.

Nach meiner Erfahrung mit alten Orgeln wäre ich also nicht dafür, mit den alten Schleifladen pneumatisches Registrierwerk zu verbinden. Sind einmal die Führungen der Registerzüge wieder in Ordnung gebracht, so gehen die Register viel leichter als jetzt.

Überdies ist ja nicht soviel Änderung der Register nötig, da die satte Schönheit des Tones zu St Jacobi gar keine vielfältige Änderung der Farbe verlangt. Zudem kommt ja für diese Orgel, wenn sie als geschichtliches Denkmal erhalten wird, nur Bachsche und Vorbachsche Musik in Frage, wo nicht soviel in Registrierung unternommen wird. Die Orgel zu St Jacobi wird dann der Organistenwelt eine Erzieherin zur richtigen Wiedergabe der alten Meister sein, indem sie ihnen zeigt, dass jene schon aus technischen Gründen sich ihm Wechsel der Register Beschränkung auferlegen mussten . . . .

5) To Axel Boberg, organist, Malmö, Sweden, from Lambaréné, 11 November 1945

Dear Mr Boberg,

What a joy for me to receive via Günsbach some news of you and of the Genarp organ! Heartfelt thanks. Just recently when writing to an organist interested in organ building in the USA, I mentioned the Genarp organ. And here you send me news of it. I am glad that this interesting instrument is being restored by you and preserved in the Malmö Museum. When shall I again get to Sweden and be able to see it once more? . . .

What always surprised me about the good Swedish organs was the waldflöte 2 on the second or third manual. I have never encountered this stop with this quality anywhere else but in Sweden. Its fullness of tone improves the forte of the second or third manuals. Here is something better than those wretched flageolets 2! Can you give me some information on the scales and characteristics of the pipes of this waldflöte 2? I would be very grateful . . . .

[Cher M. Boberg,

Quelle joie pour moi de recevoir via Günsbach, des nouvelles de vous . . et de l'orgue de Genarp! Merci de coeur. Encore dernièrement écrivant à un organiste qui s'intéresse à la construction d'orgue en USA, je lui ai parlé de l'orgue de Genarp! Et voici que vous m'en envoyez des nouvelles. Je suis heureux que cet intéressant instrument soit restauré par vous et conservé au Musée de Malmö. Quand viendrai-je de nouveau en Suède et pourrai-je le revoir? ...

Ce qui m'a toujours étonné dans les bons orgues Suédois, c'est la Waldflöte 2' sur le second ou le troisième clavier. Je n'ai rencontré ce registre dans cette qualité nulle part d'autre qu'en Suède. C'est une ampleur de son qui embellit le forte des deuxièmes ou troisièmes claviers! Voilà autre chose que ces pauvres Flagolett 2'! Pouvez-vous me donner des renseignements sur les Mensuren et qualités des Pfeifen de cette Waldflöte 2'? Je vous en serais très reconnaissant . . . .]

6) To Edouard Nies-Berger, organist, New York, from Lambaréné, 29 October 1945

Dear Mr Nies-Berger,

Thank you for your letter of 8 September 1945. I am very moved to learn that Mr Wick has collected so large a gift for my work from among the French and Alsatians of New York! ...

The Compenius organ in Frederiksborg Castle, Denmark, I have known for many years. (It is mentioned in *The Diapason* for 1 July 1945.) But I cannot say that this is an instrument which sends me into raptures. It is interesting as a step in the evolution of the organ.

The oldest organ I know is that of the village of Genarp, Sweden. When I saw it (I had to make a long journey by sleigh to get to this village) in 1923, I was completely bewildered: it was so old that it did not have tempered tuning! It was a shock for me to play on an untempered organ. It was necessary to stay in C and G! All the other keys were out of tune! It was an organ that in the old days was located in the choir of the large Cathedral of St Petri in Malmö, and was later sold to a village church. Some organist friends in Sweden write me that it has been restored and is being preserved as an antique. One manual and pedal. Remarkable sound! ...

I am enclosing stoplists for a number of organs that my son-in-law, Mr J. A. Eckert, has recently built in Switzerland for the Kuhn firm. The firm lets him build as he likes. They in no way hamper his work, which results in a staff having the qualities needed to build in an artistic way. They let him build slider chests and organs with mechanical action. The stoplists are not his own; they come from organ experts from various regions. But little by little these experts are leaning toward the old-style organ, modernized.

They have accepted the slider chest, after hesitating at first. I believe my son-in-law could not work under better conditions anywhere in the world. He is little by little beginning to train voicers (Intonateure) who are artists. But it will take time, because this art is lost. I myself still knew the voicers of the old Cavaillé-Coll firm, the Princes and the others. But all of a sudden in Paris this generation died out and was replaced by another from which people demanded speedy work rather than good work: idiotic competition brought us to that . . . .

In the specifications realized by my son-in-law in Switzerland, and drawn up and prescribed by the organ-building experts, you notice that the latter hesitate or refuse to call for gambas, cellos, voix celestes, even salicionals! They are still captivated by the idea of the (so-called) baroque organ. They forget that a trend toward building string stops is already evident in the 17th century!

All these strings are a precious acquisition for the organ, only one must do them with very large scales so that the tone is noble and round, not penetrating. What beautiful salicionals one finds in the organs built around 1880! What a resource, for giving clarity to the sound, is a lovely cello in the pedal! Why want to give that up? . . .

[Cher Monsieur Nies-Berger,
Merci de votre lettre du 8 Sept. '45. Je suis très ému d'apprendre que M. Wick a réuni un si grand don pour mon oeuvre parmi les français et alsaciens de New-York! . . .

La Compenius orgel du Château de Frederiksborg au Danemark je la connais depuis de longues années. (Il en est question de la Diapason du 1 July [*sic*] '45). Mais je ne puis pas dire que ce soit un instrument qui m'enthousiasme. C'est intéressant comme une étape vers l'orgue.

Le plus ancien orgue que je connaisse est celui du village Genarp (Suède). Quand je l'ai vu (j'ai dû faire une longue course en traîneau pour arriver dans ce village) en 1923, j'étais tout à fait perplexe: il était tellement ancien qu'il n'avait pas encore la temperierte Stimmung! C'était une grande émotion pour moi de jouer sur un orgue non tempéré. Il fallait rester en do et en sol! Toutes les autres tonalités étaient fausses! C'était un orgue qui dans les vieux temps était placé dans le choeur de la grande Cathédrale St Petri à Malmö et qui plus tard a été vendu à une église de village. Des organistes amis de Suède m'écrivent qu'il a été restauré et est conservé comme antiquité. 1 Clavier avec pédale. Le son remarquable! . . .

Je vous communique ici les dispositions d'une série d'orgues que mon gendre M. J. A. Eckert a construit ces derniers temps en Suisse pour la Maison Kuhn. La maison le laisse construire tel qu'il l'entend. On n'entrave en rien son activité qui tend de créer un personnel ayant les qualités pour construire d'une façon artistique. On le laisse construire les Schleifladen et des orgues à traction mécanique. Les dispositions ne sont pas de lui. Elles émanent de Orgelbausachverständige des différentes régions. Mais peu à peu ceux-ci tendent vers l'orgue ancien, modernisé.

Ils ont accepté la Schleiflade, après des hésitations au commencement. Je crois que nulle part au monde mon gendre pourrait travailler dans de meilleures conditions. Peu à peu il entreprend de former des harmonisateurs (Intonateure) qui sont des artistes. Mais ce sera long. Car cet art s'est perdu. Moi-même j'ai encore connu les harmonisateurs de l'ancienne Maison Cavaillé-Coll, les Prince et les autres. Mais subitement à Paris cette génération s'est éteinte et a été remplacée par une autre à laquelle on demandait de faire vite au lieu de faire bien: la concurrence idiote nous a amenés là . . . .

Dans les devis réalisés par mon gendre en Suisse et élaborés et imposés par les 'Orgelbausachverständige' vous remarquez que ceux-ci hésitent ou abstiennent à mettre des Gambes, des Cello, des Voix célestes, même des Salicionals! Ils sont encore subjugués par l'idée de la (soit-disant) Barock-orgel. Ils oublient que déjà au 17ème siècle se manifeste la tendance de construire des registres de Gambes!

Tous ces Streicher sont une acquisition précieuse pour l'orgue, seulement il faut faire des mesures très larges, que le ton soit noble et rond, pas tranchant. Que de beaux salicionals on trouve dans les orgues construits vers 1880! Quelle ressource un beau Cello dans la pédale, pour donner de la clarté au son! Pourquoi vouloir renoncer à cela? . . . .]

7) To Emilius Bangert, choirmaster, Roskilde, Denmark, from Lambaréné, 11 November 1945

Dear Friend,

. . . And my daughter married Mr Alfred Jean Eckert, an Alsatian organ builder! It is an extraordinary coincidence that I have an organ builder for a son-in-law! I met him at the organ of Notre Dame many years ago. He was then with the Cavaillé-Coll firm and was specially responsible for the maintenance of Cavaillé's organs in the large Paris churches. He had the opportunity to study in depth Cavaillé's way of building, chiefly by means of Cavaillé's documents and drawings for the work of his men. In 1942 he was hired by the Kuhn firm in Männedorf, near Zürich, where he is now technical director. In France this firm is the successor to the Merklin firm that built St Eustache. It now has its office in Lyon. And my son-in-law builds organs with slider chests, rückpositifs, tracker action, quite in line with my thinking. As the Kuhn firm has no serious competitor in Switzerland, he can allow himself to build with a view to producing good work . . . . Just now he is building a four-manual organ, with rückpositif, in the Geneva cathedral . . . .

[Cher ami,

. . . Et ma fille est mariée avec M. Alfred Jean Eckert, un alsacien facteur d'orgues! C'est une rencontre remarquable que j'ai un gendre facteur d'orgues! J'ai fait sa connaissance sur l'orgue de Notre Dame de Paris il y a de longues années. Il était à cette époque-là dans la Maison Cavaillé-Coll et était spécialement chargé de l'entretien des orgues Cavaillé dans les grandes églises de Paris. Il a eu l'occasion d'étudier à fond la façon de construire de Cavaillé, surtout aussi par les papiers et dessins de Cavaillé pour le travail des ouvriers. En 1942 il a été appelé à la Maison Kuhn à Männedorf près Zürich (Suisse) où il est maintenant Directeur technique. En France cette Maison est le successeur de la Maison Merklin qui a construit St Eustache. Elle a maintenant son siège à Lyon. Et mon gendre construit des orgues avec Schleifladen, Rückpositif, mechanische Traktur – tout à fait dans mon esprit. Comme la Maison Kuhn n'a pas de concurrent sérieux en Suisse, il peut se permettre de construire avec l'intention de fournir du bon travail . . . . En ce moment il construit un orgue de 4 claviers avec Rückpositif dans la Cathédrale de Genève . . . .]

8)   To Mr and Mrs A. J. Eckert, Männedorf, Switzerland, from Lambaréné, 22 July 1945

My Dear,

Thanks for your letter of 20 May 1945 with the very interesting details about your work in organ building and with the set of specifications of finished organs. You are kind to have taken this trouble. The specifications are interesting. Alas, they still smack of the wretched baroque organ. To begin with, they steer clear of including salicionals, voix celestes, gambas, cellos, oboes, as though it were a crime! People forget that on the great it is always necessary to have a bourdon 8 besides the other flutes. They do not call for 8-foot stops in sufficient number. How can one play any Franck on these organs? The only consolation is that these organs at least have slider chests.

Two questions about slider chests. Do your slider chests really have the effect of the old ones? How are they standing up to the heating systems found in churches?

In Schiess's specifications, one sees clearly that he is not an organist, and that he is not aware of what modern compositions require of the organs on which they are played.

An unda maris is not the same thing as a voix celeste.

I notice a waldflöte 2! This reminds me of the wonderful waldflötes 2 that I found in Swedish organs from around 1880! It gives body to the whole swell. Neither in England nor on the continent have I ever found the like. When I'm in Europe, I will try to find you the scales. They are very large.

I am surprised that Hardmeyer, who in other respects is an intelligent organist, should specify for Seebach (Zürich) a krummhorn 8 in the positif. This ghastly register does not stay in tune. Better a good clarinet. Otherwise, this specification is one of the best. It lacks, however, a bourdon 8 in the great, a gamba, a voix celeste, and in the pedal a cello 8. A gedeckt 4 in the pedal is unnecessary. So much for my grumblings. For these people Cavaillé-Coll, Merklin (who was a great builder), and other master builders between 1850 and 1880 (I think of old Walker [*sic*] and of two or three North Germans) lived in vain. And they have never bothered to go and see organs in other countries.

Now the big question. Have you managed to reform the voicing? There will lie the great difficulty. As early as 1900, voicing at Cavaillé-Coll's was obviously in decline. Mutin no longer had a sense of beauty and fullness of sonority. These organs were already dry. Think of the organ in the Salle Gaveau!

I admire you for having been able, despite the war, to find quality materials for these instruments. Bravo for doing away with zinc pipes! As for tin pipes in the façade, space them farther apart than is usually done, so that sound can the more easily get out of the organ! I know a number of organs that do not produce, because the façade pipes are too close together! Same mistake for the façades of rückpositifs. From down in the nave, it makes no visual difference at all if the façade pipes are wider apart, especially in large naves!

Already in about 1910, when they did some restoration of the organ at St Sulpice, the supple leathers that Cavaillé-Coll had at hand were no longer available. And people were very upset. I remember conversations about this with Widor. The reason was that the old tanning methods had been abandoned.

With Schiess be calm and *firm*. That is the best way to make him tractable. If they do not do a rückpositif in Basel, it will be a pity!

Enjoy being able to act as if you were head of the firm. Many builders will envy you this privilege. And don't be in a hurry to leave Switzerland. Think twice (or a dozen times!) if you are asked to take over the management of your firm's branch in Mr Valentin's town.

Well, after talking organs, some news of us. I am having to figure out a way to find food for all my people, white and black, and medicines for the hospital service – a thing nearly as difficult as providing materials for an organ-building firm. Though I may not be accomplishing the same tour de force that you are, I am nevertheless not doing too badly at extricating myself from the problem. That's something. It's just that the weather last autumn was not good for doing any planting (the rains came too early), and food supplies are short as a result. I am sick that the two nurses we are impatiently waiting for (so impatiently!) have still not been able to get here. And yet we did everything possible – and impossible. Well, our times teach patience. We must get used to it. Fortunately Miss Emma and Miss Koch are still doing reasonably well, despite fatigue. As for me, I would have an easier life if there were not so much corresponding to do. It is this that weighs on me and robs me of the hours I ought to use for my works. And to this order of things that pains me more than I can say, I do not see an end.

It is a relatively quiet Sunday morning. I was at the hospital for a while, and since then I have been able to sit at my writing table almost without interruption.

I think a lot about these grandchildren. When shall I finally see them? How can I express to both of you my delight that they are growing up in the country! . . .

Till next time. All my best wishes to you both, and to the dear children . . . .

[Mon cher,

Merci de ta lettre du 20.5.45 avec les détails si intéressants sur ton activité en construction d'orgue et avec la série des devis d'orgues construits. Tu es gentil de t'être donné cette peine. Les devis m'ont intéressé. Hélas, cela sent encore beaucoup bougrement la Barockorgel! D'abord on évite de prévoir des Salicionals, Voix célestes, des Gambes, des Cello, des Hautbois, comme si c'était un crime!! On oublie que sur le grand clavier il faut toujours un Bourdon 8 à côté des autres flûtes. On ne met pas les 8' en nombre suffisant. Comment jouer du César Franck sur ces orgues? La seule chose qui console, c'est que ces orgues ont au moins des Schleifladen.

Deux questions à propos des Schleifladen. Est-ce que tes Schleifladen ont vraiment l'effet des anciennes? Comment résistent-elles aux chauffages qui se trouvent dans les églises? Dans les devis de Schiess on voit clairement qu'il n'est pas organiste et qu'il ne se rend pas compte des besoins des compositions modernes quant à l'orgue qu'elles exigent.

Unda maris n'égale pas la Voix Céleste. Je trouve Waldflöte 2! Cela me rappelle les admirables Waldflöte 2 que j'ai trouvées dans les orgues suédoises de l'époque 1880! Cela donnait de l'ampleur à tout le récit. Je n'en ai jamais rencontré de pareilles ni en Angleterre ni sur le continent. Quand je serai en Europe je tâcherai de te trouver les Mensures. Elles sont très larges.

Que Hardmeyer, qui autrement est un organiste sensé mette pour Seebach (Zürich) un Krummhorn 8 au Positiv, m'étonne. Ce sale registre ne tient pas le ton. Une bonne clarinette vaut mieux. Pour le reste cette disposition est une des meilleures. Il manque cependant Bourdon 8 au premier clavier, une Gambe, Voix Céleste et à la pédale Cello 8. Gedeckt 4 à la pédale est inutile. Voilà les grognements que je fais entendre. Pour ces gens-là, Cavaillé-Coll, Merklin (qui était un grand facteur) et d'autres maîtres entre 1850–1880 (je pense au vieux Walker [*sic*] et à deux ou trois de l'Allemagne du Nord) ont vécu en vain. Et ils n'ont jamais pris la peine d'aller voir des orgues à l'étranger.

Maintenant la grande question: es-tu arrivé à réformer l'harmonisation? Ce sera là la grande difficulté. Déjà en 1900 l'harmonisation chez Cavaillé-Coll était manifestement en déclin. Mutin n'avait plus le sens pour la beauté et l'ampleur de la sonorité. Ces orgues ont été déjà sèches! Voir l'orgue de la Salle Gaveau!

Je t'admire d'avoir pu trouver malgré la guerre les matériaux de qualité pour ces constructions. Bravo pour la suppression des tuyaux en zinc. Quant aux tuyaux en étain en façade, fais la distance plus grande entre eux qu'on ne le fait à l'ordinaire, pour que le son puisse mieux sortir de l'orgue! Je connais une série d'orgues qui ne rendent pas parce que les tuyaux de façade sont trop serrés! La même faute pour les façades des Rückpositifs. D'en bas de la nef pour la vue cela ne fait rien du tout si les tuyaux de façade sont plus écartés, surtout pour les grandes nefs!

Quand vers 1910 on a fait des réparations à l'orgue de St Sulpice, on n'avait déjà plus les peaux souples dont disposait Cavaillé-Coll!! Et on était très ennuyé. Je me souviens d'entretiens à ce sujet avec Widor. C'est qu'on a abandonné les anciens procédés de tannage.

Avec Schiess sois calme et *ferme*. C'est la meilleure façon de le rendre souple. Si on ne fait pas un Rückpositif à Bâle, ce sera dommage! Réjouis-toi de pouvoir agir dans la Société anonyme comme si tu étais le patron. Bien des constructeurs t'envieront de ce privilège. Et ne sois pas pressé de quitter la Suisse. Réfléchis à deux fois (ou à 5 fois) si on te demande de prendre la direction de la branche de votre maison dans la ville de M. Valentin.

Donc après l'orgue, les nouvelles de nous-même. Moi j'ai à me débrouiller pour trouver la nourriture pour tout mon monde, blanc et noir, et les médicaments pour le service à l'hôpital. C'est presque aussi difficile que d'assurer les matières pour une maison de construction d'orgue. Si je ne réussis pas le tour de force de la même façon que toi, je me tire cependant d'affaire pas trop mal. C'est déjà quelque chose. C'est que la saison n'était pas bonne pour faire des plantations en automne dernier (les pluies sont arrivées trop tôt) et le ravitaillement s'en ressent. Je suis navré que les deux infirmières que nous attendons avec impatience (avec si grande impatience!) n'aient encore pu arriver. Et cependant on a fait toutes les démarches possibles et impossibles. Enfin, c'est une époque qui enseigne la patience. Il faut s'y faire. Heureusement que Melle Emma et Melle Koch tiennent encore assez bien debout, malgré la fatigue. Moi, j'aurais une vie plus facile, s'il n'y avait pas la grande correspondance à faire. C'est celle-ci qui me pèse et qui me prend les heures que je devrais employer pour mes travaux. Et je ne vois pas la fin de cet ordre de choses sous lequel je souffre plus que je ne puis le dire.

C'est un dimanche matin relativement tranquille. J'étais à l'hôpital pour un temps et depuis je puis être assis à ma table à écrire sans presque être dérangé.

Je pense beaucoup à ces enfants. Quand enfin les verrai-je? Comment vous dire mon bonheur qu'ils grandissent à la campagne! . . .

Au revoir. Toutes mes bonnes pensées à vous deux et aux chers enfants . . . .]

9)   To Bruno Walter, conductor, New York, from Lambaréné, 7 November
     1945

Dear Bruno Walter,
    . . . How often do I think of my many acquaintances from Germany who
are spending all these years abroad. What hardship so many of them have had
to endure! I consider myself undeservedly blessed, for having been allowed to
spend these years in the solitude of the rain forest doing the work I had chosen
to do . . . . Since the spring of 1939 I have not left the hospital, not even for a
day. Fortunately I can stand this climate better than other people . . . . A
thousand thanks for the greetings you sent via our helpful friend, Dr
Hume . . . . I practise on my piano every evening . . . .

[Lieber Bruno Walter,
    . . . Wie oft denke an die vielen Bekannten aus Deutschland die diese
ganzen Jahre in der Fremde sind! Wie Schweres haben so viele von ihnen
durchgemacht. Ich komme mir so unverdient begnadet vor, dass ich diese
Jahre in der Waldeinsamkeit verleben durfte in dem Wirken, das ich mir
erwählt hatte . . . . Seit Frühjahr 1939 bin ich nicht vom Spital fortgegangen,
auch nicht für einen Tag. Zum Glück ertrage ich das Climat besser als
andere . . . . Tausend Dank für die Grüsse die Sie mir durch Dr Hume, den
hilfreichen Freund, zukommen liessen . . . . Ich übe jeden Abend auf meinem
Klavier . . . .]

10)   To Carl Weinrich, organist, Princeton University, from Lambaréné,
      27 May 1946

Dear Colleague,
    It made me very happy that you illuminated and honoured my organ-
building efforts in the Festschrift celebrating my seventy years . . . . I thank
you warmly for this very kind demonstration of your interest in me.
    Widor did not want to admit that Cavaillé-Coll made a serious mistake at
St Sulpice by not using the spacious case which was already there for the
rückpositif. In one of the last years of his life, we went together to St Eustache,
where the alterations of the organ were just being completed. I played the
organ for Widor, while he listened from below. As we left he said: 'Actually
you are right in your view of the rückpositif. It lets a peculiar bright light flow
into the overall sonority of the instrument.' . . .
    I look forward to meeting you someday and to talking with you about
organ building. Alas, how many of my beloved organs in Holland were
destroyed in the war. In Denmark and Sweden also they are beginning to try
to preserve fine old organs. But how many have been torn down and replaced
by manufactured stuff! . . .

[Lieber Kollege von der Orgel,

Es hat mir eine grosse Freude gemacht, dass Sie in der Festschrift für meine 70 Jahre meine Bemühungen um den Orgelbau beleuchteten und würdigten . . . . Ich danke Ihnen herzlichst für diesen so freundlichen Erweis ihres Interesses für mich.

Widor wollte nicht zugeben, dass Cavaillé-Coll in St Sulpice einen grossen Fehler gemacht hat, indem er das geräumige für das Rückpositif vorhandene Gehäuse nicht benutzte. In einem der letzten Jahre seines Lebens gingen wir miteinander nach St Eustache, wo der Umbau der Orgel eben vollendet wurde. Ich spielte Widor die Orgel vor, während er unten zuhörte. Beim Hinausgehen sagte er: 'Sie haben eigentlich doch recht mit ihrer Verteidigung des Rückpositifs. Es lässt ein eigentümlich helles Licht in den Gesamtklang des Instruments einfliessen.' . . .

Ich freue mich in der Hoffnung einmal mit Ihnen zusammen sein zu können und mit Ihnen von Orgelbau reden zu können. Ach, wie viele meiner lieben Orgeln in Holland sind im Kriege zerstört worden. In Dänemark und Schweden fängt man jetzt auch an, darauf bedacht zu sein, schöne alte Orgeln zu erhalten. Aber wie gar manche hat man abgerissen und durch Fabrikwaren ersetzt! . . .]

11)   To Ernest M. Skinner, organ builder, Boston, from Lambaréné, 6 November 1945

Dear Mr Skinner,'

Thanks for your good letter of 2 June 1945, which took a long time to get here. I have indeed taken note of the recitals you suggest for me, and I thank you for having taken the trouble to draw up this plan. You can be sure that I will not do the tour in a hurry. That is against my principles. I allow ten or twelve hours to prepare the registration for a recital. And usually I take a young organist with me who plays the programme for me while I listen in the church and adjust the registrations!

On the other hand, dear Mr Skinner, I shall not listen to your advice about coming by air. I will come by boat. And if sailing ships still existed, I would come by sailing ship! For the days spent aboard a ship at sea are the only vacation I have had for many a long year and the only vacation I shall have until I die. All the voyages from equatorial Africa to Europe, and vice versa, I make by ship, and I always regret that the ships are steamer and not sail. But you understand my reasons . . . .

The specification of your organ for Washington Cathedral keenly interested me. Thank you for sending it to me. I am delighted to see an organ installed in a swallow's nest in the nave, as in the cathedrals of Spain and in Strasbourg.

[Cher Monsieur Skinner,

Merci de votre bonne lettre de June [*sic*] 2 1945, qui a été longtemps en route. J'ai bien pris note des récitals que vous me proposez et je vous remercie d'avoir pris la peine de me dresser un plan. Soyez certain que je ne ferai pas la tournée en courant. Ce n'est pas dans mes principes. Je compte 10–12 heures pour préparer la registration d'un récital sur un orgue. Et ordinairement j'emmène avec moi un jeune organiste qui me joue le programme tandis que moi j'écoute dans l'église et je corrige les registrations!

Par contre cher monsieur Skinner, je n'écoute pas votre conseil de venir en avion. Je viendrai en bateau. Et s'il y avait encore des bateaux à voile je viendrais en bateau à voile! Car les jours passés sur bateau en mer sont les seules vacances que j'ai eues depuis de longues années et les seules que j'aurai jusqu'à la fin de ma vie. Tous les voyages de l'Afrique Equatoriale en Europe et vice versa je les fais en bateau, avec toujours le regret, que ce soient des bateaux à vapeur au lieu d'être des bateaux à voile! Mais vous comprenez mes raisons . . . .

La composition de votre Grand Orgue de Washington Cathedral m'a vivement intéressé. Merci de me l'avoir communiquée! Ravi de voir un orgue en nid d'hirondelle dans la nef, comme dans les Cathédrales d'Espagne et à Strasbourg.]

12)   To Joseph S. Whiteford, President, Aeolian-Skinner Organ Company, Boston, from Lambaréné, 27 March 1960

Dear Sir,

Very many thanks for your letter of 18 March. I completely agree with you that the sound of today's organs is in grave danger, because the architects do not provide the location for them where their tonal effect would be best, and because much sound-absorbent material is being used in churches nowadays, which swallows the sound and destroys the magnificent resonance which stone gives to the sound of the organ. Yes, it is time that organists get together in order to meet this danger. I would like to send you a little treatise about this question, but my heavy load of work does not allow it. But you have organists who can do it also. And the question is perfectly clear. Thus I wish you luck in your fight for the organ and church music.

[Sehr geehrter Herr Direktor,

Tausend Dank für Ihren Brief vom 18 März. Ich bin ganz mit Ihnen einverstanden, dass dem Klang der Orgeln in unserer Zeit eine grosse Gefahr droht, weil die Architektur für die Orgeln in den Kirchen nicht den Platz vorsehen auf dem sie die beste Klangwirkung haben, und weil heute in den Kirchen schalldämpfendes Material in Menge verwendet wird, das den Ton verschluckt und die herrliche Resonanz die der Stein dem Orgelton verleiht vernichtet. Ja, es ist Zeit, dass die Organisten sich zusammentun, um dieser Gefahr entgegen zu treten. Gern würde ich Ihnen eine kleine Abhandlung über diese Frage schicken. Aber meine grosse Arbeit erlaubt es mir nicht. Aber Sie haben ja Organisten, die es auch gut tun können. Und die Frage liegt ja ganz klar. So wünsche ich Ihnen gut Glück in dem Unternehmen für die Orgel und die Kirchenmusik zu kämpfen.]

13) To Marcel Dupré, organist, Paris, aboard the *Foucauld* at Abidjan, French Ivory Coast, 12 July 1952

Dear Friend,

You are kind enough to play the organ for the film 'Il est minuit, Dr Schweitzer' and to extend that kindness so far as to present to my hospital as a gift what was owed to you for your collaboration! I was more deeply touched than I can say by the cheque I received, and I am writing you to express my deep gratitude. Your gift will be used to buy rice to feed some lepers (we are caring for 350). The question of feeding all these people causes me great anxiety, for lepers must stay at my hospital for a year and a half! The treatment takes that long if the disease is to be completely checked.

I am on my way to Europe. In two days I shall give a private recital on the electronic organ in the Cathedral of Conakry. I do this each time I pass through there. When the pastor thanks me, I tell him: 'No need, dear Father. In playing this type of imitation organ, I am doing penance.' It is sad to see that electronic organs are meeting with success in the colonies. Looking forward to seeing you and hearing you in October. And thanks again, in the name of my lepers . . . .

[Cher ami,

Vous avez la bonté de jouer de l'orgue pour le film 'Il est minuit' et vous poussez la bonté jusqu'à faire don à mon hôpital de ce qui devait vous revenir pour votre collaboration! J'ai été plus touché que je ne puis vous dire du chèque que j'ai reçu et je viens vous dire toute ma reconnaissance. Votre don sera employé pour l'achat de riz destiné à la nourriture des lépreux (nous en soignons 350). La question de nourrir tout ce monde me donne de grands soucis, car ces lépreux doivent rester à mon hôpital un an et demi! La cure demande à être ainsi prolongée pour que la maladie soit définitivement arrêtée. Je suis en route pour l'Europe. Dans deux jours je donnerai une audition d'orgue sur l'orgue électronique de la Cathédrale de Conakry. Je fais cela à chaque passage. Quand Monsieur le Curé me remercie, je lui dis: 'Pas besoin, cher Père. En jouant ce genre imitation d'orgue je fais pénitence.' C'est triste de voir que les orgues électroniques ont du succès en colonie. Au plaisir

de vous voir et de vous entendre en octobre. Et merci encore au nom de mes
lépreux . . . .]

14) To Archibald T. Davison, organist, Harvard University, from
    Lambaréné, 25 May 1946

Dear Mr Davison,

I read and reread the pages that you devote to me in the *Jubilee Book* and
am touched, more than I can say, by the sympathy and understanding that
you have for my effort to render Bach's music in the best way . . . .

I practise on my pedal-piano every evening (if I have not tired myself out
too much in the hospital during the day) and I delight in being able to enter
into every detail in studying a work of Bach's, without having to be finished
by a given date so as to play the piece in public.

At the end of 1936, before leaving for Lambaréné, I went to Paris for a day
just to see Widor once more. Both of us both knew that his days were
numbered. His feet were already so swollen that he could no longer put on
shoes but had to be in slippers. And we evoked once again the memories we
had in common, and we realized the great attachment we felt for each other.
And when I left him, he shook my hand and said in a low voice: 'This was our
last time together.' . . .

[Cher M. Davison,

Je lis et relis les pages que vous me consacrez dans le Jubilée Book et je suis
touché, plus que je ne puis vous dire, de la sympathie et la compréhension que
vous avez pour mon effort de rendre pour le mieux la musique de Bach . . . .

J'étudie sur mon piano avec pédales d'orgue tous les soirs (si je ne me suis
pas trop fatigué dans l'hôpital durant la journée) et je jouis de pouvoir entrer
dans tous les détails de l'étude d'une oeuvre de Bach, sans être obligé d'avoir
terminé pour une date fixe pour exécuter le morceau en public.

Fin 1936, avant mon départ pour Lambaréné je suis allé à Paris pour un
jour uniquement pour revoir encore une fois Widor. Les deux nous savions
que ses jours étaient comptés. Ses pieds étaient si gonflés déjà qu'il ne pouvait
plus mettre de souliers mais était obligé d'être en pantoufles! Et nous avons
remémoré les souvenirs que nous avions en commun et nous nous rendions
compte du grand attachement que nous avions l'un pour l'autre. Et quand je
l'ai quitté il m'a serré la main et m'a dit tout bas: 'C'est la dernière fois que
nous avons été ensemble' . . . .]

15) To A. M. Henderson, organist, University of Glasgow, from Lam-
    baréné, 24 August 1945

Dear Mr Henderson,

   ... And we have memories of Widor in common! I saw him again a few months before his death. Before leaving again for Africa I went to Paris for a few hours to see him once more. He was already very ill (heart and kidneys) and knew that he no longer had much time to live. He was very serene. In his armchair he was at work revising some of his compositions that were to be reprinted. He had a presentiment of the war, and was very grieved by the thought. We talked again of organ building. He disapproved of the departure by French organ building from the traditions of Cavaillé-Coll, and was sad that his voice was not listened to and that some of his pupils wanted to transform the lovely old organs they were in charge of. But he was certain that his works for organ would endure and influence the organists of the future.

   How often do I think of this dear master, while practising the organ here, in the African solitude, on the pedal-piano given me by the Paris Bach Society ....

[Cher M. Henderson,

   ... Et nous avons le souvenir de Widor en commun! Je l'ai vu encore quelques mois avant sa mort. Devant repartir pour l'Afrique je suis allé pour quelques heures à Paris pour le revoir. Il était déjà très malade (du coeur et des reins) et savait qu'il n'avait plus pour longtemps à vivre. Il était d'une grande sérénité. Dans son fauteuil il travaillait à revoir de ses oeuvres qui devaient être réimprimées. Il pressentait la guerre et en était très affligé. Nous parlions encore de construction d'orgue. Il désapprouvait que la construction française quittait les traditions de Cavaillé-Coll et était triste que sa voix ne fût pas écoutée et que de ses élèves voulaient transformer les belles anciennes orgues dont ils étaient les organistes. Mais il avait la certitude que ses compositions pour orgue resteraient et influenceraient les organistes de l'avenir. Que de fois je pense au cher maître en étudiant ici, dans la solitude africaine, l'orgue sur le piano avec pédales d'orgue dont la Société Bach de Paris m'a fait don ....]

16)   To Dirk Flentrop, organ builder, Zaandam, from Lambaréné, 18 April 1965

Dear Mr Flentrop,

   How kind of the International Society for Organ Building to congratulate me on my ninetieth birthday. My mind is still occupied with organ building. I still think that the pedal reeds are much too powerful in the fortissimo ....

[Lieber Herr Flentrop,

   Wie lieb von der internationalen Gesellschaft für Orgelbau, mir zum 90sten Geburtstag zu gratulieren. Im Geist beschäftige ich mich noch immer mit

Orgelbau. Noch immer finde ich dass die Zungenstimmen im Pedal im Fortissimo viel zu stark sind . . . .]

Appendix C Stoplists

Church of St Sulpice, Paris
(Aristide Cavaillé-Coll, 1862; restored, 1991)

GRAND ORGUE (II)
Principal 16
Montre 16
Bourdon 16
Flûte 16
Montre 8
Diapason 8
Bourdon 8
Flûte Harmonique 8
Flûte Traversière 8
Flûte à Pavillon 8
Quinte 5–1/3
Prestant 4
Doublette 2

POSITIF (III)
Violonbasse 16
Quintaton 16
Salicional 8
Gambe 8
Flûte Traversière 8
Quintaton 8
Unda Maris 8
Dulciane 4
Flûte Octaviante 4
Flûte Douce 4
Quinte 2–2/3
Doublette 2

Larigot 1–1/3
Tierce 1–3/5
Picolo 1
Plein Jeu V
Basson 16
Baryton 8
Trompette 8
Clairon 4

GRAND CHOEUR (I)
Salicional 8
Octave 4
Fourniture IV
Plein Jeu V
Cymbale III
Cornet V
Bombarde 16
Basson 16
Trompette I 8
Trompette II 8
Basson 8
Clairon 4
Clairon-Doublette 2

RECIT (IV)
Quintaton 16
Diapason 8
Violoncelle 8
Flûte Harmonique 8

Bourdon 8
Voix Céleste 8
Prestant 4
Flûte Octaviante 4
Dulciane 4
Nazard 2–2/3
Octavin 2
Doublette 2
Fourniture IV
Cymbale III
Cornet V
Cromorne 8
Basson-Hautbois 8
Voix Humaine 8
Bombarde 16
Trompette 8
Clairon 4

SOLO (V)
Flûte 16
Bourdon 16
Principal 8
Violoncelle 8
Gambe 8
Kérélophone 8
Flûte Harmonique 8
Bourdon 8
Quinte 5

Prestant 4
Octave 4
Flûte 4
Tierce 3
Quinte 2–2/3
Septième 2–2/7
Octavin 2
Cornet V
Bombarde 16
Trompette 8
Clairon
Trompette en Chamade 8

PEDALE
Principal 32
Principal 16
Soubasse 16
Contrebasse 16
Violoncelle 8
Flûte 8
Principal 8
Flûte 4
Bombarde 32
Bombarde 16
Basson 16
Trompette 8
Ophicléide 8
Clairon 4

Church of St Aurelia, Strasbourg
(Andreas Silbermann, 1718)

GREAT
Montre 8
Bourdon 8
Prestant 4
Flute 4
Quinte 2–2/3
Doublette 2
Tierce 1–3/5
Cornet V
Fourniture III

Cymbale III
Vox Humana 8

RÜCKPOSITIF
Bourdon 8
Prestant 4
Nazard 2–2/3
Doublette 2
Tierce 1–3/5
Fourniture III

PEDAL
Soubasse 16

Octavbass 8
Trompetenbass 8

(Rebuild, Fritz Haerpfer, 1911)

GREAT
Bourdon 16
Montre 8
Cello 8
Dulciana 8
Bourdon 8
Hohlflöte 8
Quintaton 8
Octave 4
Rohrflöte 4
Octave 2
Quint 2–2/3
Mixture-Cornet
Trompette 8

SWELL
Geigen Principal 8
Gamba 8
Voix Céleste 8

Salicional 8
Bourdon 8
Flute 8
Fugara 4
Traversflöte 4
Flageolet 2
Mixture III
Clarinet 8
Trompette 8
Clairon 4

PEDAL
Principal 16
Contrabass 16
Soubasse 16
Octave 8
Cello 8
Principal 4
Fagotto 16

'I first became acquainted with this organ in 1893,' Schweitzer recalls [Lambaréné, 7 November 1945, to J. B. Jamison, Los Gatos, California], 'after a Strasbourg organ builder of the last half of the nineteenth century had modified it and added an enclosed division of a few stops. It still had slider windchests and a rückpositif.

'Then along came central heating in the church, which split the chests and made the rückpositif unusable whenever the heat was on, since it was then out of tune with the great and the swell. The sonority of this organ was marvellous.

'When I undertook the restoration of the organ, I was forced, by the excessive way they had of heating this rather small church, to give up the idea – much against my inclination – of slider chests and a rückpositif. I was able to use most of the old pipe material. My consolation was that Fritz Haerpfer, the organ builder from Boulay (Lorraine), who had helped me faithfully restore the Silbermann in the great church of St Thomas, Strasbourg (in about 1909, I believe), would know how to recapture the beautiful tone of the old organ once again, insofar as this was possible without slider chests. I had to reconcile myself to having only a great and swell, but the swell is above the great and has a wonderful effect. As always I insisted that there be considerable space in the swell, and that there be shutters not only in front but also on both sides – and shutters well made . . . .

'This organ is so voiced as never to be shrill or harsh in the upper registers. Haerpfer's gambas, celli, voix célestes, and salicionals are wonderful! He is a magnificent voicer. But also, whenever he built an organ for which I was a member of the building committee, I set the price for the organ in such a way as to avoid any need for him to hurry the voicing for reasons of cost. A builder is an artist and, by the payment he receives for his work, should be protected from any ill-advised economies that might be forced on him by competition.'

'J'ai connu cet orgue pour la première fois en 1893 où un facteur d'orgue Strasbourgeois dans la seconde moitié du 19e siècle avait remanié cet orgue et ajouté un clavier expressif de quelques registres. Cet orgue avait encore les Schleifladen et le Rückpositif.

'Et alors vint le chauffage central de l'église qui a fait éclater les Schleifladen et qui a rendu inutilisable le Rückpositif, celui-ci durant toute l'époque où on chauffait l'église étant en désaccord avec le Grand Clavier et le Swell. La sonorité de cet orgue était merveilleuse. Quand j'ai dû m'occuper de la restauration de l'orgue, j'ai dû, à cause de la façon excessive dont on avait l'habitude de chauffer cette église pas très grande, renoncer, à contre coeur au Schleifladen et au Rückpositif! J'ai pu employer une grande partie de l'ancien matériel de pipes. Ma consolation était que Fritz Haerpfer le facteur d'orgue de Boulay (Lorraine) qui avait restauré avec moi pieusement l'orgue Silbermann de la Grande Eglise de St Thomas à Strasbourg (vers 1909, je crois), saurait assurer la belle sonorité de l'ancien orgue au nouveau, autant que cela est possible sans la Schleiflade. J'ai dû me résoudre à n'avoir qu'un grand clavier et un Swell, mais le Swell qui est au-dessus du Grand Clavier, ayant un admirable effet. Comme toujours j'ai tenu, qu'il y ait beaucoup de place dans le Swell et qu'il y ait des jalousies non seulement sur le devant mais aussi sur les deux côtés! Et des jalousies admirablement travaillées . . . .

'Cet orgue est harmonisé (intoniert) de façon qu'il n'est jamais criard ou dur dans le haut! Les Gambes, les Celli, les Voix Célestes, les Salicionals de Haerpfer sont merveilleux! Il est un intonateur splendide. Mais aussi quand il construisait un orgue où moi j'étais dans le comité de construction, je fixais le prix de l'orgue de façon à ce qu'on n'avait pas besoin d'être pressé pour l'harmonisation pour des raisons d'économie. Un facteur d'orgue est un artiste et doit être, par le paiement qu'il reçoit pour son travail, mis à l'abri de tout souci de mauvaise économie que lui imposerait la concurrence.'

Village Church, Günsbach
(Schweitzer/Haerpfer, 1932)

GREAT
Bourdon 16
Montre 8
Salicional 8
Bourdon 8
Flûte 8
Gamba 8 (swell)
Octave 4
Octave 2
Cornet III-V
Trompette 8

SWELL
Gemshorn 8
Gamba 8
Bourdon 8
Voix Céleste 8
Dulciana 8
Rohrflöte 4
Plein jeu III
Hautbois 8

PEDAL
Soubasse 16
Bourdon 16 (great)
Flute 8
Cello 8

(Revised, 1961; Schweitzer/Kern)

GREAT
Bourdon 16
Montre 8
Flûte Conique 8
Bourdon 8
Prestant 4
Flûte à Fuseau 4
Quinte 2–2/3
Doublette 2
Fourniture IV
Trompette 8

SWELL
Gemshorn 8
Bourdon 8
Gamba 8

Voix Céleste 8
Flûte à Cheminée 4
Sesquialtera II
Waldflöte 2
Plein Jeu III
Basson-Hautbois 8

PEDAL
Soubasse 16
Bourdon 16 (great)
Flute 8
Cello 8
Choralbass 4
Fourniture III
Dulciane 16

Village church, Mühlbach
(Schweitzer/Haerpfer, 1929) Schweitzer considered this stoplist ideal for a small church organ [Lambaréné, 7 November 1945, to J. B. Jamison, Los Gatos, California].

GREAT
Bourdon 16
Principal 8
Hohlflöte 8
Salicional 8 (swell)
Octave 4
Quint 2–2/3

SWELL
Gamba 8
Salicional 8
Voix Céleste 8
Bourdon 8
Flute Octaviante 4
Waldflöte 2
Mixture III
Hautbois 8

PEDAL
Soubasse 16
Bourdon 16 (swell)

Wihr-au-Val (Stoplist proposed by Schweitzer, 1950)

GREAT
Bourdon 16
Montre 8
Flute 8
Bourdon 8
Spitzflöte 8
Prestant 4
Flute 4
Doublette 2
Cornet
Mixture
Trompette 8 (soft)
Clairon 4 (soft)

SWELL
Diapason 8
Flûte à Cheminée 8
Nachthorn 8
Gamba 8
Voix Céleste 8
Salicional 8
Principal 4
Blockflöte 4
Quinte 2–2/3
Waldflöte 2
Plein Jeu III or IV
Hautbois 8

PEDAL
Soubasse 16
Flute 16
Flute 8
Cello 8
Octave 4
Basson 16
Trompette 8

The montre and diapason were to be flötenprincipals, the trumpet and clairon soft; the nachthorn was to be a cor de nuit (open), the gamba large and round, the voix céleste and salicional large, the blockflöte and the waldflöte wide-scaled, the latter to resemble the waldflötes in old Swedish organs. The cello was to be large and round, a true cello sonority. [Lambaréné, 8 January 1950, to the mayor and members of the council, Wihr-au-Val, Alsace]

First Presbyterian Church, Evanston, Illinois (Votteler-Holtkamp, 1940, rebuild of Johnson, Opus 823; Barnes Memorial Organ)

GREAT
Bourdon 16
Open Diapason 8
Principal 8
Doppelflöte 8
Salicional 8
Gemshorn 8
Ludwigtone 8
Octave 4
Flauto Traverso 4
Octave Quint 2–2/3
Super Octave 2
Mixture IV
Trumpet 8
English Horn 8
Clarion 4
Chimes

SWELL
Quintadena 16
Geigen Diapason 8
Stopped Diapason 8
Viola da Gamba 8
Voix Céleste 8
Aeoline 8
Aeoline Céleste 8
Octave Geigen 4
Flute Harmonique 4
Fifteenth 2
Mixture III
Cornopean 8
Oboe 8
Vox Humana 8

CHOIR
Viola 8
Melodia 8
Ludwigtone 8
Principal 4
Flute d'Amour 4
Fugara 4
Ludwigtone 4
Nazard 2–2/3
Piccolo 2
English Horn 16
Trumpet 8
Clarinet 8
English Horn 8
Clarion 4

PEDAL
Principal Bass 16
Open Diapason 16
Bourdon 16
Violone Dolce 16
Gross Quint 10–2/3
Flute 8
Violoncello 8
Choralbass 4
Blockflöte 2
Posaune 16
Trumpet 8
Clarion 4

Church of the Advent, Boston
(Aeolian-Skinner, 1936)

GREAT
Diapason 16
Principal 8
Diapason 8
Flûte Harmonique 8
Gross Quint 5–1/3
Principal 4
Octave 4
Quint 2–2/3
Super Octave 2
Sesquialtera IV-V
Fourniture IV
Scharf III

SWELL
Bourdon 16
Geigen 8
Viole-de-Gambe 8
Viole Céleste 8
Echo Salicional 8
Stopped Diapason 8
Octave Geigen 4
Fugara 4
Flauto Traverso 4
Fifteenth 2
Grave Mixture III
Plein Jeu III
Bombarde 16
Trompette I 8
Trompette II 8
Vox Humana 8
Clairon 4

CHOIR
Viola 8
Dolcan 8
Dolcan Céleste 8
Orchestral Flute 8
Zauberflöte 4
Trumpet 8 (unenclosed)
Clarinet 8

POSITIF
Rohrflöte 8
Principal 4
Koppel Flöte 4
Nasat 2–2/3
Blockflöte 2
Tierce 1–3/5
Stifflöte 1
Scharf IV

PEDAL
Sub Bass 32
Principal 16
Contre Basse 16
Bourdon 16
Echo Lieblich 16
Principal 8
Flûte Ouverte 8
Still Gedeckt 8
Quinte 5–1/3
Principal 4
Flûte Harmonique 4
Mixture III
Fourniture II
Bombarde 16
Trompette 8
Clairon 4

Appendix D Reverence for Life

Trained in ethics, esthetics, metaphysics, and logic at the universities of Berlin, Strasbourg, and Paris by some of the finest minds of the day, Albert Schweitzer was always to regard himself as first of all a philosopher. Out of his lifelong pondering of the great questions, moreover, he developed a world-view of unique scope and, he believed, unique applicability to the condition of modern man. Viewing civilization as decadent and perhaps headed toward catastrophe, he saw the reversal of that decadence as contingent upon a reformed ethical sense embodied in the behaviour of individual men and women. To encourage this reform, he published *The Philosophy of Civilization.*

That its conclusions did not conveniently fit into a system and were therefore sometimes disregarded by colleagues disturbed him little: he was not writing for other philosophers, but for 'thinking men and women whom I wish to provoke to elemental thought about the questions of existence.'

At the centre of his philosophy was the idea he called Reverence for Life – an idea whose ethical implications could be defended rationally, he believed, without recourse to religious tradition or to scientific knowledge, and an idea that could bring mankind into a right relationship with the world and lead to true civilization.

According to Schweitzer, 'the man who has become a thinking being feels a compulsion to give to every will-to-live the same reverence for life that he gives to his own. He experiences that other life in his own. He accepts as being good: to preserve life, to promote life, to raise to its highest value life which is capable of development; and as being evil: to destroy life, to injure life, to repress life which is capable of development. This is the absolute, fundamental principle of the moral, and it is a necessity of thought.

'The great fault of all ethics hitherto has been that they believed themselves to have to deal only with the relations of man to man. In reality, however, the question is what is his attitude to the world and all life that comes within his reach. A man is ethical only when life, as such, is sacred to him, that of plants and animals as well as that of his fellow-men, and when he devotes himself to helping all life that is in need of help. Only the universal ethic of the feeling of responsibility in an ever-widening sphere for all that lives – only that ethic can be founded in thought. The ethic of the relation of man to man is not something apart by itself: it is only a particular relation which results from the universal one.

'The ethic of Reverence for Life, therefore, comprehends within itself everything that can be described as love, devotion, and sympathy whether in suffering, joy, or effort . . . .

'Through ethical world- and life-affirmation we reach a power of reflection which enables us to distinguish between what is essential in civilization and what is not. The stupid arrogance of thinking ourselves civilized loses its power over us. We venture to face the truth that with so much progress in knowledge and power true civilization has become not easier but harder . . . .

'The ethic of Reverence for Life makes no distinction between higher and lower, more precious and less precious lives. It has good reasons for this omission. For what are we doing, when we establish hard and fast gradations in value between living organisms, but judging them in relation to ourselves, by whether they seem to stand closer to us or farther from us. This is a wholly subjective standard. How can we know what importance other living organisms have in themselves and in terms of the universe?

'In making such distinctions, we are apt to decide that there are forms of life which are worthless and may be stamped out without its mattering at all. This category may include anything from insects to primitive peoples, depending on circumstances.

'To the truly ethical man, all life is sacred, including forms of life that from the human point of view may seem to be lower than ours. He makes distinctions only from case to case, and under pressure of necessity, when he is forced to decide which life he will sacrifice in order to preserve other lives. In thus deciding from case to case, he is aware that he is proceeding subjectively and arbitrarily, and that he is accountable for the lives thus sacrificed.

'The man who is guided by the ethic of Reverence for Life stamps out life only from inescapable necessity, never from thoughtlessness . . . .

'Those who carry out scientific experiments with animals, in order to apply the knowledge gained to the alleviation of human ills, should never reassure themselves with the generality that their cruel acts serve a useful purpose. In each individual case they must ask themselves whether there is a real necessity for imposing such a sacrifice upon a living creature. They must try to reduce the suffering insofar as they are able. It is inexcusable for a scientific institution to omit anaesthesia in order to save time and trouble. It is horrible to subject animals to torment merely in order to demonstrate to students phenomena that are already familiar.

'The very fact that animals, by the pain they endure in experiments, contribute so much to suffering humanity, should forge a new and unique kind of solidarity between them and us. For that reason alone it is incumbent upon each and every one of us to do all possible good to non-human life.

'When we help an insect out of a difficulty, we are only trying to compensate for man's ever-renewed sins against other creatures. Wherever animals are impressed into the service of man, every one of us should be mindful of the toll we are exacting. We cannot stand idly by and see an animal subjected to unnecessary harshness or deliberate mistreatment. We cannot say it is not our business to interfere. On the contrary, it is our duty to intervene in the animal's behalf . . . .

'To the universal ethic of Reverence for Life, pity for animals, so often smilingly dismissed as sentimentality, becomes a mandate no thinking person can escape . . . .

'Any profound world-view is mysticism, in that it brings men into a spiritual relation with the Infinite. The world-view of Reverence for Life is ethical mysticism. It allows union with the infinite to be realized by ethical action. This ethical mysticism originates in logical thinking. If our will-to-live begins to think about itself and the world, we come to experience the life of the world, so far as it comes within our reach, in our own life, and to devote our will-to-live to the infinite will-to-live through the deeds we do. Rational thinking, if it goes deep, ends of necessity in the non-rational of mysticism . . . .

'The world-view of Reverence for Life has, therefore, a religious character. The man who avows his belief in it, and acts upon the belief, shows a piety which is elemental . . . .

'Anyone who has recognized that the idea of Love is the spiritual beam of light which reaches us from the Infinite, ceases to demand from religion that it shall offer him complete knowledge of the supra-sensible. He ponders, indeed, on the great questions: what the meaning is of the evil in the world; how in God, the great First Cause, the will-to-create and the will-to-love are one; in what relation the spiritual and the material life stand to one another, and in what way our existence is transitory and yet eternal. But he is able to leave these questions on one side, however painful it may be to give up all hope of answers to them. In the knowledge of spiritual existence in God through love he possesses the one thing needful.'

Select Bibliography

Darmstadt, Germany, Hessische Landes- und Hochschulbibliothek, Hesse papers.

Great Barrington, Massachusetts, Albert Schweitzer Centre, Schweitzer papers.

Günsbach, France, Archives Centrales Albert Schweitzer, Schweitzer papers.

Hamden, Connecticut, Albert Schweitzer Institute for the Humanities, Schweitzer papers.

Paris, France, Bibliothèque Nationale, Dupré papers.

Syracuse, New York, Syracuse University Library, Schweitzer papers.

Albrecht, Christoph (1990), 'Current Problems in the Interpretation of Bach's Organ Works', translated by Lyn Hubler, *The Diapason*, 81, January, pp. 14–15.

Amadou, Robert (1952), *Albert Schweitzer: Eléments de Biographie et de Bibliographie*, Paris: L'Arche. A fine bibliography of writings by and about Schweitzer, together with a biographical essay.

Amadou, Robert, ed. (1951), *Albert Schweitzer: Etudes et Témoignages*, Paris: Main Jetée.

Ambrosino, Jonathan (1990), 'A History of the Skinner Company', *The American Organist*, 24, May, pp. 261–68.

——— (1990), 'A History of the Aeolian-Skinner Company: The Harrison Years', *The American Organist*, 24, May, pp. 269–76.

Andersen, Poul-Gerhard (1969), *Organ Building and Design*, translated by Joanne Curnutt, London: Allen and Unwin.

Anthony, Jimmy Jess (1986), 'Charles-Marie Widor's *Symphonies pour Orgue*: Their Artistic Context and Cultural Antecedents', D.M.A. dissertation, University of Rochester, Eastman School of Music.

Anthony, John Philip (1978), 'The Organ Works of Johann Christian Kittel', Ph.D. dissertation, Yale University.

Armstrong, Agnes (1989), 'Alexandre Guilmant: American Tours and American Organs', *The Tracker*, 32 (3), pp. 15–23.

Augustiny, Waldemar (1956), *The Road to Lambaréné: A Biography of Albert Schweitzer*, translated by William J. Blake, London: Muller.

Bach, Johann Sebastian, *Complete Organ Works*, edited by Albert Schweitzer, Charles-Marie Widor (vols 1–5, 1912–13), and Edouard Nies-Berger (vols 6, 1954; 7–8, 1967), New York: Schirmer.

—— (1938–41), *Oeuvres Complètes pour Orgue*, 12 vols, edited by Marcel Dupré, Paris: Bornemann.

Barden, Nelson (1990), 'A History of the Aeolian-Skinner Company: The Post-Harrison Years', *The American Organist*, 24, May, pp. 276–80.

Barzun, Jacques (1961), *Classic, Romantic and Modern*, Boston: Little, Brown.

—— (1969), *Berlioz and the Romantic Century*, 3d ed., 2 vols, New York: Columbia University Press.

Bergel, Kurt, and Alice R. Bergel, eds and trans (1991), *Albert Schweitzer and Alice Ehlers: A Friendship in Letters*, Lanham, Maryland: University Press of America.

Billeter, Bernhard (1977), 'Albert Schweitzer und sein Orgelbauer', in *Acta Organologica*, 11, Berlin: Merseburger. Letters by Schweitzer to Fritz Haerpfer and Alfred Kern.

—— (1981), 'Albert Schweitzers Einfluss auf den europäischen Orgelbau am Beginn des 20. Jahrhunderts', in *Acta Organologica*, 15, Berlin: Merseburger.

Blume, Friedrich (1970), *Classic and Romantic Music: A Comprehensive Survey*, translated by M. D. Herter Norton, London: Norton.

Boschot, Adolphe (1937), *Notice sur la Vie et les Oeuvres de M. Charles-Marie Widor*, Paris: Firmin-Didot. An address delivered before the Institute of France, Academy of Fine Arts, 4 December.

Brabazon, James (1975), *Albert Schweitzer: a Biography*, New York: Putnam.

Brouwer, Frans (1981), *Orgelbewegung und Orgelgegenbewegung: eine Arbeit über die Ursprünge und die Entwicklung der dänischen Orgelreform bis heute*, Utrecht: Joachimsthal.

Brüllmann, R., ed. (1989), *Albert-Schweitzer-Studien*, 1, Bern: Haupt. Includes articles on Schweitzer's ethics, mysticism, Bach scholarship and its reception in France at the turn of the century, and the Paris Missionary Society.

—— (1991), *Albert-Schweitzer-Studien*, 2, Bern: Haupt. Articles on Reverence for Life, the African hospital.

Buhrman, T. Scott (1937), 'Clarity and its Development', *The American Organist*, 20, February, pp. 48–49.

Callahan, Charles (1990), *The American Classic Organ: A History in Letters*, Richmond, Virginia: Organ Historical Society. Letters to and from G. Donald Harrison, Henry Willis, Ernest M. Skinner, others.

Carl, William C. (1936), 'Alexandre Guilmant; Noted Figure Viewed 25 Years After Death', *The Diapason*, 27, June, p. 4.

Cavaillé-Coll, Aristide (facsimile, 1979), *Complete Theoretical Works*, Buren, The Netherlands: Knuf.

Cavaillé-Coll, Cécile, and Emmanuel Cavaillé-Coll (1929), *Aristide Cavaillé-Coll: ses origines, sa vie, ses oeuvres*, Paris: Fischbacher.

Cousins, Norman (1985), *Albert Schweitzer's Mission: Healing and Peace*, New York: Norton.

de Crauzat, Claude Noisette (1984), *Cavaillé-Coll*, Paris: La Flûte de Pan. Includes specifications, drawings, photographs, previously unpublished letters, and a bibliography.

David, Hans T., and Arthur Mendel (1966), *The Bach Reader: A Life of Johann Sebastian Bach in Letters and Documents*, 2nd ed., New York: Norton.

Donat, Friedrich Wilhelm (1933), *Christian Heinrich Rinck und die Orgelmusik zeiner Zeit*, Bad Oeynhausen: Theine and Peitsch.

Douglass, Fenner (1969), *The Language of the Classical French Organ: A Musical Tradition Before 1800*, New Haven: Yale University Press.

────── (1980), *Cavaillé-Coll and the Musicians*, 2 vols, Raleigh, North Carolina: Sunbury.

Douglass, Fenner, Owen Jander and Barbara Owen, eds (1986), *Charles Brenton Fisk: Organ Builder*, 2 vols, Easthampton, Massachusetts: The Westfield Centre for Early Keyboard Studies.

Dupré, Marcel (1927), *Méthode d'Orgue*, Paris: Leduc.

────── (1972), *Marcel Dupré raconte*, Paris: Bornemann. Published in English (1975) as *Recollections*, translated and edited by Ralph Kneeream, with a foreword by Olivier Messiaen, Melville, New York: Belwin-Mills; and in German (1981) as *Marcel Dupré Erinnerungen*, translated and edited by Hans Steinhaus, with a foreword by Rolande Falcinelli, Berlin: Merseburger.

────── (1984), *Philosophie de la Musique*, Tournai, Belgium: Collegium Musicum.

────── (1934), 'M. Charles-Marie Widor', *Les Nouvelles musicales*, 1, March, pp. 1–2.

────── (1937), 'Alexandre Guilmant: 1837–1911', *La Revue musicale*, 172, February–March, pp. 73–81.

────── (1947), preface to *Jean-Sébastien Bach: l'Oeuvre d'Orgue*, by François Florand, Paris: Cerf.

────── (1959), *Souvenirs sur Ch.-M. Widor*, Paris: Firmin-Didot. An address delivered before the five academies of the Institute of France, 26 October.

────── (1962), 'Alexandre Guilmant', translated by Jeannette Dupré, *The Diapason*, 53, March, p. 8.

────── (1965), 'Propos impromptu', *Le Courrier musical de France*, 11, pp. 132–35.

Einstein, Alfred (1947), *Music in the Romantic Era*, New York: Norton.

Fall, Henry Cutler (1958), 'A Critical-Bibliographical Study of the Rinck Collection', master's thesis, Yale University.

Ferguson, John (1979), *Walter Holtkamp: American Organ Builder*, Kent, Ohio: Kent State University Press.

Fisk, Charles Brenton. See Douglass, Fenner, et al., eds.

Gavoty, Bernard (1943), *Louis Vierne: La Vie et l'Oeuvre*, Paris: Michel.

—— (1955), 'Marcel Dupré', in *Les Grands Interprètes*, Geneva: Kister.

Griffith, Nancy Snell, and Laura Person (1981), *Albert Schweitzer: An International Bibliography*, Boston: Hall. Comprehensive for the years 1875–1979.

Hanheide, Stefan (1990), *Johann Sebastian Bach im Verständnis Albert Schweitzers* (vol. 25 in the series *Musikwissenschaftliche Schriften*), Munich and Salzburg: Katzbichler.

Harmon, Thomas (1973), 'The Mühlhausen Organ Revisited: Precious Clues to Bach's Preference in Organ Design and Registration', *Bach*, 4, January, pp. 3–15.

Harrison, G. Donald (1929), 'British Builder's Impressions After Two Years in U.S.', *The Diapason*, 20, November, p. 32.

Heinsheimer, Hans W. (1975), 'The Saga of Schweitzer's Bach Edition', *Music: The AGO/RCCO Magazine*, 9, January, pp. 30–31.

Henderson, A. M. (1950), 'Widor and His Organ Class Are Recalled by Friend and Pupil', *The Diapason*, 41, September, p. 16.

Hesse, Adolph Friedrich (1831), *Nützliche Gabe für Organisten*, Breslau: Förster.

Hobbs, Alain (1988), 'Charles-Marie Widor (1844–1937)', *l'Orgue: Cahiers et Mémoires*, 40, pp. 3–76.

Holden, Dorothy J. (1985), *The Life and Work of Ernest M. Skinner*, Richmond, Virginia: Organ Historical Society.

Holtkamp, Walter (1935), 'An Organ to See and Hear', *The American Organist*, 18, July, pp. 269–72.

Jacobi, Erwin R. (1975), *Albert Schweitzer und die Musik*, Wiesbaden: Breitkopf and Härtel.

—— (1984), *Musikwissenschaftliche Arbeiten*, edited by Franz Giegling, Zurich: Atlantis. Includes letters, biographical and bibliographical information, a list of concerts, and a comprehensive discography.

—— (1975), 'Zur Entstehung des Bach-Buches von Albert Schweitzer, auf Grund unveröffentlichter Briefe', *Bach Jahrbuch*, 61, pp. 141–61. Includes previously unpublished letters exchanged by Schweitzer and Breitkopf and Härtel (1900–1904) regarding his biography of Bach.

Jacobi, Erwin R., ed. (1984), *Albert Schweitzers nachgelassene Manuskripte über die Verzierungen bei Johann Sebastian Bach*, Leipzig: Breitkopf and Härtel. Schweitzer's letters to various publishers, editors, and colleagues regarding the last three volumes of the Bach edition and revisions for his biography of Bach.

Jaëll, Marie (1895), *Der Anschlag: Neues Klavierstudium auf physiologischer Grundlage*, Leipzig: Breitkopf and Härtel. An anonymous translation (1902) by Albert Schweitzer of *Le Toucher: Enseignement du piano basé sur la physiologie.*

Joy, Charles R. (1951), *Music in the Life of Albert Schweitzer*, New York: Harper; rev. ed. (1953), London: Black. Includes articles by Schweitzer, the complete organ-building essay, and excerpts from *Jean-Sébastien Bach, le musicien-poète* not otherwise available in English. Splendid translations.

Kittel, Johann Christian (facsimile, 1981), *Der angehende praktische Organist*, 3 vols, Buren, The Netherlands: Knuf. An introduction by Gerard Bal describes Kittel's personality and the significance of his work; bibliography.

Klotz, Hans (1984), *Die Ornamentik der Klavier- und Orgelwerke von Johann Sebastian Bach*, Cassel: Barenreiter.

—— (1976), 'Erinnerungen an Charles-Marie Widor', *Ars Organi*, 24, pp. 10–13.

—— (1988), 'Zur Überlieferung der Bachischen Orgelschule', edited by Hans Steinhaus, *Musica Sacra*, 108, pp. 115–120.

Lemmens, Jacques Nicolas (1862), *Ecole d'Orgue basée sur le plainchant romain*, Brussels: Schott.

—— (1886), *Du Chant Grégorien: sa mélodie, son rhythme, son harmonisation*, Ghent: Hoste. Posthumous. Includes a detailed essay on Lemmens by the Rev. Joseph Duclos.

Longyear, Rey M. (1973), *Nineteenth-Century Romanticism in Music*, 2nd ed., Englewood Cliffs, New Jersey: Prentice-Hall.

Mendelssohn, Felix (1973), *Letters*, edited by G. Selden-Goth, New York: Vienna House.

Murray, Michael (1985), *Marcel Dupré: The Work of a Master Organist*, Boston: Northeastern University Press. Published in German (1993) as *Marcel Dupré: Leben und Werk eines Meisterorganisten*, translated by Hans Uwe Hielscher, Langen bei Bregenz: Lade.

—— (1974), 'Toward Perfect Technique', *Music: The AGO/RCCO Magazine*, 8, March, pp. 36–38.

—— (1977), 'The Pure Tradition of Bach', *The Diapason*, 68, October, pp. 4–6.

Near, John Richard (1985), 'The Life and Work of Charles-Marie Widor', D.M.A. dissertation, Boston University. A thorough and discriminating study; includes a comprehensive bibliography.

—— (1993), 'Charles-Marie Widor: The Organ Works and Saint-Sulpice', *The American Organist*, 27, February, pp. 46–59.

Nies-Berger, Edouard (1976), 'The Günsbach Organ and Albert Schweitzer', *Music: The AGO/RCCO Magazine*, 10, May, pp. 50–51.

—— (1985), 'L'Odyssée de l'Edition des oeuvres pour orgue de J.-S. Bach', *Cahiers Albert Schweitzer: Publication trimestrielle de l'Association Française de ses Amis*, 59, March, pp. 16–21.

Noehren, Robert (1975), 'Notes on Bach and the Organ of his Time', *Bach*, 6, April, pp. 3–14.

—— (1975), 'Musical Expression, Bach, and the Organ', *Music: The AGO/RCCO Magazine*, 9, August, pp. 28–33.

—— (1986), 'An Interview with Robert Noehren', Phillip Steinhaus, interviewer, *The American Organist*, 20, November, pp. 52–57.

Noll, Rainer (1985), 'Albert Schweitzer als Orgelfachmann und Bach-Interpret', *Musik und Kirche*, 55, May–June, pp. 122–32.

Nye, Eugene M. (1971), 'Walter Holtkamp: A Master Organ Builder', *The Organ*, 51, October, pp. 66–77.

Ochse, Orpha (1975), *The History of the Organ in the United States*, Bloomington: Indiana University Press.

Owen, Barbara (1987), *E. Power Biggs, Concert Organist*, Bloomington: Indiana University Press.

Pape, Uwe (1978), *The Tracker Organ Revival in America*, Berlin: Pape.

Phelps, Lawrence I. (1967), *A Short History of the Organ Revival*, St Louis: Concordia. Describes the reform movements in Germany, Holland, Denmark, and the USA.

Piccand, Jean (1965), 'Trois Organistes Français', *Schweizerische Musik-zeitung*, 105, p. 89.

Pirro, André (1902), *Johann Sebastian Bach: The Organist and His Works for the Organ*, translated by Wallace Goodrich, New York: Schirmer.

Praet, Wilfried (1989), *Organ Dictionary*, Zwijndrecht, Belgium: Ceos. Organ terms, with equivalents in ten languages.

Quoika, Rudolf (1954), *Albert Schweitzers Begegnung mit der Orgel*, Berlin: Merseburger.

—— (1970), *Ein Orgelkolleg mit Albert Schweitzer*, Freising: Quoika.

Raugel, Félix (1962), *Les Organistes*, Paris: Laurens.

Rayfield, Robert (1987), 'Johann Christian Kittel's Pedaling Instructions', *The American Organist*, 21, December, pp. 68–69.

Rinck, Johann Christian (1833), *Selbstbiographie*, Breslau: Uderholz.

Roback, A. A., ed. (1945), *The Albert Schweitzer Jubilee Book*, Cambridge, Massachusetts: Sci-Art. A Festschrift honouring Schweitzer's seventieth birthday. Includes four substantive chapters on his esthetics by Leo Schrade, Archibald T. Davison, Carl Weinrich, and Alice Ehlers respectively.

Rupp, Emile (1929), *Die Entwicklungsgeschichte der Orgelbaukunst*, Einsiedeln: Benziger.

Schützeichel, Harald (1991), *Die Konzerttätigkeit Albert Schweitzers*, Bern: Haupt. An indispensable work in which Schweitzer's concerts are listed by date, city, church, and repertory, together with programmes, programme notes written by Schweitzer, and extracts from his journals and published writings. Includes registrations, stoplists, biographical notes on the composers, and an account of his interpretative and stylistic practices. Much of the information comes from primary sources; all is admirably arranged.

———— (1991), *Die Orgel im Leben und Denken Albert Schweitzers*, Kleinblittersdorf: Musikwissenschaftliche Verlags-Gesellschaft. An invaluable detailed account of Schweitzer's musical life, giving specifications of organs and biographical information about builders and musicians, together with essays on the esthetic and theological questions that informed Schweitzer's work on Bach and guided his thought in general. Comprehensive bibliography.

———— (1988), 'Albert Schweitzer und die Bachrezeption in Frankreich', *Musica*, 42, March-April, pp. 141–48.

Schützeichel, Harald, ed. (1989), *Albert Schweitzer: Briefe und Erinnerungen an Musiker*, Bern: Haupt. Selected letters, some previously unpublished, together with brief biographies of recipients, a discography, and a bibliography.

Schweitzer, Albert (1898), *Eugène Münch, 1857–1898*, Mulhouse: Brinkman; translated as 'My First Organ Teacher' in Joy, pp. 9–24.

———— (1905), *Jean-Sébastien Bach, le musicien-poète*, preface by Charles-Marie Widor, Leipzig: Breitkopf and Härtel; abridged edition (1951), Lausanne: Foetisch; excerpts translated by Joy, pp. 68–135: 'The Chorale in Bach's Work', 'The Life and Character of Bach', and 'The Symbolism of Bach.'

———— (1908), *J. S. Bach*, Leipzig: Breitkopf and Härtel. This book in German is not a translation of the preceding, but a new work incorporating new material.

———— (1911), *J. S. Bach*, 2 vols, translated by Ernest Newman, revised and enlarged by the author, London: Black, reissued 1923; New York: Macmillan, 1923; reprint, New York: Dover, 1964.

———— (1906), *Deutsche und französische Orgelbaukunst und Orgelkunst*, Leipzig: Breitkopf and Härtel; new edition, with epilogue, 1927; translated as 'The Art of Organ Building and Organ Playing in Germany and France' and 'The 1927 Epilogue' in Joy, pp. 138–76, 200–224.

———— (1924), *Memoirs of Childhood and Youth*, translated by C. T. Campion, London: Allen and Unwin; New York: Macmillan; French translation (1950), *Souvenirs de mon enfance*, Paris: Istra.

———— (1933), *Out of My Life and Thought: An Autobiography*, translated by C. T. Campion, London: Allen and Unwin; New York: Holt. A new

English translation by A. B. Lemke (1990), with a preface by Rhena Schweitzer Miller, incorporates revisions by the author.

—— (1949), *The Philosophy of Civilization*, translated by C. T. Campion, New York: Macmillan.

—— (1987), *Albert Schweitzer: Leben, Werk und Denken 1905–1965 Mitgeteilt in Seinen Briefen*, edited by Hans Walter Bähr, Heidelberg: Schneider. Published in English (1992) as *Letters, 1905–1965*, translated by Joachim Neugroschel, New York: Macmillan.

—— (1909), 'Die allgemeine Umfrage bei Orgelspielern und Orgelbauern in deutschen und romanischen Ländern', *III. Kongress der Internationalen Musikgesellschaft, Wien, 25. bis 29. Mai 1909*, Vienna: Artaria; translated as 'The Questionnaire on Organ Construction' in Joy, pp. 253–55.

—— (1909), 'Die Reform unseres Orgelbaues auf Grund einer allgemeinen Umfrage bei Orgelspielern und Orgelbauern in deutschen und romanischen Ländern', *III. Kongress der Internationalen Musikgesellschaft, Wien, 25. bis 29. Mai 1909*, Vienna: Artaria; translated as 'The Organ that Europe Wants' in Joy, pp. 255–89.

—— (1909), 'M. J. Erb's Symphonie für Orchester und Orgel', in *Die Strassburger Sängerhaus-Orgel*, Strasbourg: Manias.

—— (1909), 'Charles-Marie Widors Sinfonia Sacra für Orgel und Orchester', in *Die Strassburger Sängerhaus-Orgel*, Strasbourg: Manias.

—— (1910), 'Warum es so schwer ist einen guten Chor in Paris zusammenzubringen', *Die Musik*, 36, pp. 23–30; translated as 'The Chorus in Paris' in Joy, pp. 48–56.

—— (1927), 'Zur Reform des Orgelbaues', *Monatschrift für Gottesdienst und kirchliche Kunst*, 32, June, pp. 148–54; translated as 'Reform in Organ Building' in Joy, pp. 217–24.

—— (1930), 'Gutachten über die Orgel zu St Jacobi in Hamburg', in *Die Schnitger-Orgel der Hauptkirchet Jacobi in Hamburg*, Cassel: Bärenreiter.

—— (1932), 'Siegfried Ochs als Bachinterpret', *FestProgramm des Berliner Philharmonischen Chors*, December, pp. 11–13; translated as 'Siegfried Ochs' in Joy, pp. 186–88.

—— (1933), 'Mes Souvenirs sur Cosima Wagner', *L'Alsace française*, 25, February, pp. 124–25; translated as 'My Recollections of Cosima Wagner' in Joy, pp. 58–62.

—— (1933), 'Der runde Violinbogen', *Schweizerische Musikzeitung*, 73, March, pp. 197–203; translated as 'The Round Violin Bow' in Joy, pp. 231–40; expanded slightly as 'Der für Bachs Werke für Violinsolo erforderte Violinbogen,' in *Bach-Gedenkschrift 1950*, Zürich: Atlantis.

—— (1947), 'Zur Geschichte des Kirchenchors zu St Wilhelm', in *Le choeur de Saint-Guillaume de Strasbourg: un chapître de l'histoire de la musique en Alsace*, Strasbourg: Jung; translated as 'The Story of the Church Choir at St William' in Joy, pp. 31–34.

———— (1947), 'Souvenirs d'Ernest Münch', in *Le choeur de Saint-Guillaume de Strasbourg: un chapître de l'histoire de la musique en Alsace*, Strasbourg: Jung; translated as 'Ernest Münch, as I Remember Him' in Joy, pp. 35–45.

———— (1948), 'Souvenirs et appréciations', in *Un grand musicien français: Marie-Joseph Erb*, Strasbourg: Le Roux; translated as 'My First Concert' and 'Marie-Joseph Erb' in Joy, pp. 5–7, 183–86.

———— (1977), *Zur Diskussion über Orgelbau (1914)*, edited by Erwin R. Jacobi, Berlin: Merseburger. A previously unpublished essay of 58 ms. pages, written for *Die Orgel*, found in 1976 among Schweitzer's papers. The editor's epilogue contains information about Emile Rupp's contribution to the Alsatian reform movement.

———— (1988), *Albert Schweitzer, Aufsätze zur Musik*, Cassel: Hanheide. Reprints and translations of essays on Bach, Marie-Joseph Erb, Ernest Münch, Eugène Münch, Siegfried Ochs, Cosima Wagner, the choir of St William's, and organ building.

Schweitzer, Albert, and Franz X. Mathias (1909), *Règles internationales pour la construction des orgues, Internationales Regulativ für Orgelbau*, French and German edition, Vienna: Artaria.

Schweitzer, Albert, ed. See Bach, Johann Sebastian, *Complete Organ Works*.

Schweitzer, Albert, trans. See Jaëll, Marie, *Neues Klavierstudium auf physiologischer Grundlage*.

Seaver, George (1947), *Albert Schweitzer: The Man and His Mind*, New York: Harper; 6th and definitive ed. (1969), London: Black.

———— (1955), *Albert Schweitzer: Christian Revolutionary*, 2nd ed., New York: Harper.

Seyfried, Hans Jürgen (1965), *Adolph Friedrich Hesse als Orgelvirtuose und Orgelkomponist*, Regensburg: Bosse.

Smith, Rollin (1983), *Toward an Authentic Interpretation of the Organ Works of César Franck*, New York: Pendragon.

———— (1987), 'Alexandre Guilmant: Commemorating the 150th Anniversary of his Birth', *The American Organist*, 21, March, pp. 50–58.

Spitta, Philipp (1951), *Johann Sebastian Bach*, 3 vols, translated by Clara Bell and J. A. Fuller-Maitland, New York: Dover.

Sumner, William Leslie (1962), *The Organ: Its Evolution, Principles of Construction and Use*, 3rd ed., London: Macdonald; 4th ed. (1973), New York, St. Martin's.

———— (1969), 'The Organ in the Church of St Sulpice, Paris', *The Organ*, 48, January, pp. 97–106.

Thomson, Andrew (1987), *The Life and Times of Charles-Marie Widor, 1844–1937*, Oxford: Oxford University Press.

Vierne, Louis (1938–39), *Souvenirs*, translated by Esther Jones Barrow in thirteen monthly installments as 'Memoirs of Louis Vierne; His Life and

Contacts with Famous Men', *The Diapason*, 29–30, September–September.

Walter, Bruno (1961), *Of Music and Music-Making*, translated by Paul Hamburger, New York: Norton.

Webber, F. R. (1962), 'A Holtkamp Story', *The Diapason*, 53, April, pp. 28–29.

Weiss, Piero, ed. (1967), *Letters of Composers Through Six Centuries*, London and Philadelphia: Chilton.

Wessely, Othmar (1979), 'Albert Schweitzer: Musiker und Musikgelehrter', *Organa Austriaca*, 2, pp. 168–81.

Widor, Charles-Marie (1934), 'L'Orgue moderne', *Les Nouvelles musicales*, 1, March, pp. 5–6.

Williams, Peter (1967), *The European Organ, 1450–1850*, Nashua, New Hampshire: Organ Literature Foundation. A thoughtful and comprehensive survey; includes a glossary of stop names.

—— (1980), *A New History of the Organ, from the Greeks to the Present Day*, London: Faber.

—— (1980–84), *The Organ Music of J. S. Bach*, 3 vols, Cambridge: Cambridge University Press.

Williams, Peter, and Barbara Owen (1988), *The Organ*, Grove Musical Instruments Series, New York: Norton.

Acknowledgements

I would like to thank Rhena Schweitzer Miller and her husband, Dr David Miller, for their friendly encouragement and assistance. The passages from her father's writings are reproduced with Mrs Miller's kind permission.

Other persons close to Schweitzer have likewise helped me generously: Harold E. Robles, president of the Albert Schweitzer Institute for the Humanities; Ali Silver and Tony van Leer, of the Archives Centrales Albert Schweitzer in Günsbach; Antje Bultmann Lemke, formerly president of the board of directors of the Albert Schweitzer Centre in Great Barrington; and Elinore L. Barber, director of the Riemenschneider Bach Institute of Baldwin-Wallace College.

The excerpts from *Music in the Life of Albert Schweitzer*, by Charles R. Joy, are reprinted by permission of the copyright holders, HarperCollins Publishers, New York, and A & C Black London.

Among the many friends and colleagues who provided information and advice are Jonathan Ambrosino, G. Dene Barnard, Jacques Barzun, Luk Bastiaens, Charles Callahan, Joseph F. Dzeda, Gary L. Garber, Walter Holtkamp, Jr., Tom Johnson, Hans Klotz, Nicolas Kynaston, Arthur Lawrence, Kurt Lueders, Jerry D. Morton, Barbara Owen, Flor Peeters, William T. Van Pelt, Richard Purvis, Daniel Roth, Klaus George Roy, Mr and Mrs Carl Weinrich, Erik Wensberg, and James A. Yeager.

Paul Schwartz, Hans Steinhaus, Gila Fox, Patricia Dussaux, and Danuse Brilty Geyer gave expert help with the translations.

Thomas F. Heck, Lois Rowell Karlsberger, Lois Sims, and Stephen Rogers, of the Ohio State University Library, Columbus; Catherine Massip and the staff of the music division of the Bibliothèque Nationale, Paris; and the staffs of the Archives Centrales Albert Schweitzer, the Albert Schweitzer Centre, and the Albert Schweitzer Institute for the Humanities were unfailingly helpful, as were Ellen Keeling and Rachel Lynch of Scolar Press.

To each person, heartfelt thanks.

Index